# Employee Discipline
## How to Do It Right

# Employee Discipline
## How to Do It Right

**Louis V. Imundo**

**Wadsworth Publishing Company**
Belmont, California
A Division of Wadsworth, Inc.

Editor: Carol Butterfield
Production Editor: Vicki Friedberg
Managing Designer: Paula Shuhert
Print Buyer: Karen Hunt
Text and Cover Designer: Perry Smith
Copy Editor: Russell Fuller

Printed in the United States of America

1  2  3  4  5  6  7  8  9  10—89  88  87  86  85

ISBN 0-534-05120-0

**Library of Congress Cataloging in Publication Data**

Imundo, Louis V.
    Employee discipline.

    Includes index.
    1. Labor discipline.   2. Personnel management.
I. Title.
HF5549.5.L3I49   1985        658.3'14        85-3243
ISBN 0-534-05120-0

To Gerry for courage, strength, beauty, love, and wisdom

# Contents

**3    Determining Just Cause    61**

**4    How to Conduct a Disciplinary Interview    93**

**5    Determining the Appropriate Disciplinary Action    129**

---

**6    When Termination Is Necessary    193**

---

**7    Handling Typical Disciplinary
    Situations    225**

## About the Author

Dr. Louis V. Imundo is president of Management Perspectives, Inc., Dayton, Ohio, a successful organization and human development consulting firm. His seminars and training programs have been attended by more than one hundred thousand managers and supervisors from organizations throughout the United States and Canada.

He is the author of three other books: *The Effective Supervisor's Handbook* (AMACOM, 1980), *The Arbitration Game* (South-Western, 1982), and *Managing Your Human Resources: A Partnership Approach* (with M. P. Eisert, AMACOM, 1982). Dr. Imundo has authored numerous articles that have appeared in major academic and professional publications.

Dr. Imundo is a certified arbitrator and is listed on the Federal Mediation Conciliation Services Roster of Arbitrators as well as the American Arbitration Association's National Commercial and National Labor Arbitration Panels.

# Preface

I have written this book because I believe the subject is timely and that a comprehensive book on employee discipline is needed. I have spent many years learning about organizations and people and how to manage them. In my training and experience I received little guidance about how to effectively use discipline as a management tool. Like most people, I relied on what I saw others do and what had been done to me. I typically used punitive approaches to discipline, but more often than not these approaches failed to achieve the desired results. Failure and frustration motivated me to find better ways to use discipline. I was also motivated to find new approaches to discipline as I saw the employee rights movement taking shape more than a decade ago as a logical outgrowth of the civil rights movement and changing social values.

In my search to develop new knowledge and techniques, I decided to share and test my ideas with others. To this end, I developed a seminar on employee discipline that has now been conducted hundreds of times in the past ten years. I was also able to work directly with many executives, managers, supervisors, and staff specialists. I have learned a great deal from those who have attended my seminars and from those with whom I have worked. Much of this knowledge is presented here.

We live in an exciting, challenging, and sometimes frustrating period in history. Our economic system is changing. And along with economic restructuring, social values are changing: a new order is evolving. The employee rights movement is part of that new order. The old ways of handling disciplinary situations must give way to new ones that better fit the needs of contemporary society. In the

1980s I believe American managers have to contend with two important issues. One is the need to be more productive and thus more
competitive; the other is the need to strike a new balance between
employer and employee rights. People have come to expect their
rights as employees to be comparable to their rights as citizens in a
free society. Though the workplace is not likely ever to become a true
democracy, it will become more democratic.

I hope this book helps managers develop more productive, meaningful employee relations and helps them use discipline as a constructive management tool. I have constructed the book so that it can
be used by all levels of management in any type of organization.
Because the book has been written for supervisors, managers, executives, and staff specialists in any organization, the use of the word
*company* has been carefully avoided. Another word whose use I have
scrupulously avoided is *subordinate*. This word projects the image of
an indentured servant. Such is not in keeping with the evolving
employer-employee relationship. The word *employee* has been used in
its place. Employees are not indentured servants subject to the will of
masters. They are people who voluntarily join organizations and
contribute their skills, time, and energy in return for certain rewards.
Also, in this book I have used the term *manager* in a general sense.
Where applicable, I have referred to a specific level of management.
In its general usage, *manager* is meant to apply to those people who
supervise others and have the authority to reward and discipline or
effectively recommend such action. *Manager* may refer to a supervisor, director, manager, superintendent, officer, chairperson, president, or any other title germane to a profession or organization.

My debts as an author exceed that which can be reasonably ac-
knowledged here. I am indebted to all those with whom I have been
associated and who have influenced my thinking about employee
discipline. I am especially indebted to my wife Gerry, to whom this
book is dedicated. She encouraged me to complete this book, served
as my sounding board, and proofread the manuscript. Special thanks
goes to Sandi Marinics, who did an outstanding job following my
scratchings as she structured and typed the manuscript. I gratefully
share whatever contributions this book makes with these people.

# Introduction

This book has been written for readers whose interests and needs vary widely. Some will want to read every chapter, others will be interested only in specific chapters, and still others will use the book as a desk top reference. The following is a brief introduction to each chapter to help readers decide which chapters will be the most useful.

Most chapters conclude with a summary and outline of key points and discussion questions, and (for Chapters 3–7) case studies are interspersed throughout. The reader who does not have the time or inclination to read each chapter will find the summary and key points particularly useful. They are also useful for periodic reference.

Trainers will find the discussion questions and case studies helpful in generating discussion and in assessing how their trainees are progressing. Some of the discussion questions are open-ended, with no clear right answer, for in the workplace, managers must learn to make good judgments instead of searching for the right answer. Many of the short cases were written with the same thought in mind. Managers often will not have all the time they would like, and complete, reliable information is rarely at hand. Even if it were, subjectivity and bias would still affect interpretation. Decisions often have to be made with a certain dispatch based on what is known.

Chapter 1, "The Necessity for Just and Consistent Discipline," is essentially philosophical. It sets the stage for the remainder of the book. It begins with a look at human behavior, why people work, and what they usually expect from their jobs and employers. The need to set limits and establish guidelines for behavior on the job is presented along with the idea that treating people justly and fairly is important. Without an ongoing, concerted effort to be fair to employees, any discipline or corrective action program will ultimately fail to meet its basic objectives. The need for some form of due process as a way of ensuring that justice is served is discussed.

Readers are introduced to the broad approaches to discipline, which are expanded on in Chapter 5. The chapter closes with a discussion about the importance of being consistent while distributing discipline according to what each individual merits. Being consistent while employing the merit principle is the challenge posed to organizations and their managers. Failure to be consistent leads to employees' perceptions of arbitrariness and injustice. Failure to treat each disciplinary situation on its own merits leads to employees' feelings of unfairness, insensitivity, and injustice. If you are well informed about the aforementioned, you may wish to skip this chapter. How to develop appropriate policies and programs is addressed in Chapter 2.

Chapter 2, "Developing the Framework for an Effective Discipline Program," is a must for those readers who have policy-making authority. It is also useful reading for those in key managerial positions who must administer policies and programs. For those who do not fall into either of these categories, it may be appropriate to skip this chapter. It is recommended that all readers read Chapters 3–7.

Readers are shown the importance of having written human resources management policies and what should be considered in deciding what policies are necessary. Readers associated with small- and medium-sized organizations will find this material useful. The myriad of factors to be considered in formulating written rules, or what are referred to as employee responsibilities, are discussed.

The consistency-versus-flexibility dilemma is addressed from a policy and program perspective. Examples of highly structured, semistructured, and unstructured policies and programs are provided, and the advantages and disadvantages of each approach are outlined. Obviously, whatever types of policies and programs exist, they are useless if they do not work as they should. Readers are given guidelines on how to make them work. The chapter also discusses the necessity and importance of documentation, counseling, and due process.

Chapter 3, "Determining Just Cause," points out how the employment- or termination-at-will doctrine has been eroding for some time. In recent years this erosion has been noticeable and rapid. Employees now expect their rights in the workplace to be on a par with their rights as citizens in a democratic society.

Readers learn how to determine if just cause for discipline exists, why this is important, and how to conduct a fair and impartial investigation. Because the testimony of witnesses is often essential to making a case, readers are shown how to obtain and use testimony. Guidelines on how to obtain and use various other types of evidence are also provided. These include confessions, hearsay, records, circumstantial evidence, and expert opinions.

Chapter 4, "How to Conduct a Disciplinary Interview," focuses on this central element of the disciplinary process. Without the interview, guilt or innocence is unfairly decided without the benefit of hearing the employee's explanation and evaluating its merits. This chapter shows how to plan for, set up, and conduct a successful disciplinary interview.

Because the objective of discipline is to correct rather than punish, counseling is introduced as part of the process. In correcting, it is often necessary to get at the cause of misconduct. Although the cause may be impossible to uncover, an effort should be made nonetheless. The counseling framework and various approaches are outlined. No particular method is advocated because no single approach is best for all situations.

This chapter also addresses how to handle employees who are difficult to manage or control. For literary convenience, labels have been attached to those who exhibit certain traits and characteristics.

Chapter 5, "Determining the Appropriate Disciplinary Action," focuses on how to give discipline according to merit, that is, what each employee actually deserves, and still be consistent when compared to how other employees are treated. The many and varied forms of discipline are discussed within the framework of three general categories: punitive, punitive-rehabilitative, and rehabilitative-constructive. Readers are introduced to such forms of corrective action as the decision leave or think-it-over day, probation, retraining, and providing nothing to do.

The idea of discipline according to merit, as well as how to specifically define and determine merit, is spelled out in the bank account concept. This simple, easy to understand concept is at the heart of the individual treatment or merit concept. Readers are shown how to consider such factors as length and quality of service, seriousness of misconduct, past record, precedents, and past practices.

Chapter 6, "When Termination Is Necessary," begins by showing why termination must be done correctly, once it has been decided on. In the past, managers could fire employees at will, and the employees had little recourse available. This has all changed. Botching up a discharge can be expensive and embarrassing.

Because termination is "capital punishment," you are asked to consider if one more chance is warranted. The factors to evaluate when making such a decision are presented.

Guidelines are provided on how to prepare for and carry out a discharge in a systematic, orderly manner. Readers are shown what needs to be taken care of in the firing process, including access to personnel records, benefits eligibility, return of assigned property, and safeguarding of proprietary information.

Chapter 7, "Handling Typical Disciplinary Situations," addresses many of the common types of disciplinary situations that managers encounter. These range from habitual misconduct to incompetence, disloyalty, drug abuse, absenteeism, and medical disability. For each type of misconduct, factors to consider and guidelines to use are provided. They are not, nor were they intended to be, all-inclusive. However, most cases can be adequately handled using the information provided.

# Employee Discipline
## How to Do It Right

# 1 The Necessity for Just and Consistent Discipline

From the beginnings of civilization people have been concerned with discipline as a method and process to influence behavior. Discipline is something people must contend with throughout their lives. It can be used to benefit or to harm. Generally, discipline can be divided into two categories: self-discipline and social discipline. Self-discipline can be used by individuals to influence, reinforce, or change their own behavior. It is internally generated, based on a person's desire to do the right thing, and self-maintained without external influence. Social discipline is externally generated and may or may not be self-maintaining. Social discipline exists in many forms. It can be employed by anyone to influence, reinforce, or change another individual's behavior. In the absence of self-discipline, some form of direct or indirect influence is necessary to serve as a reminder that certain behavior is required or expected.

Any time desired, expected, or required behavior, whether internally generated or externally imposed, is not achieved and maintained, a cost results. The intensity and duration of the cost, loss, or penalty will vary depending upon the relative influences of many factors. No one person or group of people can make someone behave in a particular manner if he or she chooses not to do so. As long as a person consciously or subconsciously wants to behave in a certain way, he or she will continue to do so until some action to change is initiated and maintained. If the action to change, whether internally or externally induced, is not maintained until it becomes a matter of habit, permanent behavioral change is unlikely to result. We must recognize and accept that in some instances, regardless of the cost, even including death, certain people will be unwilling or perhaps unable to change their behavior.

This chapter will establish the conceptual framework for the remainder of the book. The following chapters will focus on how to properly develop and implement effective discipline programs. Knowing how to effectively use discipline requires working knowledge about human behavior. It is assumed that by virtue of formal education and/or life's experiences, readers are reasonably knowledgeable about human behavior. To establish a common framework, however, the following brief discussion about behavior is presented.

## The Behavior Process

All behavior can be viewed as a conscious or subconscious attempt to increase, maintain, or avoid the loss of some level of need satisfaction. A person's motivation or drive is the observed behavior of striving to satisfy a need or needs. People share a common broad range of needs, and it is difficult to identify the specific need causing a particular form of behavior and to determine how and why a person's behavior is directed toward satisfaction of that need. However, to be effective, managers must develop an understanding of the motivation process.

No two people are exactly alike; they may share many characteristics and yet be very different. People's general needs can be identified and categorized as physical, psychological, or both. They do not exist in any predetermined hierarchy; their intensity and importance can change gradually or in an instant. For example, people need food to sustain themselves. Can we conclude that eating is only a physical need? Do people eat to live or live to eat? The psychological significance of eating a particular food or a particular meal often far outweighs the physical need. People sometimes eat when they are not actually hungry or eat more than they need for physical sustenance. In the American culture, Thanksgiving, with its traditional turkey and trimmings, is a holiday where eating has been ritualized and is highly symbolic. The food's preparation, its consumption, and accompanying after-dinner rituals all satisfy both physical and psychological needs.

The following broadly lists some human needs. (They are not categorized as either physical or psychological because circumstances, perceptions, and values all interplay to make a rigidly structured classification impossible.) People have needs for food, shelter, achievement, recognition, acceptance, power, self-respect, respect from others, justice, security, opportunity, sexual gratification, peace of mind, and freedom for self-expression. The list could go on and on.

Sorting out and identifying needs that stimulate behavior or the motivational process is a difficult task, in part because behavior is shaped by various factors. First, people are not born with the same attributes and abilities. To a degree, a person's inherited traits directly and indirectly influence behavior. In addition, no two people experience exactly the same environmental influences in life. So behavior is in part inherited and in part shaped by the environment. When people work in an organization, they bring all their inherited and learned ways of behaving to the job. People are creatures of habit and, whether consciously or subconsciously, tend to repeat behaviors that are gratifying to them. It is important for managers to recognize that employees' behavior patterns are well established before they start working in organizations. The extent to which managers can change employees' behavior is limited by known and available behavior modification tools and techniques. Limitations also exist because of the law, management's skills in the application of tools, the degree of flexibility allowable in making decisions, and other factors.

How often have we heard someone say he or she is not motivated? However, when we observe behavior, we are seeing the motivational process in action. Motivation, as shown in Figure 1.1, is the action part of the needs-satisfaction cycle. People's conscious or subconscious needs at a given moment result in behavior. Some action or reaction can be associated with what is seen as eventual satisfaction of individual needs.

Behavior can be logical and rational or illogical and irrational. Furthermore, interpretation of behavior is often colored by emotional influences and by inaccurate or incomplete information. Consequently, if attempts to analyze behavior are based on what is rational or logical, the wrong conclusions can often result. People ultimately behave in ways they perceive will satisfy their self-interests, which is not to imply that one person's gain is another's loss. It *can* happen this way. But it also can happen that everyone benefits, or everyone loses. Because behavior is ultimately self-serving, it can be said that employees work for themselves rather than for their employers. Their jobs and the organizations they work for are vehicles through which they seek goals to satisfy needs. However, most and perhaps all people cannot satisfy all their needs through work.

## Figure 1.1 Needs-Satisfaction Cycle

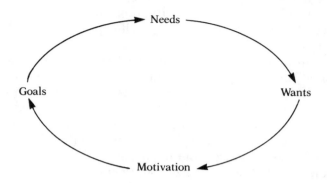

## Needs

All people have the same basic set of needs, which can be broadly classified as being either physical or psychological. Behavior results because a need (or needs) is not satisfied. When a need is satisfied, no behavior will occur. Behavior, consciously or subconsciously directed toward satisfying a need, will occur when a person feels the need strongly enough to want to satisfy it.

## Wants

As a need intensifies, it becomes a want or desire. When a person wants to either achieve, maintain, or avoid something, he or she will consciously or subconsciously engage in activities to achieve the desired goal.

## Motivation

The behavior that people exhibit, demonstrate, or perform is what is commonly referred to as motivation. All behavior, whether conscious or subconscious, is directed toward the satisfaction of needs. In effect, all behavior is goal oriented.

## Goals

When a goal is reached, a need is satisfied. The need may remain satisfied for only an instant, or it may remain satisfied for an extended period. Once a need is satisfied, no further behavior directed toward its satisfaction will occur. Behavior may continue to occur to maintain a particular level of satisfaction. Behavior changes as the priorities and intensities of needs change.

# The Meaning of Work to Employees

The importance of work activities differs among people and can change over time. These activities must compete with other interests as a means of directly or indirectly satisfying employees' needs. The commitment that employees willingly make to their jobs is a function of priorities, requirements, expectations, and the relative value of the rewards of work as compared to the costs. Rewards are defined as anything an employee views as a benefit, while costs are anything an employee views as a detriment to his or her own welfare.

Membership in any organization, whether voluntary or compulsory, usually involves some cost to the individual. This causes problems in any society where freedom, individuality, and democracy are strongly emphasized and valued. Business organizations are generally something less than democratic in their relationships with employees. Differences in job titles, compensation, working conditions, location of offices, positions on organization charts, and other so-called privileges of rank clearly illustrate that all employees do not have the same rights, privileges, power, and status.

What people willingly give up to gain the benefits from organization membership depends on many factors. What people are willing to give—economically, socially, psychologically, or physically—is proportional to what they expect in return from the relationship with the organization. Figures 1.2 and 1.3 list many of the rewards and costs associated with employment. When the expected rewards from work are fewer or less important than the perceived costs, dissatisfaction can show itself in numerous ways. The desired rewards are affected not only by the expectations present at the time of hiring but also by changes the employee perceives in the costs associated with continued employment. We could formulate a rule of human behavior that says, the higher the costs, the higher the expected rewards. A corollary is that if the rewards are not attainable in the short term, expectations are likely to increase proportionately with the passage of time.

Organizations' reasons for employing and retaining employees are also self-serving. The work relationship is a process of mutual exchange benefit. Management expects employees to make a commitment to achieving productivity goals that contribute to the organization's overall goal of survival. If an organization is to continue to retain employees, it expects employees' contributions to be greater than the costs of their maintenance. On the other hand, if organizations expect employees to maintain membership and make a

## Figure 1.2   Possible Rewards or Benefits from Working in an Organization

- Money—paycheck
- Money—benefits
- Security—steady employment
- Pleasant work environment
- Safe work environment
- Interesting work
- Challenging work
- Recognition for performance (nonfinancial awards)
- Competition
- Sense of pride in job or organizational affiliation
- Sense of accomplishment
- Job that contributes to the welfare of others
- Acquisition of status symbols
- Prestige of position or job title
- Opportunity to be promoted
- Opportunity to learn a skill
- Opportunity to acquire and exercise power
- Opportunity to participate in decision making
- Preferred work assignment
- Use of company equipment
- Discounts on company products or services
- Preference on overtime assignments
- Time off without penalty
- Discounts on used company equipment
- Bonus awards
- Opportunity to get additional training on company time at company expense
- Flexible work schedule
- Compensatory time selection
- Site visits or field trips
- Preference on office location and decoration
- Sabbatical leave with pay
- Participation by invitation in special sponsored paid activities
- Freedom to choose special work assignments
- Paid memberships in professional organizations or societies
- Paid subscription to professional publications
- Reserved parking space
- Exposure to key decision makers

## Figure 1.3  Possible Costs or Losses from Working in an Organization

- Loss of freedom to speak one's mind
- Loss of the opportunity to do something else
- Loss of the freedom to do something else
- Physically and/or psychologically hazardous working conditions
- Loss of individuality
- Too much stress
- Lack of opportunity to participate in decision making
- Lack of opportunity to advance
- Boring, disinteresting, monotonous work
- Having responsibility for the work of others

- Having to interact with others
- Being overskilled for a job
- Being underskilled for a job
- Long working hours
- Destructive conflict and politics
- Being subject to the authority of others
- Insensitive supervision
- Unfriendly associates
- Destructive competition
- No recognition for performance
- No status or prestige
- Raises based on criteria other than job performance
- Promotion based on anything but job performance

strong commitment to work, then managers must maintain an environment where employees feel that rewards exceed costs. This is no easy task, considering the high expectations of many employees and the economic difficulties plaguing some industries.

As members of a pluralistic society, people belong to various organizations. Some memberships are voluntary, whereas others are somewhat involuntary. Generally, work in industrial, commercial, or service organizations is voluntary. No employee can be forced to maintain employment. A basic liberty is the freedom to quit. But even though employees are free to leave at any time, they may still feel trapped in their jobs. Though they can quit, it often is not practical or realistic for them to do so. Economic conditions, age, family considerations, financial need, community ties, and other factors make membership in organizations for some employees more compulsory than voluntary. As long as employees feel compelled to maintain membership, they will do so. However, if employees feel locked into their jobs and the perceived rewards are fewer than the costs, they will behave in ways to change the relationship of rewards to costs.

## The Necessity for Just Discipline

Discipline is essential to all organized group action. The members of any formal or informal organization must control their individual urges and cooperate for the common good. In other words, they must reasonably conform to the code of behavior established, implemented, and administered by the organization and its managers, so that order is maintained and common goals can be accomplished.

In any formal organization, some pressures push the organization toward conformity and uniformity, while counterpressures pull the organization toward nonconformity and flexibility. The push-pull effect influences the formulation of policies, procedures, guidelines, and employees' behavior. Conformity and uniformity result in short-term high efficiency, though individuality and creativity often suffer. Nonconformity results in short-term inefficiency, though in the long term, individuality and creativity may be high. Does this mean that organizations should operate on principles of nonconformity and flexibility? Not necessarily. Too much flexibility and nonconformity without policies, programs, and procedures for guiding employees' behavior will lead to chaos. The results of chaos are collapse and failure. All organizations must develop disciplinary policies and procedures to maintain order, congruity, and continuity. When disciplinary policies, procedures, and guidelines are vague or nonexistent, employees, not knowing the boundaries of acceptable behavior, will experience anxiety and apprehension. This will lead to defensive or aggressive behavior.

When disciplinary policies or actions are perceived as being unfair, employees will develop feelings of injustice about the way they are treated. People have always been concerned about justice and fair treatment; and feelings of injustice and a sense of grievance have been the underlying causes of most if not all revolutions. It can be said that two principles have maintained the American democratic process and free enterprise system: (1) the opportunity to be upwardly mobile and share in the wealth of the nation and (2) the establishment of basic human rights, protected and maintained by legislation and due process. Managers at all levels must understand that when people believe they have been treated unfairly, they will, if their reasons are sufficiently strong, be motivated to seek redress, justice, or revenge.

It appears that a dichotomy exists in human character. To varying degrees people need structure, direction, and control in their lives, though scope and degree are influenced by many factors and conditions. Without leaders, structure, limits on behavior, and prescribed rituals, cooperation and harmony among people will decline. Eventually this will cause an erosion of the social fabric. However, excesses of structure and misuses of power eventually lead to adverse consequences. History records countless examples of people's violent reactions to abuses of power. Dictatorship in organizations can survive only by generating enough fear to quell rebellious actions. Control by rules, regulations, severe disciplinary actions, and the like is expensive and time-consuming, often at the expense of progress. Maintenance of a police state, in the long term, usually affects economic development and increases people's desire to overthrow the government. The same circumstances can arise in a business organization where management determines what is fair and just without considering employees' feelings about fairness and justice. Though managers are not deposed, their authority is reduced or circumscribed.

As this dichotomy exists in society, so also does it exist within society's organizations. As cultural values and standards change, so must the standards for behavior under which people live and work also change. Additionally, the ways in which standards are interpreted and enforced must change. What is appropriate, proper, fair, just, or correct is elusive. This is and will continue to be a matter of argument in law, philosophy, and employee relations. In the management of people, the development, implementation, and maintenance of a fair system of justice are some of the most critical and sensitive challenges facing managers at all organizational levels.

## Justice According to Merit

Justice according to merit (allocative justice) involves a proportional allocation of rewards and discipline according to policies, rules, procedures, and the facts and circumstances pertaining to each case. Each case, whether it involves a reward or corrective action, must be judged on its particular merits. A sum of money, for example, may be fixed in total, but it can be divided and allocated on the basis of merit. Corrective action, on the other hand, is in relatively inexhaustible supply. The allocation of rewards, which are partially fixed in supply, and the allocation of discipline (corrective action) must also be allocated according to merit. Rewards are proportional to what is available. Discipline must be proportional to the prevailing standards and norms, the particulars of the situation, and what has been given to others for similar actions under similar conditions.

The concept of a fair system of organizational justice and its effect on employees' perceptions of satisfaction or dissatisfaction are inter-related with many variables within the individual and the work environment. Perceptions of rewards, penalties, privileges, status symbols, and opportunities interact to produce feelings of justice or injustice. For example, office workers today often earn less than factory workers, which has led to feelings of unfairness and dissatis-faction among office workers.

Whether these feelings are defensible is irrelevant. What one group perceives to be fair treatment, another may perceive as being unfair. Government agencies, the courts, and arbitrators are overloaded with cases of perceived injustices involving compensation, promo-tions, demotions, transfers, layoffs, suspensions, and terminations.

If organizations are to function effectively and efficiently over time, the rules and regulations developed and administered must be per-ceived as fair by the majority of the organization's members. Wide-spread perceptions of unfairness or injustice can lead to some form of withdrawal or some form of aggressive behavior against the organi-zation. Antiorganization behavior can manifest itself as excessive absenteeism, slowdowns, sickouts, sabotage, theft, negligence, and even violence. It can also show itself in union organizing efforts, frequent strikes, overuse of the grievance procedure, and continual resort to the courts, government agencies, and arbitrators to settle differences. Whether such actions as unionization and seeking due process outside the organization are viewed as being antiorganiza-tion is a matter of perception. Though management might view such behavior as being negative, employees might have the opposite view-point.

## Organizational Due Process

Another aspect of justice is the due process procedure for employees who believe they have been treated unfairly or improperly under the organization's system of allocative justice. It is requisite that all formal organizations have such a system for employees. Citizens of the United States and other democratic nations have their individual civil rights safeguarded, and this country has one of the most compre-hensive due process systems in the world. Employees, whose civil rights are well protected, expect much the same level of protection for their industrial, institutional, or workplace rights. Any formal organization without a due process system for employees risks creating perceptions of unfairness and injustice. Such systems may be as informal and unstructured as an open-door policy or as formal and structured as a multistep grievance procedure.

In the absence of an organizational due process system, most employees, in time, will believe that either they or others have been treated unfairly. Authority to reward and discipline, without a system for reviewing and checking, is authority that will eventually be misused, as history has repeatedly shown. It is important to keep in mind that people react to what they perceive to be reality rather than to what others may consider reality. Grievance or complaint-handling procedures are components of formal due process systems. All such systems are designed to achieve the same goal: to review the decisions and actions initiated by others to ensure that justice prevails.

Organizational due process is necessary not only for those who are or may be directly affected but also for managers who develop and administer the reward and discipline systems. One way to measure supervisors' effectiveness as managers is to give employees the right to appeal their decisions. When supervisors' decisions are reviewed and supported by higher management, positive feedback reinforces supervisors' behavior. When higher-level managers do not support supervisors' decisions, the negative feedback can be instructive. This is part of the development of supervisors as managers.

The most common formal system for administering due process is the grievance and arbitration procedure that exists in nearly all negotiated labor agreements. The main purpose of the grievance procedure is to provide a means for review and possible modification of the allocation of rewards and penalties. For all practical purposes, what is fair will be what is agreed upon between the union and management during negotiations that take place at the various steps of the grievance procedure or what is decided by an impartial arbitrator.

Many nonunion organizations have recognized the value of a formal organizational due process system and have developed and implemented systems incorporating the spirit and philosophy of those in effect in unionized organizations. However, one feature almost always missing is the availability of arbitration as the final step for the resolution of disputes. The biggest problem in any system where management is the final authority is establishing and maintaining in employees' minds that the system is fairly administered. The question must be asked: Can management be objective when reviewing its own decisions? It's possible but difficult to accomplish. Many organizations find that such systems are not used by employees very often. The reason is not because grievances do not exist but because employees do not believe the system is fairly administered.

## The Causes of Employee Behavior Problems

Life in today's society is both stressful and complex. High rates of inflation coupled with economic downturns cause even greater stress and strain because of the anxiety produced by relative scarcity and uncertainty. Growing rates of violent crime, divorce, alcoholism and other forms of drug abuse, suicide, and mental and physical illness are in part related to the cycle of inflation and recession.

People vary in their ability to cope with stress. Under stress, a person will eventually move toward either creative or destructive solutions, and movement toward destructive solutions is likely to cause job performance problems. Proactive managers recognize when problems are likely to occur and take preventive actions. Reactive managers wait until the damage has already been done before attempting corrective action, usually in the form of warnings and threats. The proactive manager initiates positive action when symptoms show, before the problem actually surfaces.

In the job environment four major sources of disciplinary situations can be identified: (1) the kind of people hired, (2) the nature of the work, (3) the job environment itself, and (4) the philosophy and operational practices of management. No matter how refined the selection process, some people who should not have been hired will be. Second, not all jobs are "good jobs," and for some types of work it is difficult to attract or retain good people. Work environments vary in terms of physical conditions and psychological climate. Hot, dirty, dangerous, and demanding work environments may create considerable stress for employees, as do intensely competitive work climates. Under such physically or psychologically adverse conditions, the likelihood of employee behavior and performance problems increases. The way an organization or unit is structured and managed significantly affects employees' behavior.

A poorly managed organization will experience employee behavior problems more frequently than a well-managed one. This is especially true when poor supervision exists. A badly managed organization or unit may be one where supervisors and/or higher-level managers are arbitrary and dictatorial or one where inconsistency and permissiveness prevail. If misconduct is tolerated and employees obtain satisfactions from their misbehavior, the behavior will be repeated frequently. This is the case whether the situation is one of poor performance, excessive absence or lateness, or anything else.

## Approaches to Discipline

Discipline provides a means to bring about a change in behavior on the part of an individual or group based on authority or power. Disciplinary situations arise when a person or group has violated the norms of acceptable behavior of a group or organization. Norms may be implicit or explicit rules of behavior or methods of operation. Implicit norms are more subtle and often more difficult to understand than explicit norms. They can only be inferred from the behavior exhibited by others in the group or organization.

*Webster's* gives three basic meanings of the word *discipline:* (1) training that corrects, molds, strengthens, or perfects; (2) control gained by enforcing obedience; and (3) punishment or chastisement. If meanings one and two are combined, it can be stated that discipline involves the conditioning or molding of behavior by applying rewards and penalties. The third meaning is narrower because it pertains only to the act of punishing.

The first dictionary definition is treated to mean the positive, constructive, or rehabilitative approach. This is the kind of discipline that managers at all levels should strive to create. Positive discipline is actually broader and more fundamental than the dictionary definition—training that corrects, molds, strengthens, or perfects—implies. Positive discipline involves the creation of attitudes and of an organizational climate that encourage employees to willingly conform to established rules and regulations. Its application frequently requires considerable self-discipline. It is achieved when management helps the employee to change the undesired behavior and willingly accept and conform to the desired behavior. Positive or constructive discipline emphasizes internalization of the desire to do what is correct and in consonance with prevailing norms.

The second and third meanings of discipline include the use of penalties or the threat of penalties to influence people to obey orders and live up to the rules of the system. Its application always requires social discipline. Psychological and social force are universally used.

Most employees who experience problems on the job, whether the cause is job or nonjob related, are able to change on their own and avoid having management initiate disciplinary action. However, if employee behavior must be corrected and effective solutions are sought, cause and motivation for the misbehavior should be identified. This, unfortunately, does not always seem possible or worth the effort, and in such cases solutions are often directed merely at symptoms. This approach to problem solving is a hit-and-miss one that can bring about unintended side effects.

Many managers, particularly supervisors, avoid rather than address employee behavior problems because of pressure to maintain work output, concerns about lawsuits, intervention by government agencies and possible arbitration, fear of no support from higher levels of management, and even fear of physical harm.

In correcting employee misbehavior, either the positive or negative approach can be taken. Traditionally, the negative, or punitive, approach has been favored, and it is still the most widely used. The typical formal, progressive discipline in use today relies on warnings, threats, and suspensions. It is punishment oriented. The positive approach is rehabilitative and emphasizes self-control rather than punishment.

Under the punitive approach, employees learn to respond out of fear. Fear is a significant and effective influence on behavior; however, as fear diminishes, so does its effectiveness. Employees learn to avoid getting caught, or when caught they look for ways to retaliate.

Use of the positive, or rehabilitative, approach requires more patience and skill. But in the long term it often produces desired results, namely, a more permanent positive change in an employee's behavior. The positive approach uses counseling, training, retraining, probation in lieu of suspension from work, reducing or removing barriers that inhibit performance, and emphasizing the need for individuals to take responsibility. Transferring, demoting, or ignoring the employee; denying privileges; withholding merit salary increases; and the use of peer pressure can be either punitive or rehabilitative, depending on how they are applied.

## Consistency and Flexibility in Discipline

Management must establish and consistently maintain standards and expectations for conduct and job performance. Consistency does not mean that all employees must or should be treated alike. It does mean that when facts, circumstances, records of service, and other significant factors are very similar, two employees (even though they may be in different organizational units) should receive the same treatment if they are working under the same organizational policies and in similar work environments.

The matter of consistency in administering discipline is one of major concern to managers and employees. In recent years management's sensitivity to allegations of discriminatory treatment of employees has dramatically increased. In far too many instances management's fear of being charged with discrimination by employees has diluted the quality of decision making. In some instances it has paralyzed decision making.

Many managers and employees believe that everyone should be treated equally or in a like manner. This belief is frequently derived from their perceived understanding of the meaning and intent of antidiscrimination laws, most notably the Civil Rights Act of 1964. The various laws prohibiting indefensible discrimination in the treatment of employees are specific in language. However, their interpretation and application has led to considerable confusion and misunderstanding among managers and even among those in government who carry out and oversee their enforcement.

Managers, if they are to be competent and effective in their roles, must understand that differentiation or discrimination in the treatment of employees is inherent in the management process. Differential treatment based on merit is proper, legal, and defensible, but discrimination based on factors not validly related to job duties and performance is improper, illegal, and indefensible. They must understand that when job performance, records of service, facts, and circumstances differ, employees should not be treated the same. This is the essence of the merit principle. Whether managers treat all employees the same or treat them differently, they are subject to being accused of discrimination.

Sounds ridiculous, doesn't it? The following example will prove the point:

> Employees Ward and Fischer work for manager LeFever. Fischer is an exceptionally good worker and has the best performance record for the past year when compared to others in the unit. Ward, at best, is an average worker. Both employees earn about the same annual income. LeFever conducts the annual merit performance appraisal and judges Fischer high and Ward average. When the annual "merit" raises are determined, everyone in the unit, including Fischer and Ward, is given the same percentage increase.

Is this discriminatory? After all, everyone has been treated the same. No discrimination has occurred because of race, age, sex, ethnic origin, and so on. But discrimination has in fact occurred. Fischer could and should lodge a complaint with LeFever. By demonstrating high performance and making more of a contribution to the organization than Ward and others, Fischer has earned the right to a larger proportional share of the rewards available. He has been discriminated against; Ward has been favored. This example, of course, assumes that all other things are equal regarding how the two employees are treated. On the other hand, if LeFever were to give Fischer a high merit raise and Ward an average one, Ward could lodge a complaint accusing LeFever of discrimination because Fischer was given a higher raise. Ward could base the charge on any convenient factor, such as race, age, or sex. It would be up to LeFever to show that discrimination occurred because of differences in job performance and up to Ward to show that discrimination was on a different basis, one that is contrary to law.

Too often executive-level managers who have encountered problems with lower-level managers treating employees differently decide to have everyone treated the same irrespective of their service records. However, while mandating that everyone be treated alike, they will concurrently profess the virtues of merit in speeches, expound on it in training programs, and express it in writing within various human resources management policies and procedures. They feel that treating everyone the same is less risky than treating employees according to what each merits. However, as shown above, treating everyone alike can be just as discriminatory as treating each differently.

Managers must recognize and understand that people do not want to be treated alike. They want to be recognized and rewarded for their individual contributions. The importance of individuality, the pursuit of self-interest, and the rewarding of good performance is ingrained in our culture and economic system. When trust is low or nonexistent and employees believe managers are not applying merit fairly, they will react to protect themselves. This is most readily observed in unionized organizations where management's flexibility is removed or reduced by language incorporated in the negotiated labor agreement. Generally, the more provisions in the agreement, the more management's discretionary authority and flexibility are reduced. Most labor agreements stipulate that raises be given across the board and that lateral transfers and promotions be determined either solely or largely on the basis of employee seniority. Across the board raises and promotions based in whole or part on seniority are discriminatory. But they are frequently demanded by unions with strong support from the membership because the bases are readily understood and not easily manipulated. Though exclusive reliance on seniority without its being correlated with performance is inherently unfair, it is viewed as being less unfair than management's perceived arbitrariness.

Competent proactive managers will differentiate, that is, discriminate, in their treatment of employees whether rewards or discipline are being allocated. Discrimination based on performance is the most defensible of all bases on which to differentiate the treatment of employees. There is nothing in the laws, rules, regulations, and directives promulgated by governmental units that prohibits managers from using merit. However, merit must be defined, validly related to job requirements, understandable, measurable, and applied consistently and equitably. Consistency should not be confused with equality and uniformity. Nor should equal opportunity be confused with equal treatment. An exception to the above would occur when because of past injustices, government has legislatively or judicially mandated that hiring and job placement quotas be maintained or that people be discriminated for or against on bases other than job qualifications or performance. This occurred with some frequency in the 1960s and 1970s to remedy historical and existing injustices. For the most part, progress toward correcting these injustices has been made. However, if managers fail to provide for equal opportunity and do not discriminate on valid, defensible bases such as records of service, the government, courts, unions, and others will return in force in response to management's irresponsibility.

So far the discussion has pertained to rewards, but this same reasoning can be applied to the distribution of discipline. The following example will illustrate the point. Employees Ferrigan and Lafferty separately violate the same written company rule. The rule is relatively minor—not one that would warrant possible termination for a first offense. All things being equal, should the employees be given the same discipline? The answer is yes. However, in reality all other things are usually not equal. If the facts and circumstances pertaining to the misconduct, length of service, and quality of performance differ appreciably between Ferrigan and Lafferty, management would be unjust and indefensibly discriminatory in giving them equal discipline. One possible exception to the indefensibility argument would be if a highly structured, written, progressive discipline system existed that was uniformly applied in practice and accepted by employees.

Essentially for the sake of convenience, to avoid having managers use judgment, and to reduce the likelihood of challenge to imposed discipline, organizations frequently develop inflexible, structured, progressive discipline systems. If consistently followed, they establish order and uniformity in the allocation of discipline. They also eliminate managerial judgment and flexibility. The long-term result is that equal treatment prevails and equity does not. There is consistency, but there is also unfairness and injustice.

Organizations and those who manage them are challenged by the need to be uniform and consistent while retaining flexibility. This is the consistency versus flexibility dilemma. Under the guise of needing to maintain consistency and reduce the likelihood of discrimination charges, some executive-level managers will maintain highly centralized control over discipline decisions. This is accomplished in a number of ways, including the following:

1. All discipline decisions are referred to the executive management level or to the executive in charge of the human resources function, which may go under such names as Personnel, Industrial Relations, Employee Relations, or Human Resources. Because it is a staff role, when the human resources executive makes the decision, his or her latitude and authority usually are carefully shaped by the chief executive's or the chief operating officer's philosophy. Some lower-level managers may find comfort in having higher-level managers make the decisions. The burden of having to make judgments is off their shoulders, they cannot be held responsible for wrong decisions, unpopularity can be minimized or even avoided, and decisions made by the higher-ups can be criticized. Criticism of course is not without its political risks.

2. Another way to maintain consistency is to carefully prescribe process and define the degree of allowable discretion in decision making through written process and procedure. The "book" tells managers what to do and how to do it. This practice is particularly common to government, large corporations, and unionized companies of all sizes. Consistency in discipline decisions is necessary. The question is how much? This question will be examined and answered in Chapter 2.

Managers usually want to retain some flexibility in making decisions. They want to make judgments according to what they see as the particular merits of each situation. However, some managers will rationalize for themselves and attempt to convince others that whatever decision they make regarding discipline is appropriate and correct. Too much flexibility can cause more problems than treating everyone the same.

As shown, consistency and flexibility each have relative advantages and disadvantages. Do consistency and flexibility contradict one another? The answer is no. An effective discipline program must embody both concepts. Chapter 2 will show how to develop such a program.

## Summary

No matter how well managed an organization is or how good its employees, discipline situations are inevitable. Any time an employee conducts him- or herself contrary to what is required or expected, a discipline situation exists. Most people can exercise self-discipline. Social discipline, which is primarily dispensed by management, must be used when self-discipline fails. In this chapter you have learned the need to establish a discipline program that is effective and perceived as being fair and properly administered.

You have also been introduced to the idea that discipline, like rewards, should be given according to merit. While in theory merit is easy to accept, it is difficult to properly use in practice. Much of what is contained in the following chapters is designed to show how to develop an effective discipline program that embodies the use of merit and how to make it work in practice.

## Key Points

- There are two general categories of discipline. One is self-discipline, the other social discipline.
- All behavior is caused by conscious or subconscious needs.
- People ultimately behave in ways to satisfy their own self-interests as they see them.
- People's commitment to their jobs is a function of expectations, priorities, what is required, and the relative value of the rewards of work as compared to the costs.
- Discipline is essential to all group action. The members of any organization must control their individual urges and cooperate for the common good.
- When disciplinary policies or actions are viewed as being unfair, feelings of unfairness and injustice will evolve.
- Discipline must be given on the basis of merit.
- Every formal organization should have a system of due process for its members to ensure that authority is not misused.

- In every organization there are influences pushing it toward consistency and uniformity. There are also counterpressures pulling it toward flexibility and nonuniformity.
- Treating employees differently, that is, according to what each merits, is inherent in the process of managing.
- Fair and equitable discipline is consistent and based on merit.

## Discussion Questions

1. Define self-discipline.
2. Explain the meaning of social discipline.
3. Are people ultimately motivated to serve their own self-interests? If you agree, why? If you disagree, why?
4. Discuss how perceptions affect the proportional value of rewards and costs associated with work.
5. Why is work so important in our culture?
6. If employers hire only responsible, trustworthy, competent people, is there a need for written rules and disciplinary policies and procedures? Explain.
7. Why has the civil rights movement spilled over into the workplace and become the employee rights movement?
8. Why is it that what was right for employees in the past may be wrong for them today?
9. Why is it important for all employers to develop some form of a due process system for employees?
10. Discuss the basic difference between the punitive and rehabilitative approaches to discipline.
11. Discuss the problems associated with total uniformity and consistency in disciplining employees.
12. Discuss the difference between legitimate and illegitimate discrimination in managing people.
13. What are the risks associated with applying the merit principle to discipline situations?

# 2 Developing the Framework for an Effective Discipline Program

     All formal organizations, except relatively small ones, should have written personnel or human resources management policies. It can be said that organizations are managed according to the philosophy of the person who heads the organization. To varying degrees the chief executive officer or similarly titled head of an organization will exert influence over the ways employees think and act. This influence can and often does continue to exist beyond the leader's tenure in the job and even beyond his or her lifetime. Many organizations in this country, to varying degrees, are still being managed according to the philosophy of their founders. The J. C. Penney Company is a notable example. Mr. Penney stated his beliefs in writing about how a business should be managed and how employees should be treated. They were expressed in the form of commandments, or principles. Even though Mr. Penney is deceased, these principles still govern the basic way the company is currently managed.

     All organizations have character and culture, which is most readily observed by the ways employees behave in their roles. Because no two organizations function in exactly the same ways, each one develops a degree of uniqueness. An organization's culture is commonly deeply rooted in traditions and past practices. But organizations must also respond to change.

     Change is inevitable; indeed, we live in a period of accelerated change. It is a force that continually throws us off balance. Organizations and individuals are constantly engaged in trying to maintain themselves in a state of dynamic equilibrium.

Most managers are reactive rather than proactive. While the proactive manager anticipates the need to change before the need manifests, the reactive manager either cannot see the need to change or does not know how to change. The reactive manager is usually trying to catch up, while the proactive manager is trying to stay ahead. Resistance to change is more likely when things are going well.

Success frequently breeds complacency, which is dangerous in a fast-changing world. Managers, especially those whose decisions impact heavily on the way an organization functions, must remain continually alert to the need to change. Organizations and their managers, whether they effect change or are affected by it, must continually respond to it in order to regain a balance with the environment. Change per se is neither good nor bad. How it is perceived, how it is acted on or reacted to, and ultimately what results are derived from it determine whether it is good or bad. Organizations, and individuals, that cannot or will not adapt to change will face likely diminishment of power and eventual demise.

In small organizations one person can usually make all the decisions, especially when that person is aware of just about everything that is happening in the organization and the marketplace. But as an organization grows, it can become costly to have one person making all the decisions. Thus, organizations usually move toward decentralization of authority. Although this can lead to disorder and inconsistency, such problems can be avoided through written policies. But because these policies place restrictions on individual choices of behavior, they are not always welcomed by those who value individuality and independence. Fortunately, though, people also dislike instability, and when it reaches an unacceptable level, they will welcome controls.

The amount of flexibility that lower-level managers can be given in making human resources decisions is determined by the following:

- The personal security or insecurity of executive-level managers, especially the chief executive and chief operating officers
- The perceived and demonstrated competence of lower-level managers
- The impact of laws and government regulations pertaining to employment and employee relations
- The size and complexity of the organization
- The number of employees and number of different types of jobs
- The organization's philosophy, culture, traditions, and past practices

- The organization's financial health
- The prevailing relationship between managers and employees

In small organizations, such as those employing less than one hundred people, executive-level managers normally write the policies, though the services of a consultant are generally advisable. Experienced human resources consultants can help managers design policies that are comprehensive in scope, embody prevailing social values and the organization's philosophy, and do not conflict with the letter and spirit of the law.

In large organizations where a human resources function exists, the human resources executive should develop policies. The services of a consultant are again recommended. All policies should be thoroughly reviewed by executive-level management to ensure that the final policies specifically fit the organization's environment.

It is hard to believe that many organizations still do not have written human resources policies to guide managers' thoughts and actions. In organizations where authority is highly decentralized, there tend to be significant inconsistencies in the ways employees are treated, as well as pervasive feelings among employees of management's incompetence and injustice.

In organizations where written policies exist, all too often any one or a combination of the following have been known to exist:

- Policies are dated, out of touch with present conditions in the organization or with employees' values and attitudes.
- Managers, particularly supervisors, have little or no training on how to apply the policies on a day-to-day basis.
- The language used in writing the policies is not readily understood by many managers who have to use them.
- The policies are poorly written and difficult to understand.
- The policies are rarely used by middle- and lower-level managers because top management does not fully support them.
- The policies have been copied verbatim from another organization's policy manual and do not relate to the using organization's environment.
- Policy manuals are not issued to first-level managers, for example, supervisors and foremen.
- Feedback systems to assess the effectiveness of policies are nonexistent or not used.

Human resources management policies should cover all facets of employment and employee relations. Many of the policies will indirectly relate to discipline because they are preventive in nature. Figure 2.1 outlines the types of policies that should be considered for inclusion in a manual. The specific number of policies needed should be based on what top management believes is needed to guide lower-level management's behavior.

In a unionized organization many of the policies listed in Figure 2.1 would be covered in the negotiated labor agreement. It is recommended that guidelines for interpreting and complying with the provisions of the agreement be included in a policy manual.

It is important that employees understand the organization's philosophy toward them as expressed in its human resources policies. Policy manuals are rarely distributed to or even discussed with employees, so they are often ignorant of what is written in them. Policy manuals normally contain guidelines for their day-to-day use. These guidelines, which can be numerous, are of limited interest to employees. Their interests center on what the policies are and how they are affected by them. Communicating this information to employees is best accomplished by an employee handbook—an abridged version of the human resources management policy manual. Every employee should receive a copy, and supervisors should review its contents with new employees. In this way employees develop a clearer understanding of how they are to be treated, what they can expect from the employer, and what is expected of them.

As illustrated, a policy manual should cover all aspects of employment and employee relations. This information has been provided to give a picture of the scope of policies that can be written to guide management's behavior. The focus of this chapter is on those policies that pertain to discipline. The following sections provide information on how to develop an effective program that is equitable to employees, is consistent in how it is applied, and provides flexibility for managers to base discipline on merit.

## Objectives and Elements of an Effective Program

An organization's discipline program is embodied in the policies and procedures contained in its policy manual. An effective program is one that embodies or achieves the following:

- It is perceived as being fair by a substantial majority of the organization's employees, including managers.
- Its content and day-to-day application are in agreement with the letter and spirit of the law.

**Figure 2.1   Human Resources Policy Manual**

Table of Contents

Personnel Responsibilities

The Company's Human Resources Philosophy
Management's Responsibility in Carrying Out the Company's Human Resources Philosophy
The Company's Position on Union Affiliation*
Guidelines for Dealing with Organizing Activity*

Employment Practices

Equal Employment Opportunity
Affirmative Action
Occupational Safety and Health Laws
Fair Employment Practices Laws
Employment of Interns and Minors
Employment of Relatives
Employment of Aliens
Rehiring of Former Employees

Employment Policy and Procedure

Request for Personnel
Recruitment of Personnel
Selection of Personnel
Employee Orientation
Probation
Employee Classification
Change of Employee Classification
Records of Employment
Change of Employee Information
Utilization of Contract Labor
Employment Agencies and Services

Payroll Practices

Scheduled Hours of Work
Lunch and Rest Periods

---

* In a unionized company these policies normally would not be included in a manual.

*(continued)*

**Figure 2.1** *Continued*

Overtime Scheduling and Pay
Employee Attendance Record
Paycheck Calculation and Deductions
Payroll Period and Paycheck Distribution
Work Make Up

## Salary Administration and Performance Rating

Total Compensation Program
Salary Administration
Performance Assessment and Employee Development
Guidelines for Rating Each Performance Factor for Nonexempt, Nonsupervisory Employees
Guidelines for Rating Each Performance Factor for Exempt, Nonsupervisory Employees
Guidelines for Rating Each Performance Factor for Department Managers and Supervisors
Performance Planning and Appraisal for Division Officers and Branch Managers
Special Merit Performance Appraisal
Position Descriptions
Service Date
Seniority

## Absence from Work

Absenteeism and Lateness
Sick Pay
Short-Term Disability
Long-Term Disability Leave
Work Injury Leave
Bereavement Absence
Jury Duty or Court Appearance Absence
Military Duty Absence
Blood Donation Absence
Emergency Delayed Opening/Early Closing/No Opening

## Promotion and Transfer

Promotion
Transfer
Posting of Position Availability
Moving Expense Reimbursement

## Termination

Termination of Employment

## Employee Benefits

Health Protection Plan
Long-Term Disability Insurance
Basic and Supplemental Group Life Insurance
Workers Compensation Benefits
Company Officer Travel and Accident Insurance
Employee Flight Insurance
Dental Assistance Plan
Vacation
Holidays
Retirement Plan
Retirement Bonus
Profit-Sharing Bonus
Officer Physical Examination
Parking
Employee Assistance Counseling Program
Preretirement Counseling Program

## Employee Responsibilities and Services

Disciplinary Policy
Disciplinary Guidelines and Procedures
Disciplinary Employee Counseling
Procedure for Resolving Employee Concerns or Problems
Conflicts of Interest and Outside Employment
Visitor Access to Corporate Offices
Monetary Matters
Expense Advances and Reporting Procedure
Reimbursement for Loss of Personal Effects
Lost and Found Articles
Employee Improprieties
Training and Development
Employee Communications
Suggestion Program
Employees Activities Association
Employees Community Services Fund
Employees Credit Union
U.S. Savings Bond Program

- Its primary purpose is to prevent, correct, and rehabilitate instead of punish.
- It provides a framework to shape lower-level managers' thinking and guide their actions.
- It has sufficient flexibility to allow managers to apply the principles of merit and judgment in disciplinary decisions.
- It is easy to understand and apply on a day-to-day basis.
- It provides for flexible, progressive approaches to discipline.
- It stresses self-discipline and preventive measures.
- It stresses rehabilitative rather than punitive approaches to discipline.
- It supports the role of managers while simultaneously respecting and protecting the rights of employees.
- It contains a due process procedure and operates on the premise inherent in civil justice—that the employee is innocent until proven guilty.
- It requires that disciplinary action be initiated in a timely manner, usually not more than five scheduled workdays from the day misconduct was known or should have been known to have occurred.
- It requires documentation of relevant and pertinent facts and circumstances pertaining to the disciplinary situation. This includes an employee's records and information obtained from an investigation of the incident.
- It gives consideration to allowing some form of employee representation in the due process procedure.
- It provides for a limited open-door policy.
- It includes requirements for establishing just cause for discipline.
- It contains written guidelines for behavior, that is, standards of conduct or what are commonly referred to as "rules."

## Developing Written Rules, or Employee Responsibilities

Unless specifically precluded by law, negotiated agreements, or stated policy, management has the authority to prescribe necessary and reasonable rules or standards of conduct. Unless managers and employees have a common understanding of what behavior is unacceptable, problems can result. The following examples illustrate the point:

• If employees do not know the policy on maintaining confidentiality when handling certain types of information, confidences are likely to be unintentionally broken.

• Unless policies regarding access to information are known, employees will not know who is allowed to have access to what.

• Without policies pertaining to attendance, promptness in reporting to work, use of sick leave, and leaving work early, some employees will go beyond the limits of what is acceptable behavior.

• If employees do not know the requirements for maintaining safety on the job, some will inadvertently behave in ways that their bosses will decide are unsafe.

The great majority of employees will voluntarily conform to rules and standards of conduct they believe are reasonable and fairly administered. Employees expect managers to set the proper examples of behavior. They also expect management to discipline employees who break the rules. When management does so, it shows all employees that misbehavior is unacceptable and will not be tolerated. Disciplined employees learn there is a price to pay for misbehavior, and those who may be tempted to break the rules will think twice about it. Last, and most important, the majority of employees who abide by the rules develop respect for management when they see that wrongdoers don't get away with misbehavior. How management handles disciplinary situations ultimately determines the success or failure of even the best-designed program.

Every organization as part of its discipline program needs written rules or what are more appropriately called employee responsibilities. Employee responsibilities are what rules really are. The term *employee responsibilities* embodies the concept of self-discipline. Employees, as adults, should be able to control their own behavior. As adults, employees should have a general understanding of right and wrong, a desire to do what is right, and a sense of responsibility. Managers should not have to continually monitor and control employees' behavior. Of course, if everyone always behaved as they should, discipline situations would occur very infrequently. They do occur because employees misbehave out of ignorance or intent. The identification of underlying causes for misconduct is important for determining the course of corrective action.

Many organizations do not have a formal discipline program with written employee responsibilities as part of their human resources management policies. The most frequently voiced arguments against having written responsibilities are: "Discipline isn't a problem here, and we don't need written rules." "If we had written rules, it would reduce management's flexibility." Such arguments are without merit.

Without written employee responsibilities, two problems will arise. One is that employees will sometimes unknowingly misbehave and subject themselves to disciplinary action. It is grossly unfair to impose discipline on an employee for conduct he or she did not realize was unacceptable. The only possible exception is in instances where by common sense or rule of reason the employee should have known the behavior was wrong. Examples include major theft, fighting, misappropriation of funds, immoral conduct, and falsification of records. The second problem is that each manager will eventually develop his or her own rules for employees. This will cause widespread inconsistencies in the treatment of employees, which in turn will result in serious perceptions of arbitrariness and unfairness. In addition, if challenged, imposed discipline will not be defensible.

## How Many Rules Are Necessary?

In determining the number and content of written employee responsibilities, the following should be considered:

▪ Too many written employee responsibilities imply that employees need to be closely monitored and controlled.

▪ Managers and employees will have difficulty remembering a large number of written employee responsibilities. In addition, the more that exist, the greater the likelihood they will overlap. This could cause managers to cite the wrong ones when charging employees with misconduct. Misconduct must be judged on the basis of what was actually charged. If the wrong charge is made, it could mean a rescinding of disciplinary action if appealed through a due process system.

▪ Too many employee responsibilities could serve as an incentive for some employees to look for loopholes or what is commonly referred to as "walking in the cracks."

▪ Too few may provide managers with too much latitude for varying their meaning and applicability.

## Major and Minor Employee Responsibilities

**Major Rules.** Major rules are those that, if violated, could seriously affect the organization and/or its employees in an adverse way. One violation could mean possible cause for termination. Major employee responsibilities can differ among organizations. For example:

- In an oil refinery, natural gas–processing plant, or any chemical-processing plant where operations are continuous, sleeping on the job is a very serious form of misconduct. If something went wrong because of an employee's inattentiveness and it was not caught in time, operations could be seriously damaged or the facility could explode.
- Sleeping on the job would not be considered as serious in an office as in the refinery.
- In a hospital, a nurse's giving the wrong medication to a patient would be considered very serious.
- In a retail store, a clerk's giving the wrong merchandise to a customer would not be regarded with the same seriousness.
- Some forms of misconduct can be considered serious in all organizations. Fighting, physical assault, insubordination, stealing, and falsification of official records are good examples.

**Minor Rules.** Minor or less critical employee responsibilities are those for which one violation would not be cause for possible termination. Examples would include lateness, loitering, horseplay, parking illegally, discourtesy, and inappropriate business attire. As will be discussed in subsequent chapters, cumulative or repeated violation of minor employee responsibilities could subject an employee to termination.

## What Else Should Be Considered?

- Employee responsibilities may be categorized under general subject headings such as welfare and safety, professional and personal responsibilities, attendance, solicitation, and distribution of promotional activities.
- Employee responsibilities may be written in descriptive paragraph form or as specific statements.
- In developing employee responsibilities, management must consider employees' values, attitudes, concerns, and feelings.
- Management must also give consideration to prevailing social, business, and community values, standards, or norms. For example, the term *appropriate business attire* is difficult to define. As social values have changed, the meaning of appropriate business attire has

also changed. In the past, women were often required to wear dresses or skirts. Slacks and especially jeans were out of the question. For men in management, suits, white shirts, and wing-tipped shoes constituted appropriate dress. The norms regarding grooming have also changed. Beards, mustaches, and long hair have become acceptable. As values continue to change, what is and is not acceptable attire and grooming will also change. However, the degree of change varies among organizations.

Unless management has legitimate defensible reasons, employees cannot be required to act in ways that significantly differ from what society defines as acceptable and normal. Dress codes and specific ways of acting can be required if the reasons for them are based on legitimate considerations such as safety, image, customer relations, or employee relations.

• Written or implied rules of conduct for employees must conform to the law and society's perceptions of reasonableness.

• Rules must be communicated to employees. As appropriate, employee handbooks, orientation programs, house organs, and bulletin board notices should be used.

• Whenever new employee responsibilities are written or existing ones revised, the reasons for the new or revised ones should be communicated.

• Indirect or direct employee input into the formulation of written employee responsibilities should be considered. However, it is management's responsibility to make the final determination of their form and content.

• In unionized organizations, union representatives should be indirectly involved in the formulation of employee responsibilities. When a cooperative relationship exists between organized labor and management, unions can provide valuable input to the process. When union viewpoints are not considered, the likelihood of employees voluntarily accepting the employee responsibilities is reduced. Even where union-management relations are less than harmonious, the union should be informed in advance of any new or revised employee responsibilities. Circumventing the union is tantamount to a psychological slap in the face. The union can be expected to retaliate.

No matter what is written into policies, they must be applied in ways they are intended and be perceived as fairly administered by employees. One of the major challenges faced by management is being consistent and equitable.

# Maintaining Consistency in the Program

In any discipline program it is essential that *all* employees who work in similar job environments or under the same policies and procedures be judged by the same employee responsibilities. This does not mean that discipline must be applied equally to employees.

The simplest way to ensure consistency in the ways employees are disciplined is to establish a progressive discipline system similar to the one shown in Figure 2.2.

The system is highly structured, thus ensuring that everyone is treated about the same. Managers can exercise very little independent judgment in varying the type and degree of discipline to impose on employees. In addition, the types of discipline, warnings, and suspensions are strictly punitive. To be effective in the long term, a discipline program must include both rehabilitative and punitive approaches. The wide variety of actions to choose in disciplining employees will be discussed in Chapter 5. The discipline system shown in Figure 2.2 is commonly used in unionized organizations.

Because the differences in the way unionized and nonunionized organizations are managed are much smaller than what managers usually believe them to be, progressive discipline programs similar to the one shown in Figure 2.2 are common to both types of workplaces. The system appears to be nondiscriminatory. However, it is highly discriminatory because it requires that unequal situations be treated equally. As stated, unions frequently support and even push for such systems. Because their distrust of management tends to be high, unions seldom want systems that provide for the use of merit and judgment. It would be unfair to say that all unions think this way. While unions want management to be consistent and treat everyone alike, they will frequently press for exceptions, especially when an employee is terminated. Even though the terminated employee has been properly processed through the progressive disciplinary levels or steps, union representatives or anyone else representing the employee will introduce all kinds of information to have the termination rescinded or reduced. Examples include the employee's length of service, quality of work, mitigating or extenuating circumstances, and how other employees have been treated under similar circumstances for the same type of misconduct. This is nothing more than use of the merit principle.

The example below (see p. 40) illustrates how uniform application of a rule would result in injustice:

## Figure 2.2  Employee Responsibilities with Structured, Progressive Discipline

Key to Symbols: V—Verbal Warning; W—Written Warning;
3,5—Suspension Days; D—Discharge

| | Offense | | | | |
|---|---|---|---|---|---|
| | First | Second | Third | Fourth | Fifth |
| 1. Absenteeism | | | | | |
| a. Excessive or habitual absenteeism for reasons not acceptable to the company. Excessive or habitual absenteeism is defined as the second day (or equivalent partial days) of absence within an employee's sixty (60) workday period for reasons not acceptable to the company. | V | W | 5 | D | |
| b. Absence from overtime assignment, for reasons not acceptable to the company, after having accepted the assignment. | W | 5 | D | | |
| 2. Tardiness | | | | | |
| a. Excessive or habitual tardiness for reasons not acceptable to the company. Excessive or habitual tardiness is defined as the third tardiness within an employee's twenty (20) workday period for reasons not acceptable to the company. | V | W | 3 | 5 | D |

|  | Offense | | | | |
|---|---|---|---|---|---|
|  | First | Second | Third | Fourth | Fifth |
|    b. Returning late from lunch. | W | 3 | 5 | D | |
| 3. Leaving without permission | | | | | |
|    Leaving the plant, work station, or work area without proper permission is not allowed. Failure to return to work after the lunch period is a part of this rule. | W | 5 | D | | |
| 4. Loafing, loitering, etc. | | | | | |
|    Do not loaf, loiter, or engage in unauthorized visiting during working time. It is not allowed. | W | 5 | D | | |
| 5. Sleeping, reading | | | | | |
|    Sleeping during working time and reading of materials other than those pertaining to an employee's work are prohibited. | W | 5 | D | | |
| 6. Solicitations | | | | | |
|    Employees may not solicit for any purpose or sell anything during their working time or in working areas. Solicitation, selling, and distribution of literature are prohibited at all times on company property. | W | 3 | 5 | D | |
| 7. Unsanitary conditions | | | | | |
|    Do not create unsanitary conditions in any way in any place in the plant or on the premises. | W | 5 | D | | |

*(continued)*

**Figure 2.2**  *Continued*

| | Offense | | | | |
|---|---|---|---|---|---|
| | First | Second | Third | Fourth | Fifth |
| 8. Disorderly conduct | | | | | |
| a. Disorderly conduct during working time or on company property, including fighting and threatening or abusing any other employee, is prohibited. | 5 | D | | | |
| b. Horseplay | 3 | 5 | D | | |
| 9. Intent to harm | | | | | |
| Acts during working time or on company property intended to destroy property or to inflict bodily injury, whether or not the destruction or injury actually occurs, are prohibited. | D | | | | |
| 10. Drinking | | | | | |
| a. Unfitness to work as a result of excessive drinking of alcoholic beverages is not allowed. | 3 | 5 | D | | |
| b. No employee is allowed to possess or drink alcoholic beverages on company property. | 5 | D | | | |
| 11. Gambling | | | | | |
| Gambling is not permitted on company property. | 5 | D | | | |

|  | Offense | | | | |
|  | First | Second | Third | Fourth | Fifth |
|---|---|---|---|---|---|
| 12. Narcotics | | | | | |
| a. Possession or use of narcotics on company property, or attempting to bring narcotics onto company property, is prohibited. | D | | | | |
| b. Appearing for work under the influence of narcotics is prohibited. | D | | | | |
| 13. Explosives and firearms | | | | | |
| a. Possession of explosives or firearms on company property is not allowed. | D | | | | |
| b. Attempting to bring explosives or firearms onto company property is not allowed. | W | D | | | |
| 14. Safety | | | | | |
| Guidelines for your continued safety at work are a separate set of rules. Violation of these rules, as posted by the company, or a violation of general safe practices in the performance of work for the company or in the use of the company's facilities for any purpose is not allowed. Penalties for violations of these rules are as shown opposite this paragraph, except for the "No Smoking" rule. | W | 3 | 5 | D | |

*(continued)*

**Figure 2.2** *Continued*

| | Offense | | | | |
|---|---|---|---|---|---|
| | First | Second | Third | Fourth | Fifth |
| 15. Smoking<br>Employees may not smoke in areas where smoking has been prohibited by local authorities or by management. | W | D | | | |
| 16. Negligence<br>The commission of negligent or careless acts during working time or on company property that results in personal injury or property damage, or that cause expenses to be incurred by the company, is not allowed. | 5 | D | | | |
| 17. Stealing<br>Stealing is absolutely prohibited. If the violation occurs during working time or on company property, the employee will be discharged. | D | | | | |
| 18. Unauthorized possession of company property<br>Unauthorized possession or use of any company property, equipment, or materials is prohibited. | D | | | | |
| 19. Falsification of records<br>Falsification of time cards, job cards, or other company reports or punching another employee's time card is not allowed. | 5 | D | | | |

| | Offense | | | | |
|---|---|---|---|---|---|
| | First | Second | Third | Fourth | Fifth |
| 20. Fraudulent statements | | | | | |
| Fraudulent statements of any nature are prohibited. | 5 | D | | | |
| 21. Performing other than company work | | | | | |
| All work performed on the premises must be for the direct benefit of the company, unless otherwise authorized. Performing work on the company's premises other than officially assigned duties is not allowed. | W | 5 | D | | |
| 22. Unauthorized work | | | | | |
| You are not allowed to start work before regularly scheduled hours of work or work overtime without the permission of a supervisor. Do not punch in more than thirty (30) minutes prior to your regularly scheduled starting time. If you do work other than authorized hours, you will not be paid. | N/A | | | | |
| 23. Insubordination | | | | | |
| a. Refusing to accept work, refusal to perform work in accordance with the instructions furnished by a supervisor, or refusal to otherwise cooperate with management is prohibited. | D | | | | |

*(continued)*

**Figure 2.2** *Continued*

| | Offense | | | | |
|---|---|---|---|---|---|
| | First | Second | Third | Fourth | Fifth |
| b. Threats or intimidation of management personnel are not allowed. | D | | | | |
| 24. Slowdown, willful holding back, slowing down, hindering, or limiting production is not allowed. | W | D | | | |
| 25. Encouraging violation of rules | | | | | |
| Do not encourage, coerce, incite, bribe, or otherwise induce any employee or employees to engage in any practice in violation of these company rules. If you do, the discipline imposed for such violation of this rule will be the same as that specified for a violation of the rule or rules in question. | N/A | | | | |

Employees O'Brien and Schultz get into a fight. No one saw who started it and each accuses the other. O'Brien has been with the company for twenty years and has a good service record. He has never been in trouble. Schultz has been with the company for less than two years. His service record is not good, and he has been disciplined a number of times for a variety of rule infractions. The company has a rule against fighting, and one offense means automatic termination. Both were observed fighting and management decides to uniformly apply the rule and fire both employees.

The action would be unfair because the differences in their service records were not considered. The example assumes everything else is equal. If it was known who started the fight, a higher degree of guilt

| | Offense | | | | |
|---|---|---|---|---|---|
| | First | Second | Third | Fourth | Fifth |
| 26. Multiple violations<br>Violation of three or<br>more separate work<br>rules (numbers 1 to 25<br>above) during one<br>twelve-month period,<br>where the disciplinary<br>action for any two of the<br>violations was a suspen-<br>sion from work, will<br>result in immediate dis-<br>missal of the employee. | N/A | | | | |

The policy concerning prior disciplinary action is as follows: all written warnings or disciplinary suspensions not exceeding ten (10) working days shall be considered null and void twelve months from date of issuance.

The above twelve-month cutoff period shall include all time during which the employee is listed as an active employee on the payroll of the company, except time lost by him or her due to disciplinary suspension and/or due to any consecutive absence exceeding thirty (30) days no matter what the reason. Any time lost due to layoff is also excluded from said twelve-month cutoff period.

Adapted from material provided by Dresser Industries, Inc., Wayne Division.

would be assigned to that person. The importance of considering service records and other factors will be expanded on in Chapter 5.

In unionized organizations union advocates often succeed in having arbitrators reduce termination to lesser discipline by invoking the merit principle. This happens even if the system is similar to the one shown in Figure 2.2. It is especially likely to happen if management has not considered all relevant facts and circumstances. Management is more likely to succeed in having terminations upheld by arbitrators and others if they have applied the principle of merit and have done so in writing as part of the disciplinary actions. Those readers from organizations that do not have unions and arbitration as part of due process may be saying to themselves, "We do not have to worry about this type of problem." While nonunion employees do not have the protective umbrella a union may provide, they do have redress through internal due process, if such exists, and external due process in the courts and government agencies. Union-represented employees may also take their grievances to the courts or government agencies in addition to using the negotiated grievance procedure.

Executive-level managers frequently contend with instances where lower-level managers either are lax on requiring employees to conform with the employee responsibilities or fail to initiate corrective action against those who do not. Because managers' personalities and relationships with employees differ, some will be more tolerant than others of employee misconduct. The result is indefensible inconsistency in the enforcement of employee responsibilities. The following example illustrates the point:

> Employee Corwin has been late for work four times in the past month. This exceeds the written standard of three per month. Corwin, who has been counseled and forewarned that lateness was becoming a problem, now receives a written warning. On receiving the warning, Corwin seeks to have it rescinded through the due process (grievance) procedure. She names half a dozen employees in other units covered by the same lateness policy who have been late for work more often in the past month than she has been and have not received any comparable discipline. Her supervisor answers, "They don't work for me, you do. I can't control what goes on in their units. You have to live by the rules and that's that."

Is the supervisor's position correct? Will the written warning be sustained if Corwin appeals it through successively higher levels in the organization under the due process procedure? The supervisor's position is correct, but the warning will not be upheld if management is fair to the employee, because the lateness policy is being inconsistently enforced. If other employees are not being disciplined for lateness and management knows or should know about it, enforcement of the policy is indefensibly discriminatory. Assuming there are no valid special considerations for not disciplining other employees and singling out Corwin, whose record is no better or worse than the employees she named, management cannot justify disciplining her and not the others. A dilemma exists. If the actions of conscientious managers are not supported when they enforce written employee responsibilities and related policies, how can respect for managers be maintained with employees who conform to the employee responsibilities? Also, how can lower-level management's morale and loyalty be maintained when correct decisions and actions are not supported? Some readers will feel the supervisor in this case should be supported. However, to do so would be quite unfair to Corwin. Had management disciplined all employees covered by the program whose lateness exceeded the standard's upper limit, the disciplinary action would have been fair and proper, assuming that the standard itself is reasonable. The responsibility lies with executive-level management to ensure that lower levels of management consistently enforce the rules.

As a defensive tactic, it is not uncommon for a disciplined employee to cite instances where other employees misbehaved and were not caught. This tactic will fail if management has conscientiously attempted to enforce its employee responsibilities and related policies and programs since it would be unreasonable to expect management to know about every instance of misconduct by employees. Because one employee got away with something does not give all other employees the right to misbehave. But if numerous instances of others getting away with something are known and management has done little if anything to correct the situation, then those who are caught cannot legitimately be disciplined for similar misconduct. The exception to this would be if management announced that a new policy of enforcement was being put into effect and then some were subsequently caught.

The most effective way to ensure that standards for behavior are consistently maintained is to train managers in how to carry out policies, monitor their behavior, reward those who do it right, and take corrective action against those who do not. Many executive-level managers fail to take necessary actions to correct the behavior of lower-level managers who do not follow policies. This is especially true when the manager is a high producer or popular with associates and bosses.

Should professionals working in offices be treated differently if such is noted in applicable policies or is commonly accepted practice? For example, in a research and development unit where work is unstructured, work schedules may be more flexible than those in a data-processing center, an accounting office, or an assembly line. As another example, take scheduled break times. If the policy states that the morning coffee break is from 10:00 A.M. to 10:15 A.M., then all employees would be expected to take their break during this period. Would it be appropriate to impose this requirement on all employees if some are assigned to field service work? Imagine an employee driving down a busy highway at 10:00 A.M. Should the employee pull over and take a break? The obvious answer is no. However, if the employee took a break at another time, he or she would be violating policy. In this example the employee clearly should be allowed more flexibility in scheduling his or her break time. However, the employee should not be allowed to take a break for longer than fifteen minutes.

If explanations for varying applications of certain policies, procedures, and employee responsibilities are not provided, misunderstanding, confusion, resentment, and perceptions of unfairness will surely result. Written and verbal explanations that are sincere and honest will greatly reduce the occurrence of problems. It should be noted that most written rules will apply uniformly throughout the entire organization. However, the specific discipline imposed on employees could and should vary.

Whenever some employees are exempted from following a policy meant to apply to all employees, such as break time, the reason should be noted in writing. The language may be narrow or broad in scope. A key point to remember is that no employee, irrespective of position, power, or popularity, should be beyond reproach for misconduct. All employees must be subject to discipline for theft, being under the influence of intoxicants, negligence, insubordination, stealing, incompetence, and fighting. If managers are allowed to go undisciplined for misconduct, respect, trust, and credibility will be diminished. Because managers are leaders, they should be held to higher standards of conduct than other employees. This should be stated as a matter of policy. Misconduct by managers, especially if it adversely affects the organization, should be subject to strong disciplinary action.

## Incorporating Merit in the Program

Developing a discipline program that provides for flexibility, the practice of the merit principle, and the use of judgment is possible. Its format could be similar to the one shown in Figure 2.2 except that the progressive discipline steps could be modified to include greater flexibility and more varied courses of action. It could be similar to the one shown in Figure 2.3, where employee responsibilities are categorized and no specific disciplinary courses of action are outlined. Or it could contain a policy statement and guidelines to follow, as shown in Figure 2.4.

It is difficult to make any program that embodies merit work equitably and consistently. However, the long-term benefits make it well worth the effort. A note of advice and caution is in order. This type of program should be reconsidered unless executive-level

# Figure 2.3   Disciplinary Policy—All Employees

## Policy Statement

To a large degree the success of the company is directly related to the quality of its employees. The company has traditionally tried to be selective in extending offers of employment. Management believes that the majority of employees are dedicated people motivated to do what is expected of them.

However, whenever people work together, the necessity arises to establish certain limits to or guidelines for behavior. These behavioral limits are commonly referred to as guidelines or rules. Failure to observe the rules of a game usually results in a penalty. In the same way, failure to observe the company's rules will result in management's taking disciplinary action.

Management recognizes that only a small number of employees occasionally break rules. This point should be constantly emphasized to the vast majority of our employees performing loyally and efficiently. It should also be stressed that the company's rules, which management prefers to call employee responsibilities, are few in number and are the outgrowth of management's concern to provide for an efficient and safe work environment. It is the intent of the company to regard this disciplinary policy as a positive instrument for helping employees to develop rather than simply to punish them. Employees, both as individuals and as a group, will adhere to the desired standards of behavior because they understand, believe in, and support them. This policy is intended to help the employee develop an understanding and an attitude of adherence to these employee responsibilities.

Whenever possible, reinforcement and encouragement should be given to those employees performing loyally and efficiently. However, when employees break rules, disciplinary action must be taken with the objective of influencing the employee to change his or her behavior. This means that disciplinary action must be carried out in a supportive and corrective manner. Vindictiveness has no legitimate place in any disciplinary action.

A necessary prerequisite for this positive approach is for the supervisor to help employees understand what is expected of them. In creating a climate of positive, helpful discipline, supervisors must seek to help employees build a sense of personal responsibility and self-discipline. Therefore, supervisors must apply principles of positive motivation and good leadership. They must also recognize individual differences and when necessary vary the approaches to discipline.

Employees' work-related responsibilities are few in number. They can be clustered into the following four categories:

1. Attendance
2. Professional and personal responsibilities
3. Solicitation, distribution, and promotional activities
4. Employee welfare and safety

Adapted from material provided by Erie Insurance Group.

---

### Figure 2.4   Guide to Positive Discipline—Hourly Employees

I. Policy

The normal standards of good conduct and acceptable job performance apply to all hourly employees. It is the policy of company
management to provide a positive, supportive environment in which
employees can perform to their greatest ability and the organizational goals can be attained. To this end, it is necessary to have
guidelines for both management and employees to follow in the
pursuit of their common interests.

II. Purpose

Occasionally an employee may develop a performance problem. A
performance problem is the difference between the performance expected and the employee's actual performance. Counseling by the
supervisor will usually correct the undesired performance. However,
if counseling fails, the following positive disciplinary procedure has
been established.

III. Procedure

A. Step One—Oral Warning

The oral warning is a documented conversation between the supervisor and the employee about a performance problem. It is the
first step of the positive discipline program.

The purpose of the oral warning is to correct a performance problem by bringing it to the employee's attention in a friendly but
serious manner.

The employee will sign and receive a copy of an oral warning
notice. This notice is to ensure that the employee understands the
infraction and that corrective action is to be taken by the employee. This notice will be kept in the employee's department file.

B. Step Two—Written Warning (Related Offense)

Should the same problem continue or a serious problem develop
that requires immediate attention due to its severity, the employee will be given a written warning by the immediate supervisor. The employee will be asked to sign the written warning,
which will be forwarded to the employee relations department to
become a part of the employee's record. Should the employee
refuse to sign the written warning, it will be necessary for a third
party to verify the reprimand in the presence of the employee. The
employee's signature is not an admission of guilt.

---

C. Step Three—Decision Leave (Related Offense)

If the employee has not corrected the problem after receiving a written warning, the employee will then receive a decision-making leave. The decision-making leave is one day off *with pay* (including shift premium). The purpose of the decision-making leave is to provide the employee the opportunity to decide whether he or she wants and is able to continue working for the company—which means following *all* the rules and doing a good job.

D. Unrelated Offenses

If an employee's conduct is unacceptable in two or more unrelated areas, the following steps of the positive discipline program will apply:

1. First offense—oral warning
2. Second offense—oral warning
3. Any third offense—written warning
4. Any fourth offense—decision leave
5. Any fifth offense—discharge

*Example:* John Smith has three attendance infractions in a thirty-day period and receives an oral warning. Three weeks later, Mr. Smith is found working without safety glasses. He now receives another oral warning for this infraction. Two weeks later Mr. Smith leaves fifteen minutes early to clean up for lunch break. For this violation of company policy he receives a written warning. Mr. Smith would then receive a decision leave for any fourth violation and would be discharged for any fifth violation.

E. Timeliness

For maximum effectiveness, disciplinary action should be taken as soon as a problem is identified. Warnings and decision leaves will normally be issued within three (3) working days of the infraction. If it is necessary to suspend an employee during working hours, the decision as to the type of disciplinary action that will be taken (decision leave or discharge) will be made within twenty-four hours (or the next working day) of the suspension. The employee will be informed as soon as the decision is reached. Time on suspension is unpaid.

F. Voiding of Disciplinary Actions

Each step of the positive discipline program provides a time limit after which a specific previous disciplinary action taken cannot be used for consideration in future steps of the disciplinary procedure. The following is the length of time each disciplinary action will remain in effect.

*(continued)*

---

**Figure 2.4** *Continued*

Oral warning—three (3) calendar months
Written warning—six (6) calendar months
Decision leave—nine (9) calendar months

*Example:* Oral warning effective date March 1, 1985, will become void on June 1, 1985, if no other disciplinary action has been necessary.

IV. Responsibilities

*Supervisors/general supervisors* will identify problem areas, counsel employees, and initiate disciplinary action. Will submit a status change requesting pay for a decision leave in a timely manner.

*Employee relations* counsels supervisors regarding problems of conduct and job performance and methods of discipline in order to ensure fair, equal, and consistent corrective action through the company.

*Oral warning* requires supervisor and manager approval.

*Written warning* requires supervisor, manager, and director approval.

*Decision leave* requires supervisor, manager, director, and employee relations approval.

*Discharge* requires supervisor, manager, director, and employee relations approval.

---

Adapted from material provided by Smith Tool Division, Smith International Inc.

---

management is fully committed to it, willing to put the resources into it to make it work, and patient enough to wait until it becomes part of the organization's culture before it pays dividends.

In the short term, the structured, inflexible, uniformly consistent type of program is the simplest to develop, implement, and administer. But in the long term, its use can be very costly and damaging to employee relations. Unfortunately, too many managers think only in the short term and take the course of least resistance. The relatively unstructured, flexible type of program is not without its potential risks. Once developed it cannot be forgotten. It does require continual monitoring, training in its use, guidance of users, reinforcement, and occasional control from executive-level managers. Failure to maintain the effort will cause erosion from misapplication and will eventually damage employee relations.

Within the extremes of highly structured and highly unstructured programs are countless combinations. Most organizations should provide some structure to the types and degrees of discipline that can be imposed for various forms of misconduct. Without some structure, managers will judge similar situations so differently that in time employees will perceive management as being arbitrary in dispensing discipline. Structure limits discretionary judgment and brings about more uniformity and consistency. With some structure, perceptions of arbitrariness are less likely to arise. For each particular rule or general category of employee responsibility, whichever way they are written, a range of positive and negative types of discipline with guidelines for their usage should be written. The various types of disciplinary action, how to determine which is appropriate, and how to apply them will be discussed in Chapter 5.

## Guidelines for Making a Program Work

For organizations that have used either structured, relatively inflexible discipline programs or where executive-level managers have made all discipline decisions, changing to a less structured, decentralized, merit-oriented program must be carefully planned and made operational in stages. It would be unwise for executive-level managers to abruptly relinquish control or dismantle a highly structured program. Doing this would place authority and responsibility in the hands of managers who have not been properly prepared to accept and effectively use it. Undoubtedly some managers could adapt quickly and perform well. Most could not, and this would cause many problems. The new program would eventually collapse, and executive-level management would likely return to the old way and be less willing to risk another change.

To avoid this scenario, the following guidelines for implementing a flexible program based on the use of the merit principle and judgment are suggested:

- All levels of management should be thoroughly trained in the system's philosophy, policies, and procedures.
- Training should be experientially oriented, with group involvement and case studies similar to ones likely to be encountered. Nothing turns trainees off more quickly than cases they perceive as not being relevant to their environment and experiences.
- If employee misconduct isn't a serious and pervasive problem, the program's introduction should be low key and positive.

• For at least the first year, supervisors and perhaps even middle-level managers should not be given unilateral authority to determine and impose discipline. Initially their role should be one of developing the case and recommending courses of action. If the recommended action is consistent with the program's philosophy and guidelines outlined in the policies, it should be approved. The authority to approve or reject recommended discipline should reside with either the head of the human resources function or a top-level operations manager. If the recommended action is inconsistent with the program and/or with how similar cases have been handled, the recommendation should be disapproved and the reasons carefully explained.

• As managers learn to think and act within the program's framework, they should be given the authority to make discipline decisions without advance approval from higher authority.

• The more managers develop competency and proficiency in handling disciplinary situations, the more authority they should be given to act independently within the program's framework. However, written records must be maintained, and summary reports should be prepared for review by higher authority.

• Under no circumstances should individual managers be given the exclusive authority to terminate or demote employees. Both types of discipline are most serious, and it is best for all concerned to have input from executive-level management and/or human resources function specialists to ensure that just cause exists and the severe discipline is warranted.

• The human resources function should be the central depository for all official information pertaining to employees' records. Analyses of disciplinary actions for all employees should be on a continuing basis to ensure that different organization units are consistent in their applications of discipline. In other words, if two supervisors in separate units are given the same case to decide, each should independently arrive at the same or similar decision.

• Results of analyses pertaining to how to handle cases and how cases have been handled should be communicated to managers.

• Feedback obtained from meetings, suggestion programs, due process procedures, and other forms of upward communications should be reviewed to determine if the program is working properly.

• Occasions will arise when an exception to the application of a rule will occur. These must be infrequent, and the reasons for the exception should be documented. It is important to remember that the more exceptions are made to rules, the more diluted and unenforceable the rules become.

## Considerations for Applying Merit

In Chapters 1 and 2 the terms *flexibility, judgment,* and *merit principle* have been used. Before opening the book, you had some understanding of their meanings. *Merit, flexibility,* and *judgment* are terms frequently used in all types of organizations. Most organizations and their managers profess to give rewards (raises, promotions, privileges) on the basis of merit. As stated before, the merit principle should be applied to the discipline process. The merit principle is at the heart of any equitable program. In judging merit the following factors should be weighed and questions answered:

1. Has just cause for taking disciplinary action been established?
2. Has the employee violated a major or minor employee responsibility?
3. What general approach—rehabilitative, punitive, or some combination—should be used in this case?
4. What are the types and degrees of disciplinary action that can be used?
5. What specific types of discipline—written warning, transfer, suspension, decision leave—should be considered in this case?
6. What is the employee's past disciplinary record?
   a. Frequency or pattern of misconduct
   b. Seriousness of misconduct
7. What is the employee's record of service?
   a. Length of continuous service
   b. Performance as compared to standards
   c. History of raises and promotions
   d. Attendance as compared to standards
8. What changes in behavior have been demonstrated by the employee as a result of previous disciplinary action being imposed?
9. What are the organization's past practices in administering discipline?
10. What are the organization's present policies and practices?
11. Why did the employee engage in misconduct?

12. How have other employees with similar records or similar facts and circumstances been treated?

13. If discharge is being considered, can the employee be easily replaced?

14. What is the employee's position and what are his or her responsibilities?

15. What will be the reaction of other employees if this employee is discharged? Will the action increase or decrease respect for management?

16. What extenuating or mitigating facts or events in the employee's job or personal life are affecting his or her behavior? This includes the employee's physical and emotional health.

17. Is the case against the employee strong enough to sustain a review by others either internal or external to the organization?

While various approaches to discipline may be used, their application should be progressive in severity. All things considered, the degree of discipline must fit the seriousness of the misconduct. Exceptions to the application of progressive discipline should only occur in cases where employees know or should have reasonably known that one violation could mean possible termination. Examples would include dishonesty, disloyalty, immoral or indecent conduct, fighting, deliberate destruction of company assets, possession of weapons or explosives, possession or use of drugs.

## Documentation

In any disciplinary situation management must show that reason or just cause for discipline existed and the action taken was appropriate. Documentation is essential to ensure fairness to the disciplined employee and to defend the case through either internal or external due process proceedings. Documentation of misconduct is obvious. Less obvious is management's responsibility to maintain accurate, up-to-date records of the positive as well as the negative aspects of employees' job-related behavior. Managements all too often lose cases they should not because of poor documentation, failure to properly consider the employee's record of service, and poor preparation for due process proceedings.

Before actual discipline is imposed, the employee must be properly charged and given an opportunity to present information that may bear on the situation. Remember, the employee is innocent until proven guilty.

In some instances, however, suspension from work may occur before a formal disciplinary interview is conducted. An example would be an employee who works with children and is accused of child molesting. Allowing the accused employee to continue to work could jeopardize the children's welfare, anger parents, damage the organization's image, and increase the risk of lawsuits. This illustrates the importance of prompt investigation. The employee is living under a cloud of suspicion. Even if the employee is later found to be innocent, the cloud of suspicion may not disappear if it lingers too long. Other examples would be an employee who handles money and is charged with misappropriation or embezzlement, a law enforcement officer who is charged with using excessive force, and a medical practitioner who is being charged with malpractice.

In any situation where an employee charged with misconduct is subsequently found to be innocent, he or she is entitled to have the suspension rescinded and to be paid for lost income. In some cases a public apology may be warranted. A wrongfully charged employee who can prove damage to his or her reputation can bring suit against the employer. Damage awards can be substantial.

In organizations where employees are represented by a union, the union should be kept informed about disciplinary action being considered against a member. Copies of any written warnings should be given to the union.

## Counseling

Counseling is an implicit part of any discipline program. Management must help the employee help him- or herself to change behavior. Management must also forewarn employees of the possible consequences for continued misconduct. Counseling will be further discussed in Chapters 4 and 5. Whenever an employee is forewarned, a written record should be made. It may be written in detailed or summary form, but it should be shown to the employee, and, if requested, a copy should be given to him or her. Written records corroborate what was said and serve as a data base for determining possible future actions.

## Due Process

No discipline program, irrespective of its philosophy, policies, and procedural format, can be equitably and fairly administered if employees do not have the right to appeal imposed discipline through a due process mechanism. Generally, the procedure should be written and have some structure. In the unionized organization such mechanisms are known as grievance procedures; in nonunion organizations they are usually titled differently. They usually serve a similar purpose as a negotiated grievance procedure. These procedures are typically called open-door policies. Other titles are the "I Am Concerned Program," "Employee Speak-Up Program," and "Employee Problem-Solving Procedure." Though an appeals process should exist separately from the discipline program because its scope and coverage goes beyond disciplinary action, it is an integral part of any disciplinary program. The reason it should exist separately is that it serves many other purposes in addition to due process. A due process mechanism also:

- Allows upward communications of matters of concern or interest to employees

- Allows downward communications from management when more traditional channels should not be used

- Provides a safety valve through which employees can express their feelings in a neutral environment

- Keeps supervisors and higher-level managers cognizant of the employee relations aspects of their jobs

- Encourages managers at all levels to take the initiative in solving problems

- Provides executive-level management with firsthand knowledge of what may be occurring on a day-to-day basis in the workplace

Many nonunion organizations still do not have formal mechanisms or procedures for resolving employees' concerns or complaints. They are essential in today's work environment. The civil rights movement has spilled over into the workplace and affected all employees, including managers. All employees expect their rights in the workplace to be as well protected as their civil rights. Feelings of mistreatment, abuse of power, and injustice are the main reasons why employees form or join unions. They are also the major reasons why in unionized organizations adversarial relations continue to persist. An effective due process procedure is one of the best ways to reduce the likelihood that employees will seek redress from the courts or government for perceived injustice. Even when cases are brought before outsiders (unemployment insurance referees, workers' compensation boards, human rights agencies, National Labor Relations Board administration law judges, arbitrators, and the courts), managers are in a better position to defend their actions if an equitably administered due process procedure was used.

The two main differences between a due process or grievance procedure in unionized and nonunion organizations are: (1) employees' right to have representation and (2) binding arbitration as the last step. In unionized organizations a major responsibility of the union is to represent its members' interests in matters relating to the employer-employee relationship. Those employees represented by the union are entitled to have union leaders represent them in attempts to have grievances resolved. When grievances are being discussed at lower organizational levels, employees' representatives are usually elected or appointed union officials who are also employees of the organization. When grievances are discussed at higher organizational levels, union representatives who are not employees usually participate in the process. Much has been written about the relative advantages and disadvantages of having others represent aggrieved employees' interests. The disadvantages for management in allowing employees the right to representation slightly outweigh the advantages of having them represent themselves. This is primarily because the relationship between the person representing the aggrieved employee and management becomes a factor in addressing the issue. This can complicate matters and cause management to take positions they might not take if a third party were not involved. If representation is provided for, employee representatives should always be elected by employees and not appointed by management.

In unionized organizations nearly all negotiated grievance procedures provide for an appeal to arbitration as the final step to settle the matter. Arbitrators are people mutually selected by the parties to the grievance who hear the case and render a final and binding decision. The arbitrator's authority to render a binding decision is derived from language written into the negotiated grievance procedure. Most managers, particularly those in nonunion organizations, do not relish the idea of having an outsider make decisions that may greatly affect their authority and flexibility. It is very unusual for due process procedures in nonunion organizations to provide for an appeal to arbitration. The final level of appeal is normally the chief executive or chief human resources officer. Some organizations use employee fact-finding boards as a prefinal step. Board members are usually nonmanagement employees who review the case and make a nonbinding recommendation to executive-level management. When no provision exists for appeal to a neutral third party, a tremendous burden is placed on all managers, particularly executive-level managers, to maintain employees' confidence in the system's fairness. Regretfully, employees with or without substantive proof too often believe that open-door policies swing only one way. Once a due process system loses credibility, it is not likely to be regained.

Though the right to appeal to arbitration is an effective means of ensuring justice to aggrieved employees, arbitration is not without its disadvantages. First, it is an admission by the parties that they could not resolve the matter among themselves. Second, the arbitrator could render a decision that neither party likes. Where arbitration is available it should be used infrequently. This places the responsibility on management and labor to work cooperatively instead of adversarially. Where arbitration is not available, the due process procedure can work quite well if management continually strives to maintain a climate of mutual trust, confidence, and respect with employees. A due process procedure exists as a communication tool and as a safety device to avoid potential problems and resolve existing problems, not to create or perpetuate them.

## What Should Be Included in a Due Process Program?

A formal written procedure for resolving employees' concerns, complaints, criticisms, grievances, and so on, whether it is called a grievance procedure, open-door policy, or whatever else, should contain the following elements:

1. It should stress the importance of attempting to resolve grievances informally at the first level of management.

2. It should provide the necessary form for formally writing grievances that cannot be settled informally.

3. Once a grievance is put in writing, all responses from management should also be in writing.

4. The various levels or steps should be identified.

5. The titles of those responsible for handling grievances at the various steps should be identified.

6. Time limits for the filing of a grievance and processing it through the various levels must be established and strictly adhered to unless both parties agree to a waiver.

7. Adequate opportunity to investigate a grievance should be given to those concerned.

8. Information should be made available on a need-to-know basis. Care must be taken to avoid releasing confidential and sensitive information to those not needing it.

9. Provision should be made for handling priority issues such as termination.

10. Provision should be made in nonunion procedures for employees to bring the grievance directly to executive-level management. Executive-level management must use discretion and judgment in determining when employees can bypass their supervisors and the human resources function and take their grievances directly to top management. Allowing employees complete freedom to go right to the top anytime they so choose could undermine the role of lower-level managers. It could also cause executive-level management to become overly involved in matters that could best be handled by lower-level managers.

## Summary

As internal and external conditions change, new policies and procedures must be developed and existing ones must be either changed or scrapped. The intent of this chapter has been to guide readers in developing a new discipline program or changing an existing one.

No single program is best for all organizations. The scope, content, and structure of a program will be influenced by many factors. Some of these are the following:

- *The type of people employed.* Some people, by virtue of their values, attitudes, and experiences, are more prone than others to becoming discipline problems. The employee who has had recurring difficulties with authority figures (teachers, parents, police, previous bosses) is more likely to be a discipline problem than the employee who has conformed to required standards of conduct. The employee who is frustrated by a lack of success in trying to work within the system is more likely to be a discipline problem than the employee who has achieved success from working within the system.

- *The types of jobs in the organization.* Where work environments are highly regulated by law, processes are integrated, and uniformity and consistency are required, jobs are likely to be structured. The more jobs are structured, the more people must be required to conform to prescribed ways of working. The job of a research chemist is likely to be far less structured than that of an assembler on an integrated assembly line. The chemist would have more flexibility than the assembler in determining how work should be done.

▪ *The environment in which work is done or business conducted.*
When competition is keen, pressure to meet deadlines intense, resources limited, and client demands high and their loyalty low, tension in the workplace tends to be high. When stress is high, anxiety
and apprehension can also be high. In such environments conflict
and confrontation are more likely to occur. The possible result is a
more frequent need to discipline. The same can be said of organizations where gamesmanship and political backstabbing are the norm.

▪ *The numbers of people employed.* The larger an organization, the
greater the likelihood of inconsistencies in applying top management's philosophy and policies. Structure becomes necessary to ensure a measure of uniformity and consistency.

▪ *Management's philosophy toward employees.* Where management
views employees as just another resource to be used and disposed of
when it's worn out, the attitude will be reflected in relationships with
employees.

▪ *Top management's philosophy toward dispersing authority and
their confidence in lower levels of management to properly use authority.*
An effective program is one that accomplishes what it is designed to
do and is perceived as being equitable and fairly administered by a
majority of employees. In view of the evolving employee rights movement, managements are being called on to restructure their traditional approaches to discipline. The most difficult aspect of making a
merit-based program work is being consistent while retaining flexibility. While most managers would prefer to have considerable flexibility in applying discipline, they recognize the need to be consistent.
The right balance will vary from organization to organization.
Though management will shape the organization's program, employees and society will ultimately sanction what exists or force change.

Chapter 3 addresses the first step in applying discipline, namely,
the determination of whether substantial cause for discipline exists.

## Key Points

▪ Change is inevitable. Managers must continually respond and
adapt to it.

▪ Change per se is neither good or bad. How it is perceived, how it
is acted on or reacted to, and ultimately what results are derived
from it determine whether it is good or bad.

▪ As an organization grows, the number of employees increases,
and authority is delegated to more people, the likelihood of incon-

sistencies in decisions also increases. To avoid or reduce the probability of this occurring, written policies, procedures, and programs should be developed.

- Written, publicized employee responsibilities (rules) should exist in all formal organizations to establish what is generally unacceptable behavior.
- No specific number of rules is best for all organizations. Rules may be specific or general.
- Standards of conduct should be based on prevailing social values and legitimate business interests.
- Highly structured, progressive discipline programs ensure consistency and all but eliminate the need for judgment. Such programs are inherently unfair to employees because unequal situations are treated equally.
- Semistructured, progressive discipline programs can provide for consistency and flexibility to apply the merit principle.
- Discipline should be given according to what the recipient merits. Merit means a number of factors should be weighed in determining the form and degree of discipline.
- Different standards of conduct could exist for employees in different job environments within the same organization.
- Charges of misconduct should be substantiated by documentation.
- All formal organizations should have a system for due process. Free of fear of reprisal, employees should have the right to question actions taken against them. Without internal due process, employees are more likely to perceive mistreatment. Furthermore, employees will be more inclined to seek redress outside the organization.
- Due process systems can be as informal as the open-door policy or as structured as the negotiated grievance procedure common to virtually all labor agreements.
- Counseling should be part of any discipline program. A basic objective of counseling in discipline situations is to get the employee to act responsibly and practice self-discipline.

## Discussion Questions

1. Explain why traditions and past practices can often be difficult to change.

2. Why does success so often cause complacency?

3. Discuss the advantages and disadvantages of centralizing authority.

4. Why should rules be written and publicized?

5. How does one determine which rules are the major ones, where one violation could mean termination?

6. Under what circumstances would a highly structured, progressive discipline program be appropriate?

7. Under what conditions would such a program adversely affect employer-employee relations?

8. Discuss the problems likely to be encountered in administering a flexible discipline program.

9. How can these problems be avoided or minimized?

10. Why must management be consistent in enforcing standards of conduct?

11. How can management justify requiring some employees to start work at a specific time while allowing others to have flexible start time?

12. How is merit built into a discipline program?

13. What are the two basic differences between most union-negotiated grievance procedures and employer-initiated due process programs?

14. Discuss what factors should be considered in developing a due process program.

# 3 Determining Just Cause

Our country was founded on principles of individuality, free enterprise, and personal liberty. As citizens our personal liberties are among the most respected and best protected in the world. Laws guaranteeing individual rights, including free speech, systems and procedures for ensuring due process, overlapping court jurisdictions, and social values supporting equitable justice and fairness, have served to guarantee the protection and maintenance of democracy and individual liberty. However, with respect to personal liberty, there has been a basic incongruity between the ways society and corporations function. It is unlikely that business organizations will ever be truly representative democracies.

But our society is in the midst of major social, economic, political, and technological changes. These changes have been evolving during the past twenty years and longer. For many reasons, especially financial self-interest, far too many managers observed but did not see, heard but did not listen to, the forces of change. Now these managers must recognize that the ability to adapt to change is essential to survival and prosperity. Proactive managers anticipate and respond to change before the need is clearly present. Reactive managers act after the fact.

Through the 1980s and beyond, managers will have to find ways to effectively cope with and even capitalize on a variety of far-reaching changes. One such change is the employee rights movement. Employees are now demanding that their institutional, industrial, and organizational rights, or what can be called workplace rights, be on the same level as their civil rights. Outside the workplace people's civil rights are well respected and protected. But work environments, particularly business corporations, have historically operated in a highly authoritarian way compared to government. Historically, people have left many of their rights behind them when they became employees of some organization. For example, employees are rarely free to openly criticize their employer and bosses without risking reprisal, while as citizens they can criticize the government, its laws, and elected officials. In business, where loyalty is highly regarded, open criticism, especially if it occurs outside the organization, is often *perceived* as disloyalty, though sometimes this perception is wrong.

Today, even the most basic tenets of the traditional employer-employee relationship are being challenged. Though, as mentioned above, it is unlikely that business organizations will ever be truly representative democracies, their top-down authoritarian approach to managing people, as well as the relative absence of workplace rights and systems for ensuring due process is out of touch with contemporary values and must change.

Many have advocated democracy in the workplace as a way to humanize jobs. However, participation, which is often confused with democracy, is perhaps a more practical approach. With participation, employee involvement is considered, but management still retains the authority to accept or reject, while in a democracy, majority rule prevails and each person has an equal vote. Management by the democratic process is usually a cumbersome, inefficient, and impractical way to manage a business. Employee participation in decision making, however, can be useful under the right conditions:

- If employees want to be involved
- If employees possess the skills and experience to make contributions
- If management is sincerely interested in listening to and considering employee input

## The Evolution of the Employee Rights Movement

The 1930s was a period of major social and economic change. Many laws pertaining to the employer-employee relationship were passed during the 1930s, including the Fair Labor Standards Act, the Davis-Bacon Act, the Norris LaGuardia Act, and the Wagner Act. The significant and dramatic changes that occurred in a relatively short span of time had been evolving for nearly forty years. As history shows, the period proved to be tumultuous for both employers and employees. During this time, those employees most directly affected by the changes were the so-called working class. These were the hourly wage earners in lower-level jobs primarily centered in the nation's factories, mills, and mines. The sweeping reforms to a far lesser degree affected professional, technical, service, clerical, and administrative personnel.

In the 1960s we again witnessed many changes in the areas of employer-employee relations and workers' rights. The most comprehensive piece of legislation passed during this period was the Civil Rights Act of 1964. Title VII of the act (as amended in 1972) is known as the Equal Employment Opportunity Act. The 1964 act created the Equal Employment Opportunity Commission (EEOC). Title VII of the act prohibits employers from refusing to hire, fire, or otherwise discriminate against any person with respect to compensation, terms and conditions of employment, or privileges because of race, color, religion, sex, or national origin. The EEOC was empowered to investigate complaints and ensure compliance with the law.

Though many of the laws enacted during this period were primarily aimed at correcting social injustices, business organizations were directly affected. The civil rights movement spilled over into the workplace and became the employee rights movement.

From a primarily agricultural economy, we evolved into a manufacturing economy. For the first half of this century, smokestack industries dominated the American business scene. In the 1950s and 1960s we evolved into a service economy. In the 1970s and 1980s energy, high technology, and information have been the growth areas. With these changes have come changes in the structure of the workforce. With the growth of service industries came increased numbers of white-collar jobs. In the mid-1950s the number of white-collar workers surpassed the number of blue-collar workers, and the gap has been widening ever since. In the 1970s the overall demand for technical and professional workers outpaced the demand for all other types of skills. The effects of the silicon revolution are just starting to be felt.

For a number of reasons today's employees are significantly different from their counterparts of the thirties, forties, and fifties. Of particular importance is their difference in attitude toward authority, work, relationships, and rights. We have become an increasingly rights-conscious society. Unions and their members achieved protection under the law and collective bargaining rights in the 1930s. Minorities achieved meaningful protection from wrongful discrimination under the Civil Rights Act of 1964 and companion laws of the period. The evolving concern is for the workplace rights of all employees, particularly those who are nonunion and nonminority. The so-called new breed of employees, namely, those born during the baby-boom period of the 1940s and later, now constitutes the majority of workers. As a group they are less willing to accept the authority of others without first knowing the "hows" and "whys." They are also more vocal and demanding, have higher expectations, are more sensitive about their rights, and have shown a greater willingness to do something about perceived injustices. Organizations and their managers have often had a difficult time understanding, relating to, coping with, and accepting these values and attitudes.

Those organizations and their managers who are unwilling or unable to accommodate, compromise, and in part accept these new values and attitudes into the corporate culture, operational policies, procedures, and systems will experience increasingly costly adverse employee relations. It is interesting to note that many of the highly successful, rapid growth, high-technology organizations that conduct business in highly competitive markets have developed and implemented some of the most innovative management practices and progressive personnel policies. For example, the management philosophy and practices of Intel, IBM, Hewlett-Packard, Proctor & Gamble, Black & Decker, Texas Instruments, and Motorola are far more innovative and progressive than those of many companies in the automobile, steel, and public utility industries. Deteriorating organizations and industries are often the ones that have not adapted to change and have clung to traditions and past practices that have outlived their usefulness.

When cooperative employee relations exist and employees implicitly trust managers to act responsibly, they are less willing to form or join unions, quit, or turn to the government or the courts to seek redress for perceived injustices. When adversarial relations exist and trust is absent, employees will take whatever action they deem appropriate to protect themselves. Figure 3.1 shows examples of such actions.

Why has it taken most managers so long to recognize the significance of the employees' rights movement? And why is it that many still do not? At the risk of oversimplification, the most probable reason is that economic necessity has not mandated change. Though economic interests are important organizational values, a number of factors, some already mentioned, provide incentive for managers to address the employee rights issue. They are as follows:

- Influence of unions in unionized organizations

## Figure 3.1 Ways Employees Can Retaliate against Supervisors or the Organization

- Forget to do something the supervisor told him or her to do
- Do a halfway job or as little as possible
- Fake illness or injury on the job
- Plan days to be absent, especially during critical work periods
- Work in slow motion, stall, or waste time
- Misplace parts or work orders
- Repeatedly ask questions about how to do something or why it needs to be done
- Steal something of value
- When asked to do something, contend that it is not in his or her job description
- Complain about anything and everything
- Refuse to comply with directions
- File individual and group grievances
- Sabotage or destroy something that belongs to the organization or the person who is causing problems
- Give dirty looks, be disrespectful, and do other things to generally keep the person who is exploiting him or her in a state of anxiety
- Complain that it is not his or her turn and that he or she is being singled out for harassment purposes
- Accuse his or her supervisor of prejudice, racism, bigotry, and the like
- Spread rumors that are untrue
- Make frequent trips to the bathroom

- Fear of being unionized in nonunion organizations
- Enactment of civil rights and companion legislation
- Examples of how successful competitors, particularly foreign competitors, manage their employees
- Increased litigation by employees and court decisions supporting employees' complaints
- Declining productivity, profitability, and economic order
- Recognition that employees' values have changed
- Changing values of managers

The concept of employee rights has many components. The major ones include reasonable written rules; limits on management's authority; rights to privacy; freedom to speak openly without fear of reprisal; promotion, raises, and other rewards distributed on the basis of merit; just cause for discipline; and a fairly administered due process system.

In organizations where employees are represented by a union, the negotiated grievance procedure provides employees covered by the labor agreement with the right to file grievances and process them through the procedure's various steps. Nearly all negotiated grievance procedures provide for impartial arbitration as the final step. For readers unfamiliar with the arbitration process and the role of arbitrators, the following brief explanations are provided.

## The Arbitration Process

An arbitration proceeding is a relatively informal, quasi-judicial hearing. Representatives from labor and management present their respective positions in regard to an unresolved issue to an impartial outsider or panel. The individual or panel is asked to render a decision to settle the matter. More than one dispute may be presented at a hearing, and a dispute may involve more than one issue. The arbitrator may be one person or an odd-numbered board, generally not more than three. Anyone can call him- or herself an arbitrator. However, nearly all labor dispute arbitrators are selected from lists of names provided by either the Federal Mediation and Conciliation Service (FMCS) or the American Arbitration Association (AAA). Obtaining recognition or certification by either or both of these organizations requires considerable demonstrated competence and experience in labor relations. Impartiality, professional and personal integrity, common sense, sensitivity, and other qualities are essential for maintaining acceptability with labor and management. With infrequent exceptions, arbitrators are mutually selected by the parties to a dispute rather than being appointed by either the FMCS or AAA.

Arbitrators get their authority to decide issues presented to them from language contained in the negotiated labor agreement. In the private sector arbitrators' decisions as stipulated in the agreement are almost universally binding on the parties. In the public sector some agreements stipulate that an arbitrator's decision is not binding and management still retains the final authority to accept or reject the arbitrator's decision.

Provisions do exist under the law for the courts to overturn arbitrators' decisions, though the bases for such action are limited.

Since the U.S. Supreme Court's celebrated Lincoln Mills case of 1957 (353 U.S. 448) and the Steelworkers' Trilogy of 1960 (363 U.S. 564, 363 U.S. 574, and 363 U.S. 593), where the Court affirmed the process of arbitration and the role of arbitrators in settling grievances raised under the collective bargaining agreement, courts have shown considerable reluctance to overturn arbitrators' decisions. The principal reason for the courts' reluctance is their recognition that arbitrators usually possess unique knowledge about workplace environments and employer-employee relations not generally possessed by judges.

However, in recent years courts have become increasingly involved in employee relations issues. Where arbitration is available to employees, discipline cases most commonly end up in court either concurrently with or after arbitration because allegations of discrimination based on race, sex, age, misrepresentation by the union, or other criteria covered by law are involved. The result is that a case may be tried through the grievance procedure and again in court. Discipline cases may also end up before government administrative agencies such as the Equal Employment Opportunity Commission (EEOC), the National Labor Relations Board (NLRB) or their state-level equivalents, and civil service commissions.

In nonunion organizations discipline cases may end up in the courts and/or government agencies for the reasons cited above. The likelihood of this occurring increases significantly if an organization does not have a formal due process system or has one that is known to be unfairly administered.

Employees at all levels, including managers, are increasingly demanding that their workplace rights be protected on a par with their civil rights. Because employees are more inclined to seek redress for perceived injustices, organizations must be prepared to defend decisions regarding how employees are treated. They must be able to defend actions whether the matter is being pursued through internal or external due process. This responsibility does not reside with attorneys, personnel, or human resources function specialists. It resides with managers at all levels. Legal counsel or staff support should be used for guidance and assistance and not for assuming full responsibility.

## Establishing Just Cause to Discipline

Some readers may now be saying to themselves, "Wait a minute, why do I have to defend my actions? I am responsible for maintaining an efficient operation and a safe workplace. It's my prerogative to manage and, when necessary, discipline employees. If an employee is unhappy with my action and lodges a complaint, he or she, as the plaintiff, must show that I am wrong."

As a matter of well-established practice, management has the responsibility to first present testimony and evidence to prove the disciplined employee was guilty of misconduct. The rationale for this is as follows:

- Our culture and social values require that the accused is presumed innocent until proven guilty by the charging party.

- Management initiated the disciplinary action for reasons known to the employer. If the employee had to first prove innocence, he or she would have to show no guilt for anything at anytime.

- Requiring that managers show substantive reasons for discipline is a highly effective way to minimize the misuse of authority. Managers who can impose discipline without having to account for it are more likely to abuse their authority than those who must give an accounting.

- Proving cause for discipline is the first step in moving toward the goal of constructive discipline.

- Showing cause significantly reduces the likelihood that disciplined employees will become martyrs among their peers.

- Being able to demonstrate cause can be used to strengthen employee relations.

- Proving cause facilitates the justice process and the fair treatment of employees.

- As a defensive act, proving cause can be used to support a position if the matter is referred to third parties.

- In unionized organizations, most agreements contain a provision requiring that just cause for discipline exist before any action is taken.

In unionized organizations, where formal due process procedures almost always exist, managers have usually had more experience in proving cause for discipline than managers in nonunion organizations. Discipline cases are the ones most frequently heard by arbitrators. Over the years the published decisions of arbitrators have established a foundation of knowledge to guide managers in substantiating just cause for discipline. Managers in nonunion organizations must recognize and accept that the principles, standards, guidelines, and criteria used by arbitrators and managers in unionized organizations to show cause will increasingly be applied by external authorities to nonunion cases brought before them. In fact, judges and government administrative officers will apply even stricter stan-

## Case Jean Sims

Jean Sims, a supervisor at the local sporting goods company, is faced with a problem. Recently, while on her lunch break, she overheard several employees discussing the results of the weekend football pool. One of the men had won $150 and was bragging about his ability to pick the winners.

Gambling, games of chance, and lotteries on company time or premises are strictly forbidden. The minimum discipline that may be given is a three-day suspension from work.

Although she witnessed only a few employees participating in the football pool, she knows others are involved. She believes that she must discipline the ones she saw but is unsure about how to handle those she has not seen but knows are involved.

### Questions

1. What advice would you give to Jean to help her handle the matter?
2. Should Jean get involved or turn her back on the matter? Why?

---

dards, because many either have training in the law or are responsible for interpreting and enforcing the law. They will tend to draw on that knowledge and on perceptions of their roles in making judgments. This will be especially true if they are unfamiliar with the "common law of the shop," which is simply the employer-employee relations environment and framework.

In addition, the standards employed by arbitrators largely reflect prevailing social values and employee perceptions of fairness. I'm not suggesting that managers in nonunion organizations adopt arbitration as part of due process or rigidly adhere to the general standards employed by arbitrators in discipline cases. Arbitrators themselves vary somewhat in how they apply the standards that have taken shape over the years and will continue to evolve as changes occur in social values and the law. I do suggest that to be in consonance with prevailing values, the law, and employee expectations, managers use the standards to guide thoughts and actions, primarily to ensure a high degree of fairness to all concerned. Another sound reason for doing so is to be on solid ground if the matter cannot be satisfactorily resolved through internal due process and is appealed to third parties, in which case managers will be called on to defend their actions. It should be remembered that in discipline situations, especially where termination is involved, courts and government agency administrators tend to be more sympathetic to employees than to employers.

Many reasons account for this prevailing sentiment. The two most significant are (1) management's track record of mistreating employees and (2) changing attitudes about the employer-employee relationship. If managers improve on their record of fairly and equitably treating employees, the current sympathetic attitude toward employees will be tempered. But this will not happen overnight. Therefore, for the foreseeable future, managers must overcompensate by ensuring they have properly applied discipline. The first step in defending an action is to convincingly demonstrate that sufficient reason to initiate discipline existed.

Though the primary burden of proof properly rests with management, disciplined employees cannot idly maintain their innocence of any wrongdoing. Irrespective of who is judging the matter, employees, like managers, must present oral testimony, as well as written and other evidence, to support their position. They may claim complete innocence, partial guilt, or that imposed discipline is overly severe.

## Considerations for Determining Just Cause

To help managers determine if sufficient reason to take disciplinary action exists, the following guidelines are provided:

1. Employee responsibilities or standards of conduct should be known and understood by employees. Employees cannot be expected to observe required standards of conduct if they are unaware of them or do not understand them. Ignorance of a rule is occasionally a legitimate defense. The following example illustrates this point:

> Sally Abrams makes a personal long-distance telephone call on a company telephone. She notes the time and charges and intends to reimburse the company. Before she does so, however, the call is discovered and she is reprimanded by her boss. The company has an unwritten policy prohibiting employees from using company telephones for per-

sonal business. Sally contends that she was unaware of the rule. Her boss says that ignorance is no excuse, even though he admits the policy is unwritten, has not been formally communicated, and is probably not widely known. Unless management can apply the principle of common sense, Sally has a good case to get the discipline rescinded.

It must be pointed out that ignorance as a defense can be used only in situations where management has failed to make the rule known and where, by virtue of common sense, employees could not be expected to have known such behavior was unacceptable.

2. The written employee responsibilities should be directly related to the nature of the organization's operations and business environment. Employees cannot be required to conform to rules that are neither relevant nor make common sense. However, employees can be required to conform to limits on dress, hair styles, and activities if such requirements are legitimately defensible for legal, safety, or business considerations.

The following example shows how the same rule can be appropriate in one organization and inappropriate in another. The rule is: male employees cannot have beards or mustaches. The executives of both organizations are conservative and do not personally approve of beards or mustaches. The community is also very conservative. Organization no. 1 is the local police department. Organization no. 2 is a factory doing business nationwide through local distributors. Most employees have no direct contact with customers.

In the police department the rule would be appropriate because management could easily show that the community would react negatively to beards and mustaches. In the factory employees having beards and mustaches would not adversely affect business; therefore, the rule could be judged as unreasonable. An exception could occur if safety considerations were used to defend the rule.

3. In relatively minor instances of misconduct where only a verbal reprimand is warranted, no formal written warning should be issued. However, a record of the verbal warning and resulting discussion should be made.

4. Whenever a formal change of misconduct is warranted, any and all charges must be clearly stated in writing. Whenever possible, the specific written rules violated should be cited.

5. Employees who fail to abide by the rules must be forewarned of the possible consequences for continued misconduct. They must clearly understand that a positive change in behavior is expected and that action will be taken if it is not forthcoming. Exceptions to the

necessity of forewarning are for such misbehavior as immoral conduct, fighting, falsification of records, coming to work or working under the influence of drugs or intoxicants, major theft, and gross insubordination. In such cases, by virtue of common sense, employees should know that one violation could result in discharge. The word *could* instead of *would* or *may* instead of *will* should be used. Words like *would* or *will* leave no room for flexibility and thus the ability to apply judgment. When flexibility is absent, choices do not exist. If a rule states that any employee who uses, possesses, or is under the influence of any intoxicant will be fired regardless of quality and length of service, management is bound to fire anyone who is caught breaking the rule. Any exceptions would cripple the rule's enforceability. The following example illustrates how such a strict policy could have a disastrous effect:

> Chuck Askew has been with the company for thirty years. He is a hard-working, loyal employee. One day he comes to work stone drunk. He is caught and fired because the rule provides for no exceptions.

Obviously, the effect of such strict enforcement is disastrous. Askew will become a martyr among his peers. Rumors will spread and respect for management will erode. In this case it would have been wise for management to make an exception and not fire Askew.

Occasions certainly exist, however, where strict enforcement of a rule becomes necessary. The following example makes the point:

### Notice to All Employees

> It has come to management's attention that a serious safety hazard for all employees has not been alleviated because of employees' using and/or being under the influence of intoxicants on company premises in violation of publicized rules and regulations. Discipline short of discharge has not been effective. Therefore, effective the date of this notification, any employee found in violation of Rule 8 ("Use, possession, or being under the influence of intoxicants, narcotics, or any hallucinatory drugs on company premises") will be discharged regardless of length of service and/or past record.
>
> Please take this matter seriously. We hope that understanding the seriousness of this rule will solve our problem. Please keep in mind that there will be no exceptions to the discharge.

Notice that management said why stricter enforcement of the rule had become necessary. Leniency had not worked and the problem had to be controlled. Under these circumstances the no-exception policy would be appropriate. Now what if this policy were in effect and the employee referenced in the previous example was caught. Would the effect of his discharge be any different? The answer is yes and no. He might still become a matyr. However, because abuse of the rule had gotten out of hand and lesser discipline had failed to control it, many employees would understand and accept that extreme action as proper. Furthermore, if the action were appealed, it would likely be upheld. Again, a legitimate basis existed for taking extreme action.

6. Except for instances where immediate action is required, a fair and impartial investigation of the employee's alleged misconduct should be carried out in a timely manner. When immediate action is required, the best procedure is to suspend the employee pending the results of the investigation. Suspension during an investigation would be proper, for example, where an employee responsible for handling finances is accused of misappropriation or embezzlement. If the investigation shows that the employee is completely innocent of any wrongdoing, compensation for all losses incurred should be made. A timely investigation is one conducted within three to five workdays from the date misconduct occurred. Most investigations can be completed within a week, although some will take longer. Facts, testimony, and other evidence should be obtained while they are fresh. In addition, it is unfair to an employee charged with misconduct to have to undergo the stress associated with delayed investigation.

7. The documented results of any investigation must produce sufficient evidence or proof of guilt to support charges and impose discipline. The degree of proof required is proportional to the seriousness of the misconduct, the employee's overall record of service, and related factors. Misconduct that could result in termination and seriously impair the employee's chances for future employment should require proof of guilt beyond reasonable doubt. This is not to imply that the rigid standards of absolute proof required by courts for criminal law cases must be met.

8. In order to effect discipline, the organization's expressed standards of conduct must have been consistently enforced. This does not mean that because certain employees may have eluded discipline for known misconduct or misconduct that management *should* have known occurred, an employee now charged with the same or similar misconduct cannot be disciplined. It means, instead, that management cannot legitimately apply and enforce rules on a selective or subjective basis.

## Case  Paul Conlon

Paul Conlon has been an average worker at the company for the past fourteen years. He is in his late fifties and in failing health. Though reputed to be a heavy drinker, he has never been observed to be under the influence of alcohol on the job. Except when he walked off the job without permission eight years ago, he has never received any discipline. He was placed on probation for six months and suspended for a week without pay.

Four years ago Paul contracted tuberculosis and a circulatory disease. As a result he was off work for two years on a medical disability leave. The disease caused him to lose two toes. Paul is also handicapped, having lost an arm many years ago, and wears a prosthesis.

The company has a written rule stating that leaving work without permission is a major infraction that could result in discharge. Three years ago the problem of employees violating this rule became so serious that management issued a policy saying that any employee who left work without permission would be considered to have voluntarily resigned. Since its issuance, three employees have left work without permission and were considered to have resigned. All appealed, but none was reinstated.

This morning, close to starting time, Paul's supervisor saw him enter the building and hurriedly go to the second floor, where his time clock and work area are located. The supervisor said, "You're cutting it close, buddy." Paul muttered something inaudible. About half an hour later, the supervisor learned that Paul had left work. It appeared that after Paul got to his work area, a couple of his cowork-

## Determining the Extent of Proof Required to Show Just Cause

Whatever misconduct an employee is accused of, evidence must substantiate the charges and the extent of any action taken. Although this may be intuitively obvious, too many managers still impose discipline in the mistaken belief that facts are not required to support actions. The question is: How much evidence or proof of wrongdoing

ers hassled him for not having brought in donuts for everyone. A check of Paul's time card showed he clocked in four minutes late and clocked out three minutes later. The company allows employees to clock in up to three minutes late before they are charged with being late and docked pay. If they are more than three minutes late, employees are docked fifteen minutes' pay. Paul will not be paid for the time he spent at work.

The supervisor wants to process Paul out of the company as a voluntary quit under the policy. He also wants to charge Paul under the Job Abandonment Rule.

## Questions

1. What is the correct course of action to follow at this point?
2. To what extent should Paul's physical condition affect the disposition of this case?
3. To what extent should Paul's service record affect the case?
4. What if Paul is fired and it is subsequently learned that prior to coming to work, he learned that a good friend had died during the night?
5. Should an exception to processing him out as either a voluntary resignation or a discharge be made? Why? What are the possible consequences of either course of action?

is needed to support specific degrees of discipline? In the prosecution of criminal cases in the courts, standards of proof under criminal law are required. In addition, technical rules of evidence are strictly applied. Some believe the same standards should be applied to the disciplining of employees, especially when termination occurs. Though much can be learned from the standards of proof required and rules of evidence used in the courtroom, strict adherence to them is impractical and unsound. The relationship between managers and employees is not quite the same as the relationship between prosecutors and defendants. The employer-employee relationship is broader, extending to all employees and lasting over time.

Managers should be guided by the following principle: the more serious the misconduct, the higher the degree of proof required to impose extreme forms or degrees of discipline. Serious discipline, including termination, should require proof of guilt beyond reasonable doubt before any final action is taken. Where less serious discipline is involved, somewhat lesser degrees of proof should be established. The literature on discipline and arbitrators' decisions commonly contains such phrases as "clear and convincing" and "preponderance of the evidence" in addition to "beyond reasonable doubt" when discussing degrees of proof.

The terms *preponderance, clear and convincing,* and *beyond reasonable doubt* are somewhat vague. *Preponderance* simply means that sufficient information is known to indicate the employee probably engaged in the misconduct for which he or she has been, or is going to be, charged. In effect, the greater weight of the evidence leans to probable guilt. Proof of this nature is usually sufficient to sustain minimal to moderate degrees of discipline. *Clear and convincing* means that management has obtained sufficient evidence in any one or a combination of forms—testimony, confession, expert opinion, documents, records, physical evidence—to be convinced that the suspected or accused employee is guilty of misconduct. If any doubt exists, it is clearly minimal. Such proof would probably support all degrees of discipline except termination for (1) reasons that would damage the employee's moral character, (2) ones that would seriously adversely affect the employee's emotional or physical well-being, (3) ones that would severely limit opportunity for future employment, or (4) ones where the employee could face prosecution under criminal law. Proof *beyond reasonable doubt* simply means that management is fully convinced the suspected or accused employee is guilty.

## Objectives of an Investigation

The objective of any investigation involving employee misconduct is to gather sufficient information relevant to the situation or incident in order to:

1. Determine whether a basis of fact exists to formally accuse the employee

2. Serve, if an accusation has already been made, as the basis of

fact for determining if the accusation was warranted and if warranted, as the basis for initiating some type of discipline

3. Serve, if some type of disciplinary action has been effected, such as a suspension from duties pending the outcome of an investigation, as the basis for either sustaining or rescinding the action

4. Determine if a basis of fact exists for imposing discipline over and above what already may have been given relative to the misconduct investigated

## Conducting an Impartial Investigation

Any investigation should be conducted in a systematic and timely manner. The following reasons mandate this requirement:

- First and foremost, any employee living under a cloud of suspicion or the burden of accusation is entitled to an impartial hearing where guilt or innocence can be determined. The stress and anxiety associated with being suspected or actually accused can do serious emotional and physical damage to the employee and his or her family. Even if the accused employee is subsequently found to be guilty, the damage caused by unwarranted delays in investigations and other aspects of due process could be far more serious than any discipline imposed after guilt has been established.

- Keeping in mind that discipline should be used to strengthen employee relations, unwarranted delays will only serve to weaken them.

- The American system of civil justice dictates that the accused is entitled to timely due process. For reasons already discussed, the justice system in the workplace must operate on similar principles. In unionized organizations labor agreements typically stipulate three to five scheduled workday limits for management to initiate discipline against an employee for misconduct that is known to have occurred or management reasonably should have known about. This clause prevents management from initiating discipline at its convenience and minimizes the time an employee must live under the cloud of suspicion or accusation without resort to trial through due process.

- As children we are taught to tell the truth. We also learn not to snitch on others. Testimony given by employees is often necessary to making management's case. When delays in conducting an investigation occur, employees' recollection of what they heard or saw can fade. In addition, the accused or others can directly or indirectly use considerable peer pressure to silence witnesses. Before memories fade or stories change, management must get information germane to the case into the record.

▪ Whether due process occurs inside or outside of the organization, the disposition of a case is largely determined by the quality and quantity of oral testimony and written evidence submitted by the parties. Because management shoulders the primary responsibility to make its case, it is requisite that the case be prepared and presented on the basis of information learned from a thorough and impartial investigation.

In conducting an investigation, management should attempt to reconstruct as completely as possible the facts and circumstances that (1) preceded the situation or incident, (2) occurred during its course, and (3) took place after it occurred. Management should also attempt to learn about all mitigating facts and circumstances that have a bearing on the case. The investigation should provide answers to the following questions:

1. Who was involved? The identities of all people directly and indirectly involved in the matter should be established. Whatever they know, saw, or heard should be recorded for purposes of assessing the situation, identifying causes and effects, and determining possible courses of action.

2. What happened to cause the situation to become a disciplinary matter? Did it progress in stages over time or quickly arise?

3. Does the matter pertain to or involve any one or a combination of the following: the employee's relationship with his or her peers and supervisors, the employee's position responsibilities, the employee's physical or emotional health, the employee's life outside the workplace?

4. When did the incident occur? Specific times, dates, and locations must be established.

5. Is the employee's misconduct a singular act or part of a pattern? To what extent, if any, are the employee's associates or supervisors factors?

6. Why did the misconduct occur? Was the employee's misbehavior intentional or unintentional? Did the employee act in good faith? Were his or her actions justified, partially justified, or totally unjustified? To what extent, if any, did management knowingly or unknowingly contribute to the employee's misconduct?

7. Is the employee repentant, and, if so, is it because of being caught or for other reasons?

The answers to these and other questions should be used not only to establish just cause but also to help management determine the appropriate type and degree of corrective action. Answers to the aforementioned and other questions, and how they should influence the determination of specific discipline, will be discussed in Chapter 5.

Information used for carrying out discipline should be documented and be able to withstand careful scrutiny. Written records should be made because they have an important advantage over verbal testimony. Time and circumstances tend to affect perceptions and memory, and written records reduce the likelihood of this occurring. Records compiled during or after an investigation should be witnessed and signed if they will be directly or indirectly used to provide a basis for disciplinary action. Written records should also be systematically developed in sufficient detail so as to clearly communicate the intended information and meaning.

## Guidelines for Using Witnesses

During the course of an investigation, it is not uncommon for accusations to be made. Regardless of their source, all accusations should be examined to see if they are supported by facts. The various sides to

---

## Case   Ed Lundquist

Ed Lundquist is manager of the claims division for a regional insurance company. This evening, after a long day at the office, he returned to his favorite chair to read the evening paper. As he read the paper, he came across a story about one of his department supervisors, Hank Wilson. The story told how Wilson got into a fistfight with the estranged husband of Mary Price, one of his employees. Ed had heard that Hank was seeing Mary since she became separated.

Ed leans back and thinks, "I wonder what I should do?"

### Questions

1. What should Ed do the next day and why?
2. Can Ed discipline Hank and Mary for their relationship?

any story should be learned and reviewed to ensure impartiality. Personal bias and unsubstantiated allegations should be filtered out of the process. Cases are partly and sometimes totally based on the testimony of employees. Though most people are basically honest, circumstances can cause people to withhold and distort information. In some instances even honest people will lie. Further, except in cases of very serious and/or socially reprehensible misconduct, employees are usually reluctant, even under pressure from management, to volunteer damaging information about a fellow employee. This is especially true if the suspected or accused employee is popular or politically influential. Getting employees to testify against one another is complicated by the widely held notion that people are not supposed to tattle on one another. It is often difficult for people to sort out their feelings in regard to getting involved, telling the truth, and snitching. A further complication exists when employees fear retaliation by others if they give damaging testimony.

If employees eagerly volunteer damaging testimony about someone or a group, management should carefully assess their motives and thoroughly review what is learned before using it in the case. This is not to imply that whenever employees voluntarily give information it should be suspect. When a high level of trust and confidence exists between employees and managers, employees tend to be very cooperative and supportive of the organization.

Managers frequently ask: How can we get reluctant employees to come forth and give us information essential to our case, especially in instances where retaliation is feared? Unfortunately, there is no formula or system that will always remedy this problem. However, application of the following guidelines should prove helpful:

• A high degree of mutual trust, confidence, and respect between employees and managers will do much to avoid or remedy this type of problem. However, even in the best of relationships, the problem can still occur.

• In interviewing witnesses, or those who are believed to have knowledge that could affect the outcome of a case, interviews should be conducted in a private, nonthreatening environment. For example, interviewing in your office from behind a desk could intimidate an already apprehensive employee, who is at a psychological disadvantage while sitting in front of you.

• Generally, interviews should be conducted one on one. The interviewee is apt to feel intimidated if he or she is being interviewed by a number of people at one time. If these people are strangers to him or her and the setting is unfamiliar, anxiety will be heightened.

- Remember, the interviewee would probably prefer to be somewhere else instead of giving testimony.
- Management should understand the interviewed employee's value system. Appealing to a person's value system—sense of responsibility, protection of self-interest, identification with family, relationship with peers, professionalism, moral code, patriotism, or loyalty to the organization—may be an effective way to get him or her to volunteer information.
- Avoid tape-recording interviews. People tend to either play-act for the recorder or, more often, clam up. If a recorder is used, the person giving testimony should be so informed. Never secretly record testimony.
- If possible, avoid taking notes during an interview. This allows you to pay full attention to the employee's responses, including body language. It also seems to reduce the employee's anxiety. After the interview is completed, dictate or write out in detail the results of the meeting.
- Most interviewers do not possess sufficient skill to conduct a lengthy interview without taking notes. If note-taking is necessary, the interviewee should be told why. Do not attempt to capture every word spoken. Some testimony can be summarized, though some may require exact recording of what is said.
- The summary document containing the results of the interview should be reviewed with those who gave testimony to ensure its completeness and accuracy. The final document should be signed by all involved and the signatures witnessed.
- As appropriate, peer influence can be used to get a reluctant witness to testify. This should be done with caution. It can be accomplished in various ways. For example:

1. Employees can be told that if no one comes forth, the case against the accused employee will be dropped because of insufficient evidence and the allegedly guilty person will go free.

2. Employees can be told that all will be held responsible for the misdeed unless the guilty ones are identified.

3. Employees can be asked to talk to the unwilling associate to find out why he or she is unwilling to give testimony.

- If a witness fears serious retaliation from others for having given testimony, he or she should be given anonymity. However, those accused should have the right to face their accusers and cross-examine them. Forewarning those who may be tempted to initiate or participate in acts of retaliation what will happen to them usually dissuades all but the most determined. Withholding a witness's identity to the last possible moment can also be effective. In extreme situations, where serious retaliation is likely, the identity of witnesses should be withheld. In unionized organizations where arbitration has been called for, testimony by witnesses may be given in private to the arbitrator. Cross-examination by a union representative will also be done in private. Union representatives understand the reasons for this and, in such extreme cases, understand the importance of withholding identities. In addition, many states have laws giving arbitrators the authority to subpoena witnesses. Subpoenaed witnesses must appear and testify. If they do not, the court can be called on to enforce the subpoena. Being subpoenaed affords them some degree of protection from peer retaliation.

• Another possible way to handle these unusual and rare situations is to ask the police to talk with those most likely to start trouble. The police may even recommend issuance of a peace bond.

## Types and Uses of Evidence

In the courtroom strict rules of evidence are applied. In less formal, quasi-judicial proceedings, such as an arbitration hearing, strict adherence to such rules is not essential. A proceeding internal to an organization will tend toward minimal, if any, adherence to rules of evidence. But managers should give some consideration to legal rules of evidence. This will strengthen the intended fairness of internal due process and strengthen management's position should the matter end up in an external forum.

Because organizations are each unique and the way in which they handle discipline will vary, no one set of guides for using evidence can be provided to suit everyone's taste or fit their needs. The following information is meant to serve as a framework from which managers can choose how best to evaluate and use evidence. It is not meant to be all-inclusive.

### Evaluating the Merit of Conflicting Evidence and Testimony

On occasion, people will suffer a lapse of memory, shade the truth, or unintentionally or intentionally lie to protect themselves or others. Also, people may sincerely interpret what they saw or heard in one way, while others will have an entirely different interpretation of the same events. In these and similar instances, fact must be sorted from fiction to reach the truth. Oral testimony, written information, and other forms of evidence must be credited and discredited.

Conducting a complete and objective investigation is the most effective way to minimize the presence of conflicting testimony in a hearing. Careful review of documents, records, and physical evidence for accuracy, competency, and relevancy facilitates evaluation. Planned, systematic, and thorough direct and cross-examination of oral testimony will yield a clearer picture of what is fact and what is fiction. In direct examination, and particularly in cross-examination, the character, social-political relationships, and motives of witnesses should be learned. Witnesses' records of integrity will also affect the perceived credibility of their testimony. The testimony of witnesses with records of untrustworthiness will tend to carry less weight than that of witnesses with well-established credibility.

Another point to consider in evaluating the credibility of testimony is that employees who have much to lose from being disciplined have an obvious incentive to maintain innocence and stretch the truth. This is not to say that all employees who face serious discipline will perjure themselves. Most people are basically honest.

In situations where it is a supervisor's or higher-level manager's word against that of an employee or group of employees, managers tend to back the supervisor or higher-level manager. It is unwise to automatically conclude that managers always tell the truth or are accurate in their recall. Though a supervisor's testimony will usually be credited over an employee's, if it is shown or known that a supervisor or higher-level manager has a reason to set up an employee or get him or her in trouble, that person's testimony should be carefully scrutinized.

In nonunion organizations, where management almost universally has the final internal authority to decide discipline cases, the highest degree of character and a strong belief in being fair are generally necessary for the manager judging the case to discredit the testimony of another manager. This is most likely to pose a problem if the person who should be discredited is a friend or has political power. Remember, if managers don't police themselves, they risk having someone else do it for them.

In unionized organizations, when arbitration is used, the arbitrator, who has no vested financial or political interest in the organization, must finally decide whose testimony is credible or incredible. Competent managers, like competent arbitrators, should use their perceptual and analytical skills to consistently make good decisions.

To effectively weigh the relative merit of conflicting testimony, the following factors should be considered: (1) the character of witnesses, (2) social-political relationships, (3) records of trustworthiness, (4) motives to withhold or distort information, (5) correlation of body language with spoken words, (6) consistency of testimony, (7) degree of sincerity and conviction, (8) quality of recall, (9) quantity of recall, and (10) voids or gaps in testimony.

Most people, when they do not tell the truth, are poor liars. They get nervous and display such physical symptoms as avoiding eye contact, fidgeting with their hands, foot tapping, frequent shifting of body position while sitting, cracking voice, and playing with jewelry. Incompetent liars frequently answer the same question differently each time it is asked, especially when the question is phrased differently.

It is not unusual for lapses of memory to occur, especially when events under discussion occurred some time in the past. However, a pattern of selective lapses or gaps could indicate untruthfulness. On the other hand, the witness who can recall every detail of something that happened long ago may also be lying.

## The Use of Confessions

Obviously, a confession of guilt is strong evidence to support a case against an employee. However, for a confession to be used properly, the following conditions should be met:

1. The confession should be voluntarily given. Coercion, threats, intimidation, or promises of leniency should not be used to get a confession.

2. The confession should be recorded on tape and/or in writing, and it should be witnessed. The person confessing should say that admission of guilt is being freely given.

3. The employee must understand what he or she is confessing to and that the confession will be used against him or her.

## The Best Evidence Rule

In preparing and presenting its case, management should use the best evidence available. Evidence (whether oral, written, physical, or other) that substitutes for better evidence, which for lack of good reason is withheld, could hurt a case.

When oral testimony is used, the people who originally gave the information should be called to testify in the hearing. A written transcript of testimony given as part of an investigation should be used in conjunction with live testimony. An authentic recording can be used if, for valid reasons, the person who gave it is unavailable. Sole use of written or recorded testimony, when the person who gave it is available, would not be considered best evidence.

When written records (such as reports, letters, memoranda, work records, receipts, and invoices) are part of a case, the original record or verified photocopy should be submitted as evidence. Merely saying that applicable information is in the records while failing to produce the records themselves would violate the best evidence rule. This could hurt management's case. Whenever the best evidence available is not used, management should have good reasons for not producing it.

## Illegally or Improperly Obtained Evidence

Management should avoid violating employees' constitutional rights when trying to obtain incriminating evidence. Further, management should not deliberately attempt to entrap a suspected employee. Entrapment would occur, for example, if management suspected an employee of theft and deliberately left money in a place and at a time when the suspect could readily walk off with it without obvious notice by anyone. However, planning to catch someone in the act of wrongdoing and using covert surveillance are proper if sufficient valid reasons exist. The fewer the number of employees singled out for surveillance or for searches of desks, lockers, files, work areas, and even personal possessions, the more defensible the reasons should be. Management should use good judgment and exercise prudence in searching employees' personal possessions and possibly violating privacy rights.

Some organizations use polygraphs (lie detectors) as evidence in determining guilt or innocence. Polygraph tests are not recommended, for the following reasons:

- The skill of the machine's operator can affect the results and their interpretation.
- The reliability of the equipment itself is questionable.
- The physical condition and emotional state of mind of the person being subjected to the lie detector can affect responses to posed questions.
- Courts have often refused to accept polygraph results as evidence.
- More effective, less dramatic and traumatic ways of determining guilt or innocence are likely available.

▪ The reactions of employees to the use of a polygraph are usually negative. This could adversely affect the employee relations climate and even cause employees to be sympathetic to those subjected to it, irrespective of their guilt or innocence.

Again, common sense should prevail in obtaining evidence. Sometimes anger and frustration cause managers to go to extremes to catch suspects. But the more extreme the action, the more questionable it becomes, the more likely it is to upset other employees, and the more likely it is to be judged improper or illegal. Though the workplace is not the courtroom, managers should appreciate the courts' views regarding the admissibility of improperly obtained evidence. However, managers do not have to strictly adhere to the law, as do the police when they carry out investigations and obtain evidence.

## Hearsay and the Relevance of Evidence

The use of hearsay or secondhand information, whether oral or written, should be avoided because the accused cannot directly question the truthfulness or accuracy of it. Hearsay occurs when one person recalls something said by another person who is unavailable to testify. Sometimes its use cannot be avoided, but when it is used, management should have a valid reason for using it. Hearsay evidence is not as strong as firsthand evidence, and it is usually inadmissible in a court. In an arbitration proceeding, arbitrators recognize the difficulty in keeping it out and usually accept it into the record, prefacing acceptance with the words *for what it's worth*. That *worth* is almost always not very much. Affidavits or sworn declarations can be used, but they are similar to other forms of hearsay because the people who gave them are not present for cross-examination.

Regardless of its form, format, or substance, evidence that is brought into a case should be logically related to that case. Indirect evidence can be used to lay the groundwork for what is forthcoming or to develop a clearer picture of the situation and conditions surrounding or pertaining to it. An employee's past record of conduct and service may be used if it can be shown that it is being or was considered in determining discipline. Past records of misconduct more than two to three years old should only be used to show a continuing pattern of misconduct. More will be discussed on the use of past records in Chapter 5.

## Official Records, Performance Reviews, and Physical Evidence

Accurate official records relevant to the case are admissible evidence. In discipline cases such records may include prior discipline, compensation changes, changes in job status, performance reviews, and medical records. With respect to performance reviews, most do not accurately reflect employees' actual performance. The performance appraisal process usually fails because of the following reasons:

1. Managers do not develop adequate standards or measures of performance.

2. Performance reviews are not correlated with actual performance.

3. The forms and format are poorly designed.

4. Managers fail to document performance.

5. Managers do not take the process seriously.

6. Rewards (raises, promotions, privileges) are not tied to performance.

7. Inadequate performance is not confronted until it becomes acute.

8. Managers are not properly trained to conduct performance appraisals with their employees.

If past performance—which typically includes conduct under such headings as work habits, attendance, adaptiveness, cooperativeness, and interpersonal relations—is being considered in present discipline, the recorded performance reviews had best support any action taken. A history of inflated performance reviews in an employee's personnel file will weaken management's case if it is contended that the employee has a history of misbehavior.

Many managers still do not even bother to give formal periodic reviews. In the absence of any negative information about an employee's performance and behavior, his or her record is considered to be at least adequate, especially if the employee has received regular average salary increases and promotions. Managers should also recognize that an employee can use inflated past performance reviews to establish a longstanding record of good service for consideration when discipline for current misconduct is determined.

When lateness and absence are involved in discipline cases, employees frequently use written medical excuses to legitimize their behavior. A medical statement can be used to show that treatment was sought for an actual illness or an illness that the employee believed existed. However, a medical excuse should not automatically protect an employee from possible discipline for excessive lateness or absence. Employers have a legitimate right to expect employees to conform to reasonable attendance standards, and they may properly take disciplinary action if an employee cannot consistently meet the standards.

## Expert Opinions as Evidence

If experts are used, their qualifications should be established. Professional opinions and/or conclusions may be used as evidence. In discipline cases, expert medical opinion is often relied on when an employee's health or abilities are in question. When medical questions arise, managers tend to rely on the opinions of the organization's medical staff, while employees usually seek the opinions of non-company-employed licensed medical practitioners. These may include physicians, osteopaths, chiropractors, podiatrists, psychologists, and others from whom treatment has been sought. It is not unusual for the opinions of medical experts to differ, especially when mental health is at issue. Though the organization's medical personnel may know more about the jobs and work environment, it could be argued that their views are not objective because they too are employees and owe their loyalty to the organization. On the other hand, it could be argued that an employee's medical counselors lack familiarity with his or her job and the work environment and so cannot properly assess whether the employee is able to properly do his or her job. It can further be argued that these practitioners are not objective because the employee is their client and provides a source of income. When expert opinions disagree, it is best to call on a neutral medical expert to evaluate the employee's condition. A neutral expert is one mutually agreed to by management and the employee or by the organization's and the employee's medical advisor.

## Circumstantial Evidence

Sometimes physical evidence, witnesses, documents, and records are either unavailable or insufficient to show with certainty that the accused is guilty. In such instances, management may have to rely on circumstantial evidence. The appearance of guilt does not necessarily establish proof of guilt. However, enough circumstantial evidence may be presented to convince the person deciding the case that the accused is probably guilty.

# Summary

The employee rights movement started taking shape in the 1930s when the government's attitude toward collective bargaining changed from tolerance to encouragement. The result was a wave of union growth and more aggressive collective bargaining. Two notable collectively bargained accomplishments for organized labor were (1) the establishment of due process, that is, grievance procedures with binding arbitration, and (2) the agreement that discipline occur only for just cause. These provisions in labor agreements afforded covered employees some protection from possible mistreatment; however, most employees were not covered by negotiated labor agreements.

The Civil Rights Act of 1964 and the Age Discrimination Act of 1967 increased the government's influence over employee relations matters and gave protection to many employees who, heretofore, had none. The government's intervention continued in the 1970s with enactment of the Occupational Safety and Health Act (OSHA) of 1971 and the Pension Reform Act (ERISA) of 1974. These reforms and protections altered the nature of the employer-employee relationship. People's perceptions of how they should be treated by employers changed. Employees became increasingly concerned with their rights to fair and equitable treatment by their employers. In effect, the civil rights movement had spilled over into the workplace.

Through much of the 1970s the courts, with few exceptions, upheld the common law doctrine of employment or termination at will. However, as the courts became increasingly involved in employee relations matters because of laws enacted in the 1960s and 1970s, a shift in thinking took place. The common law doctrine was outliving its usefulness. Judges began to refuse to uphold the employment- or termination-at-will doctrine and required that managements show just cause for discipline. This trend will continue to gain momentum during the 1980s. All employees are being afforded some measure of protection from arbitrary actions by employers.

Aside from the fact that managements will have to adapt and conform to the legal and social changes occurring regarding employee rights, it is good management practice to require that proper cause for discipline exists before any action is taken. From an employee relations perspective, a well-managed organization is one that sincerely attempts to be fair with employees. Showing just cause for discipline is basic to the notion of fairness.

The material presented in this chapter provides guidelines for

determining if just cause exists. Readers should now be more knowledgeable about how to carry out an investigation, obtain and evaluate evidence, and handle witnesses. The information can be used to
determine whether formal charges are in order and, if accusations
have been made, to determine if guilt exists. This sets the stage for
imposing discipline.

## Key Points

- The employee rights movement will continue to gain momentum
  through the 1980s.
- The notion of employee rights has many components, including
  reasonable written rules, limits on managerial authority, rights
  to privacy, freedom to express views without fear of reprisal,
  rewards based on merit, just cause for discipline, and timely due
  process.
- Employees' rights must be carefully balanced with employers'
  rights. Employers can rightfully expect employees to be at work
  when they are supposed to, do a fair day's work for their pay,
  cooperate with others, and be reasonably loyal.
- The work relationship is symbiotic, based on mutual exchange
  and benefit.
- Management carries the primary burden of proof in showing
  cause for discipline.
- Management has the responsibility to communicate required
  standards for behavior to employees. Employees are responsible
  for complying with reasonable standards.
- Whenever formal charges of misconduct are made, they should be
  clearly stated in writing, and specific rules or standards violated
  should be referenced.
- Employees should always be forewarned of the possible consequences for continued misconduct.
- The degree of proof required to substantiate discipline is directly
  proportional to the seriousness of the misconduct: the more serious the misconduct, the more proof is required.
- Where proof is lacking, the benefit of the doubt should be given to
  the accused. Circumstantial evidence can be used when it
  strongly supports the allegation or charge of misconduct.
- Generally, investigations should be quickly started once miscon-

duct is known. Delays in completing investigations should be avoided.

- Investigations of disciplinary matters should be impartial and thorough.
- In conducting an investigation, management should attempt to reconstruct as completely as possible the facts and circumstances that (1) preceded the situation or incident, (2) occurred during its course, and (3) took place after it occurred.
- Information obtained from an investigation should be substantiated and documented.
- Witnesses' testimony should be obtained while memories are fresh.
- In disciplinary matters, it is not uncommon for people to shade what they saw, know, or heard to suit their own purposes. Managers must learn to recognize credible and incredible information.
- Firsthand information is always better than secondhand information.
- Evidence must be obtained legally and properly.
- As appropriate, employees' official records should be used to support disciplinary action.

## Discussion Questions

1. If employees can still terminate their employment at will, why shouldn't employers have the same right to end the work relationship at will?
2. Identify some of the reasons why managers are now addressing the employee rights issue.
3. Why does the primary burden of proof in disciplinary matters reside with management?
4. Discuss the tests for just cause.
5. What do the terms *preponderance of the evidence, clear and convincing evidence*, and *proof beyond reasonable doubt* mean? Why is it impossible to define them with precision?
6. Why should an investigation into a disciplinary matter be expeditiously carried out? What are the dangers of doing it too quickly?
7. Why are employees usually reluctant to give damaging testimony about a coworker?

8. How can managers get reluctant witnesses to testify?
9. What are the potential problems in having a number of managers collectively interview witnesses to others' misconduct?
10. What methods and techniques can managers use to assess the credibility of testimony?
11. Why does a supervisor's or higher-level manager's word often carry more credibility than an accused employee's? Under what circumstances is the opposite likely to exist?
12. What conditions should be met in using confessions?
13. When can circumstantial evidence suffice in deciding whether guilt exists?

# 4 How to Conduct a Disciplinary Interview

The disciplinary interview is a central element of the discipline process. Without it, guilt or innocence is determined without the benefit of hearing the employee's position and weighing its merits. If the employee is judged guilty, discipline is imposed without proper evaluation of factors and/or conditions in his or her favor. If no internal procedure exists for seeking redress, the employee is denied the right to due process within the organization. The employee must then choose between accepting management's decision or taking the matter outside the organization and pursuing due process in another forum.

In theory, seeking due process in another forum is relatively simple. In reality, it can be sufficiently intimidating to dissuade all but the most determined. Though growing numbers of employees have recently shown the willingness, many are still reluctant because of the mental anguish and financial expense that can be associated with the process. For example:

- Delays caused by backlogs of cases can run into years.
- Continuing to work for the same organization and managers party to a suit or action does not make for the best working relationship.
- Friends and associates can be lost because of fear of what could happen to them if it appeared they supported or sympathized with the person who initiated an action or suit.
- Attempting to find employment with another organization while involved in a suit or action with a former employer can be difficult if not impossible.

• Even if the suit or action is won, remaining with or returning to the organization can be difficult.

• If the suit or action is lost, remaining with the same employer or finding another job can be difficult.

• Marital relations and financial resources can be strained.

On the other hand, if a third party decides in favor of the aggrieved employee, a number of undesirable consequences for the organization can result. For example:

• Management's credibility with the aggrieved employee and others can be seriously damaged.

• Adverse publicity in and outside the organization can affect image, customer relations, and even sales. If the organization's action is upheld, the publicity can benefit, but it can also hurt.

• Respect for management can be weakened.

• The cost for attorneys, management's time taken from more productive activities, compensatory and possibly punitive damages awarded can be considerable.

• Losing a major case can serve as an incentive for other employees to look for or even create issues.

• After seeing that the organization can be successfully challenged, other employees with past or present grievances may be tempted to take action.

If internal due process does exist, the employee must decide if it is worth the effort to pursue the matter. Though the responsibility to show cause for discipline and appropriateness of any action taken rests with management, managers in some organizations do not always see it this way. The employee who has already been judged guilty must now convince management to rescind or modify the decision.


## Purpose and Benefits

For all concerned it is best to allow the employee to have his or her "day in court" before passing judgment on the matter and taking corrective action. Furthermore, giving the employee the opportunity to respond to charges before judgment is passed, determining what action (if any) is appropriate, and deciding what needs to be done to prevent a recurrence cannot be properly accomplished without discussion with the employee. If properly planned and carried out, the interview or meeting can:

- Foster the notion of personal responsibility and self-discipline
- Facilitate improved communication by clearing the air of possible misunderstandings
- Ensure that the employee's rights are safeguarded
- Serve to more accurately determine the employee's innocence or degree of guilt
- Promote good employee relations
- Provide a forum for the employee to explain the reasons for whatever caused the disciplinary matter
- Serve as a basis for determining the appropriate corrective action

If handled badly, the disciplinary interview can:

- Erode respect, trust, and confidence for specific managers, management at large, and even the organization itself
- Fan the fires of discontent
- Serve to make the disciplined employee a martyr with his or her peers
- Damage interpersonal relationships
- Temporarily and even permanently injure the employee's pride, dignity, and sense of self-worth
- In extreme cases, precipitate a serious and possibly violent confrontation

## Management's Responsibility

People inherently are neither good nor bad. They have a tremendous capacity to help or hurt one another. Emotions affect behavior and behavior affects emotions. A disciplinary situation arouses feelings and evokes responses from all who are touched by it. No one can be totally neutral or nonjudgmental about a disciplinary situation when in some way he or she is involved with it.

Most of us believe that a disciplinary interview and the act of administering discipline are unpleasant tasks that we would prefer to avoid. However, even in the best-managed organization, discipline situations are inevitable. Further, intervention by management is called for when employees are unable or unwilling to practice self-discipline. A manager who becomes involved in the discipline process can view the situation as: (1) an opportunity to take responsibility, (2) an opportunity to demonstrate management skills and attempt corrective action, or (3) an opportunity to show power and put the screws to someone. This last attitude is most likely to exist when the employee has been a recurring problem. Executive-level managers cannot dismiss this possibility or condone such when it is known to exist.

Management's general attitude and the attitude of those directly involved in the process are important factors in determining how a disciplinary interview will be conducted. Managers should be able to control their own thoughts, feelings, and actions. If managers cannot meet the organization's expectations and conform to what is required, then they should be subject to disciplinary action. To a degree, managers can influence the suspected or accused employee's behavior.

## Planning a Disciplinary Interview

Every disciplinary interview should be thoroughly planned. Managers should prepare facts, documents, and records and be aware of attitudes. The manager calling for the meeting may feel frustrated, angry, sympathetic, vindictive, or something else. The employee may feel guilty, indignant, persecuted, hurt, helpless, anxious, flip, cavalier, or belligerent. To increase the chances that an interview will be a positive experience, managers should observe the following guidelines:

▪ Organize and review all relevant and pertinent information obtained from the investigation, including documents, records, and testimony.

▪ Set a time and place for the meeting. The meeting should be private, face to face, and attended by as few people as possible—preferably one on one.

▪ Give the employee at least a day's advance notice about the meeting's time, place, and purpose.

▪ Keep in mind that conducting the meeting in the manager's office puts the employee at a psychological disadvantage. Unless a psychological advantage is desired, consider holding the meeting in a more neutral place, such as a conference room.

▪ Consider the effect the arrangement of chairs, desks, spatial distance, and even ventilation and lighting could have on attitude and behavior.

## Case   Ann Williams

Recently you have noticed a change in behavior in one of your staff. As her supervisor, you are concerned. Ann Williams has been working on an important project for you, which requires that she gather data from the production, accounting, and materials purchasing departments. At the beginning of the project, Ann seemed to be doing quite well and had been ahead of schedule. But that was four weeks ago. About two weeks ago, Ann started slowing down and barely met the project deadlines for weeks three and four. This week Ann has been late for work twice, and you feel she will more than likely fail to meet the next deadline.

In addition, you have noticed that Ann's appearance and demeanor have changed for the worse in the past week. Ann looks haggard, and she has been seen snapping at the people she works with and at people in other departments. Her normal demeanor and positive attitude have been replaced by a sullen, withdrawn look and pessimistic attitude toward her work. This morning you heard some grapevine gossip from your secretary. She told you that Ann has had some kind of problem at home and she's taking it out on her associates. On hearing this, you decide to ask Ann to your office to talk over the situation.

### Questions

1. What type of behavior has Ann been exhibiting when she snaps at her fellow workers?

2. As it turns out, Ann and her husband have separated, causing Ann a great deal of emotional stress. Upon confiding in you, Ann says that she will try to improve her work. As her supervisor, what risks do you incur by becoming personally involved in Ann's problem?

3. During the next week, Ann stops by your office several times to talk. Her work seems to be progressing and she is looking better, but you find these interruptions are delaying your own work. What should you do?

4. Are there alternatives to using your own time to counsel an employee with a problem?

- Learn as much as is relevant and realistically possible about the employee's background, record of service, character, and attitude. This information should be used to plan the physical and psychological climate for the meeting.

- Remember the purposes of the meeting, despite frustration or anger:

1. To outline the problem and whatever charges have been made.

2. To present the known facts pertaining to the matter.

3. To give the employee an opportunity to explain his or her position and/or views.

4. If possible at the time, to decide on the employee's degree of guilt or innocence. If the matter needs to be given further thought or a reinvestigation is called for, judgment should not be passed during the meeting.

5. To decide corrective action if the employee is judged culpable.

6. To work out an approach to constructively resolve the matter and avoid recurrence.

- Remember that judgment of guilt or innocence should not be made until the employee has been heard and listened to. Though it may be impossible not to have some feeling about the employee's guilt or innocence prior to the interview, prejudgment is a miscarriage of justice.

- Control his or her own emotions and actions when conducting the interview.

- If the employee is known to be hostile, intimidating, or a hothead, steps should be taken prior to the meeting to induce the employee to exercise self-restraint or change. Let the employee know that if such behavior is shown it will hurt his or her case.

- It is more common for an employee accused of misconduct—be it for breaking a rule, absenteeism, poor performance, or anything else—to feel anxious. This is not bad, especially if the employee knows that he or she is guilty. Guilt can serve as an effective incentive to change behavior. So can fear. However, behavioral changes arising out of fear work only if the fear is maintained. If an employee is extremely anxious, nervous, or depressed, he or she needs to know that the world is not coming to an end. Even if termination is possible, the employee's dignity and sense of self-worth do not have to be destroyed in the process. Employees need to understand the purposes of a disciplinary interview and be convinced of management's belief in rehabilitative discipline.

# Guides for the Interview's Setting

The following are offered to guide managers in creating the type of mood and setting that will best serve their purposes. There is no one best way for each employee or form of misconduct. Many factors will affect the setting and climate. Some of these are:

- The sense of urgency
- The manager's preferred style
- The employee's personality, character, and temperament
- The employee's record of service and conduct
- The seriousness of the misconduct
- The frequency of misconduct

How the employee is handled in advance of the meeting will affect his or her attitude. What is said, when, how, and by whom can evoke feelings ranging from curiosity to fear. For example, the manager can go to the employee and say:

- "Joe, do you have some time for me this afternoon? I would appreciate a few minutes to discuss some of your work."
- "Joe, see me sometime this afternoon. I want to discuss some aspects of your work."
- "Joe, I have scheduled a meeting with you at 3:00 P.M. in my office. Bring your work records; I want to discuss your recent performance."
- "Joe, I want to see you as soon as possible. It's important and it's about your work."

Instead of going to the employee, the manager can summon the employee to his or her office, demonstrating control. However, note that summoning the employee could put him or her on the defensive. The manager can call the employee, thereby maintaining distance and avoiding direct contact. This can be useful where it is felt that advance direct contact could precipitate a confrontation. The manager can also have a secretary go to or call the employee to inform him or her that the boss has scheduled a meeting.

As soon as the employee arrives for a scheduled meeting, the manager can do any of the following:

- Greet the employee in a formal or casual manner. Formal: "Ms. Sobel, would you have a seat." Informal: "Hi, Chris, come on in and make yourself comfortable."

• Stand up and remain standing while staying behind the desk. This communicates authority and power. It also puts the employee somewhat on edge because the manager is looking down at and not across to the employee.

• Remain seated and avoid eye contact by reading a document. Keeping the employee waiting is a sign of power and control.

• Look the employee straight in the eye and authoritatively tell him or her to sit down.

• Get up, come out from behind the desk, and greet the employee in a warm, friendly way. This can signal openness and receptivity.

The arrangement of information on the manager's desk can affect the psychological climate. The manager whose desk is orderly, with necessary records close at hand, projects the image of a person who is organized, prepared, and in control. To the employee this can be assuring or intimidating.

The manager, whether male or female, who wears a suit jacket and addresses the employee as Mr., Mrs., or Ms. instead of by first name establishes a formal atmosphere. The manager whose jacket is off and shirt sleeves rolled up, and who goes on a first-name basis, creates an informal setting.

The soft light of a desk lamp creates a different mood than harsh, overhead fluorescent lights. Drawing office blinds or drapes can make the employee feel comfortable or uncomfortable. How close the manager sits to the employee while conversing can affect the meeting. The closer the manager is to the employee, the more likely he or she is to feel anxious.

If the employee's situation is not serious, the meeting should usually be informal, low key, and friendly. The manager should not stay behind the desk and should sit three to five feet from the employee. Strong words and emotions should be avoided. The tone of conversation should be nonthreatening, one of discovery and examination. Taking written notes during the meeting is optional; making mental notes is essential.

When the employee's situation is serious, the meeting should usually be direct and formal. The manager will likely stay behind the desk and even stand while the employee is seated. The agenda should be thoroughly planned, and a wider range of feelings should be displayed. The seriousness of the matter should not be understated. The employee should understand the consequences for failure to change. Note-taking is suggested as long as it does not interfere with listening. No matter how serious the matter, common courtesy should be extended and maintained.

# Conducting a Successful Disciplinary Interview

Managers should always start a disciplinary interview with a positive attitude. Opening remarks may be of a general nature, those typically used in starting a conversation, but remarks not related to the purpose of the meeting should be kept to a minimum. Their only purpose is to allow the employee to become acclimated to the setting and, if possible, to be somewhat at ease. Once the employee is acclimated, the manager should state the purpose of the meeting. In general, the manager should tell the employee:

- *Why the meeting has been called.* Do not assume that the employee fully understands why. Even if the reason is known, restating it will ensure that everyone is addressing the same issue.
- *What specifically he or she has been charged with, accused of, or suspected of.* If it's a job performance problem, identify the specific deficiencies believed to exist. If it's an attendance problem, state the specific amount of absence and/or lateness. If it's a violation of employee responsibilities and/or standards of conduct, state the specific improprieties.
- *That a decision will not be made until after relevant facts have been examined and views expressed.* If information is brought to light that changes the substance of the case, a decision about the employee's innocence or guilt may not be possible or feasible at the end of the meeting.
- *If it is decided that misconduct has occurred, the objective of any corrective action is to avoid a repetition of the situation, incident, problem, or issue.*

Throughout the course of the interview, pay careful attention to the employee's spoken and body language. Nonverbal communication often tells a lot more about what someone is thinking or really means than what is actually said. Though no one nonverbal signal will likely communicate all that a person is thinking, a steady flow of such signals will often show a pattern of thinking. Managers must sense if the employee understands what is being said. Assurance that understanding exists requires listening to what is said and seeing if nonverbal communication supports and reinforces it. The degree of correlation between verbal and nonverbal communication indicates the employee's degree of understanding and willingness to comply.

In evaluating nonverbal communication, pay attention to the following:

- *Facial expressions.* During the course of an exchange, facial

## Case   Dick Underwood

Dick Underwood is a supervisor of twenty-eight people in your division. He has been a supervisor for four years and has consistently met or exceeded job requirements. About eight months ago, Dick became extensively involved in physical fitness activities. He jogs five miles every day, frequently plays racquetball, and now eats only organic foods. Meat is no longer part of his diet. He usually eats lunch at his desk. He eats wheat germ, soybeans, bran, nuts, fruits, and an assortment of other nonmeat foods purchased from area health food stores.

On occasion, when you have visited Dick at his desk or while he has been in your office, you have noticed an odor about Dick similar to that of decaying vegetables or feces. Your first notice of the odor corresponds roughly with the time Dick started changing his eating and exercise habits. Until now, you have not said anything to Dick or anyone else.

In the past couple of months, you have overheard various

expressions will change as the employee reacts to what is said. The smile, frown, pursed lips, scowl, raised eyebrows, thrusting chin, angle of the head in relation to the body, yawn, lip biting, and sneer all convey information.

• *Body posture.* During the course of a conversation, posture and body movement will change. Slouching may indicate disinterest, while erectness could mean anxiety. Folded arms could show defensiveness. Crossed legs, clasped hands, and fingers playing with a piece of jewelry all convey information.

• *Gestures.* Most people have certain hand movements they regularly use when talking. Some may be idiosyncratic, while others have universal meaning.

• *Eye contact.* Eye contact is an important facet of communication. Eye contact and expressions shown in the eyes, coupled with facial expressions and other nonverbal communication, are strong signs of feeling. Avoidance of eye contact can signal shame, guilt, anxiety, insecurity, resentment, or fear. Eye contact can also signal when to talk, when the other person is about to speak, or when to keep quiet.

disparaging comments from other people about the odor that lingers around Dick. Phrases like "the flag is up," "stay downwind from Dick," "a farting horse never tires," and "all employees should be issued gas masks" have caught your attention.

On three different occasions this week, Dick's employees have complained to you about the situation. You have decided to talk to Dick, who has just entered your office and sat down in a chair.

### Questions

1. As Dick's supervisor, what will you say to him?
2. Should you have discussed the matter with Dick sooner?
3. What will you tell Dick's employees?

---

Intense, prolonged eye contact (approximately ten seconds or longer) can show very strong positive or negative feelings.

A well-developed ability to read nonverbal communication will help managers anticipate what the employee is going to say and how he or she is likely to act on what has been said.

Keep emotions under control. Letting emotions overtake logic, reason, and judgment is a major reason why disciplinary interviews fail to serve their intended purpose. Maintaining control over emotions does not mean being devoid of emotion. Be sensitive to overreacting or overexpressing yourself. Be honest and sincere yet tactful. If you are not, it will show in speech and body language. The employee will be quick to sense it and will react in a self-protective way.

Once it is determined the employee understands the nature and purpose of the interview, present the facts at hand. It is most important to stick to the issue and facts; avoid rambling or talking about unrelated issues. If the situation involves patterned or cumulative misconduct, make reference to the continuing problem. Use caution, however, because the employee may be innocent or only partially to blame. Proceed to tell the employee what facts, records, documents, testimony, and so on have been obtained to indicate cause for discipline.

Remember that the employee may not accept the fact that a problem exists. The employee may view his or her behavior as being normal or something that management is making an unnecessary big deal about. It is important that you take the time to help the employee understand that a problem or potential problem is believed to exist. If the employee admits, or prior to the meeting has admitted to, misconduct, it is not necessary to present all the information that has been obtained. There is no need for overkill. Present enough information to show that relative to the seriousness of the matter, sufficient reason exists for taking corrective action.

After the evidence of specific misconduct has been presented, or if charges have already been substantiated, the employee should be given the opportunity to respond. If the employee admits to wrongdoing, the case is made and the next step is to find out why it happened. If the employee proclaims innocence of any and all wrongdoing, he or she now bears the burden of proof. If partial responsibility or culpability is admitted, the employee must explain why. Again, the employee now has the responsibility to present a defense.

Listen carefully with an open mind to what the employee has to say. If necessary, take notes. It is not unusual for the employee's and manager's interpretations of the "facts" to differ. Avoid getting into an argument or debate. The employee may say that information was overlooked, relevant factors and conditions were ignored or not properly considered, the record is wrong, or others have not told the truth. The employee's defense can include just about anything and everything. This is where the value of knowing the employee and having done a thorough investigation are most important.

If the employee's understanding of the matter differs from your own, clarify the areas where agreement exists and the specific areas where there is disagreement. Again, avoid getting defensive and emotional; neither will be productive. Stick to the issue and the facts. It's easy to go off on tangents, talk about vague and nonrelated issues, and even get into an argument.

Most employees will be sincere and honest. They will honestly believe that they are right in their opinions and beliefs. It is essential to have well-developed interpersonal skills to work through this part of the interview without damaging relationships. Remember, only a small percentage of employees are real troublemakers and are prone to be argumentative, dishonest, deceptive, aggressive, or to otherwise cause problems. I will discuss handling these types of employees later in this chapter. Here the discussion concerns the basically good employee, who with counseling and constructive discipline is likely to self-correct. Remember, the purpose of discipline is rehabilitative. Only a small percentage of employees are destined for termination.

If what the employee has said causes you to doubt the accuracy or credibility of your position, tell the employee you need to do some further investigation. Close the meeting and let the employee know you will be in touch within a specified time period.

If you are convinced that the employee's position lacks merit, tactfully but firmly say so. Help the employee see that his or her position is contrary to what you believe are the correct facts. If it appears the employee is not listening or that an argument is in the making, back off and bring the discussion to a close. Assuming that an internal due process system exists, the employee has the right to appeal your action if he or she is dissatisfied with the outcome of the meeting and subsequent action.

## Counseling as Part of the Interview

Managers use counseling in the disciplinary interview to attempt to learn the reason(s) why misconduct occurred and to work toward resolving the matter to limit the chances of recurrence. If the incident is the latest in a series with a discernible pattern, counseling is an attempt to uncover why previous efforts have apparently failed and what options are available to deal with the situation.

To effectively use counseling at this stage of the process, the following conditions should be satisfied:

• The employee has recognized and accepted that he or she is completely or partially at fault for the disciplinary matter.

• The employee has expressed an interest or desire in wanting to remedy the situation and avoid further discipline.

• The situation apparently or actually was precipitated by things that are partially or fully controllable.

• The interview has proceeded well to this point.

If the employee has become defensive and either is not listening or has become argumentative, it probably will not do any good to start counseling at this time. In this type of situation, the time to employ counseling would be after discipline has been determined and imposed.

If the employee is extremely nervous or anxious about the specific discipline he or she might receive and likely would not respond well to counseling at this time, it should be postponed and rescheduled. Regardless of the type of discipline the employee may receive, counseling should be included as part of the corrective action process. Counseling serves two important purposes: (1) to discover the cause(s) for misconduct and (2) to facilitate the employee's recovery to proper behavior.

A disciplinary interview is not particularly enjoyable; it can be an unsettling experience. But most disciplinary interviews do not end up in emotional confrontations. Most employees really want to do the right thing. For the employee who is truly sorry for the misconduct and wants to avoid a repetition of discipline, counseling is likely to yield positive results.

## The Importance of Counseling

Counseling can determine the extent to which the employee's misconduct occurred for controllable, semicontrollable, or uncontrollable reasons. For example, failure to complete assigned work on time could have been caused by the employee's taking a day off to play golf or go fishing or shopping—a controllable reason. It could have resulted because certain information or materials did not arrive in time—perhaps a partially controllable reason if the employee could have sought it from other sources or advised others it was needed by a particular time. Or the problem could have happened because the employee was not directed to do the work, never received any training, or was required by a sudden family emergency to be somewhere else—all of which are probably uncontrollable. The determination of specific discipline should be influenced by evaluation of the degree to which the employee could have controlled the situation. It would be unfair to discipline an employee for something over which he or she had little or no control.

Counseling can also determine if the employee's misconduct occurred out of ignorance or intent. Willful and knowing misbehavior is more serious than misconduct due to misunderstanding or lack of knowledge. On occasion, an employee will claim ignorance as a reason for misconduct. Ignorance cannot be accepted if the employee violated a written rule, a well-established common understanding, something that is considered common sense, or something that is common knowledge to the industry, profession, or organization.

Discipline problems sometimes stem from causes indirectly related to the act or result of the wrongdoing itself. An employee's excessive absence or lateness is caused by something. If the cause(s) can be identified and removed or controlled, the problem will be resolved. Similarly, a job performance problem is caused by something. Most managers are reactive rather than proactive, and it often takes a crisis to stimulate them into taking corrective action. In addition, they are often impatient; they want instant solutions to complex problems. Disciplining an employee without looking for the causes is superficial treatment and a short-term cure. Sometimes this works; often it does not.

The underlying causes for discipline usually stem from any one or a combination of (1) the employee's work, (2) the organization's environment, and (3) the employee's situation outside of work. Figures 4.1, 4.2, and 4.3 can be used as references in helping managers identify possible causal factors. However, it is not always possible or feasible to identify direct and underlying causes. In such instances the symptoms must then be treated. But treating symptoms is likely to be a hit-and-miss proposition; the risk of failure is high because the source still exists. Managers should try to identify causes before taking the easier approach of treating symptoms.

If the employee is responsible for the misbehavior, counseling is important to help him or her exercise self-control and self-discipline. The employee who is unwilling or unable to maintain self-control requires continual monitoring and control by management. Though only a fraction of employees fall into this category, they can be found in nearly all organizations. There are limits as to how far management should go to help a problem employee change behavior. (I will

---

**Figure 4.1   Possible Causes of Job-Related Discipline Situations**

- Inadequate capability, intelligence, training, or job knowledge
- Boring, uninteresting, monotonous work
- Being overskilled or too qualified for the job
- Uncertainty about job responsibilities
- Having responsibility for the work of others
- Inability to effectively cope with the stress inherent in the job
- Lack of clear direction
- Not having the proper equipment, materials, and other resources
- Unrealistic deadlines
- Inability to measure progress and results
- No control over work activities

---

---

**Figure 4.2   Possible Causes of Job Environment Discipline Situations**

- Hazardous working conditions
- Lack of opportunity to participate in decisions
- Lack of opportunity to professionally grow within a particular job
- No opportunity to be promoted to higher-level positions
- Destructive infighting and politicking
- Ineffective supervision
- No recognition for performance and contributions
- Inadequate or nonexistent job security
- Erratic production or work schedules
- Having to work on rotating shifts
- Excessive heat, inadequate ventilation, poor lighting, excessive noise
- No opportunity to have contact with other people
- Inability to get along with supervisors
- Inability to get along with associates
- Raises based on criteria other than job performance
- Promotion based on anything but job performance
- Too much overtime
- Dated personnel policies and practices or none at all
- Favoritism, nepotism, paternalism, good-ole-boyism
- "Use them or lose them" sick day policy
- Thursday payday—Friday absence
- Dissatisfaction with compensation

---

address just how far management should go in subsequent chapters.) If the employee is worth keeping and sincerely wants to change, management should provide guidance, coaching, and other forms of assistance. Management should even consider offering assistance to the employee who does not want to change. However, if the employee shows no real progress toward improvement, counseling should be cut back and eventually ended. In all counseling, monitoring behavior and documenting progress are recommended.

## Documenting Counseling

Documenting counseling is important for establishing a record of what has been done to help the employee help him or herself. Because counseling may continue over time, it is important to have a record of

**Figure 4.3   Possible Causes of Non-Work-Related Discipline Situations**

- Personal business
- Moonlighting
- Drug addiction
- Marital problems
- Illness of employee or family member
- Injury or accident to employee or family member
- Child-care conflicts
- Weather conditions
- Transportation problems
- Inconvenient shopping and banking hours, causing absence and lateness
- Care of parents or relatives
- Religious beliefs
- Legal, economic, or social problems
- Looking for another job
- Dental, eye, hearing, or prosthesis problems
- Conflict with leisure activities
- Lifestyle that conflicts with job responsibilities
- Lack of sense of self-discipline and personal responsibility

what's being done and the results attained. As part of counseling, the employee must understand the consequences of his or her behavior and assume responsibility for them. If management's and the employee's efforts succeed, the record can be analyzed to learn what techniques and approaches are best used for specific types of situations. This can be done without violating confidentiality. If a technique that worked with one employee is used in another case, there is no need to say where the approach came from or why it was decided on. Without being specific, the manager could say, "We have had success with this approach in similar types of cases." If results are less than what is desired, analysis of the steps taken can help identify the extent of what is or is not working. If the efforts fail and the employee resigns or is terminated, analysis of counseling records may reveal why they failed.

Additionally, should a terminated employee pursue internal or external due process, the manager can use counseling records to defend disciplinary action. The manager should use his or her judgment in deciding whether to take notes during counseling. Certainly, key points and critical comments should be noted, but tape-recording should be avoided because people fear that anything they say may be held against them. After the interview is completed, the manager should write out all notes in detail. It is recommended that the manager share information pertaining to achieved results and agreed courses of action with the employee. If the employee disagrees with the record, an attempt should be made to reach a common understanding. If such cannot be reached, the employee should be advised to put his or her comments in writing. Judgment should be used in deciding whether to share written impressions and opinions not based on fact with the employee. Keep in mind that whatever is not supported by fact should not be part of the employee's permanent record or be used in determining specific disciplinary action.

## The Manager's Style of Counseling

The ways that people act and relate to others are shaped by many factors. Some facets of behavior are determined by genetic programming, as well as electrical and chemical balances in the body. Much of behavior is influenced by environmental conditioning. Over time, training, influences of others, and personal experiences help shape behavior patterns. Managers develop ways of acting and interacting with bosses, peers, and their staff. Rarely does a manager's style fit any particular textbook definition. Most managers use a variety of styles. A manager's style at any one time or in any specific situation is largely dictated by circumstances; however, managers tend to behave in ways they find comfortable. This is often apparent when a manager must function as a counselor because he or she must simultaneously play the roles of disciplinarian and confidant.

Communication is inherent to counseling, and how a manager communicates is inherent in his or her style(s) of managing. For example, the controlling type of manager will have a directive style of communicating and counseling. A participative type of manager will be more receptive to listening to and considering others' viewpoints. He or she is likely to employ a nondirective approach to counseling. Some managers really do not manage; they function as caretakers. They are inclined to avoid responsibility and communication beyond what is minimally required. Their style of counseling is likely to be one of avoidance and shifting the responsibility to someone else.

## Approaches to Counseling

The many approaches to counseling range from highly directive to totally nondirective. Basically, the more directive approaches are characterized by giving advice, asking questions, making a diagnosis, and providing answers and solutions. The nondirective approach

## Case   Carla Gilray

Carla Gilray is an electronic parts assembler in your department. She is part of a seven-person team. Carla has worked in your department for four years and is a good worker. She is the mother of two young children and is legally separated.

It is common knowledge that Carla has dated a number of the men in the company, some of whom are married. In the past week, you have received two telephone calls about her. One was anonymous and the other was from the wife of one of your employees. Both complained strongly about Carla's behavior with men.

You have decided to have a talk with Carla. After a few minutes of social amenities, Carla says that she knows you are going to talk to her about her relationship with some of the men in the department. She tells you it's none of your business—her personal life is hers to live as she chooses.

### Questions

1. Were you correct in calling Carla into your office for counseling?
2. What should you do at the moment?
3. What, if anything, should you say to the male employees who have been involved with Carla?

focuses on the employee's discovering the cause of difficulties and deciding on the proper course of action. The manager refrains from giving advice, making a diagnosis, and imposing solutions.

No single approach fits all situations. Each manager will eventually use the methods he or she is most comfortable using. Before deciding on the initial approach, however, consider the following:

- The employee's personality and attitude
- The nature of the problem being addressed
- The seriousness of the situation
- The amount of time you are willing to give to counseling
- The organization's support system for handling employee problems

- The degree of success experienced with other employees in taking a particular approach to counseling

## The Counseling Framework

Implicit to counseling is the willingness and ability to empathize with the employee. Empathy should not be confused with sympathy or agreement. In empathizing the manager seeks to understand the employee's feelings. The manager who can see things from the employee's viewpoint is likely to establish rapport. After rapport is established, communication is likely to be more free-flowing. Rapport involves three elements: (1) an understanding manager, (2) a physical and psychological nonthreatening climate, and (3) an employee who is willing to accept counseling.

Counseling of personal problems must be conducted in an atmosphere of confidence. Only in exceptional cases, such as that of a seriously maladjusted person, are confidences revealed. For example, confidence should be broken in the case of an employee who carries a firearm and is predisposed to violence or in the case of an employee with strong sexual perversions who works with children. In such cases, more harm could be done if the maladjusted person is allowed to continue functioning in environments where there is considerable risk to others.

Good listening habits are critical to counseling's success. Perhaps the most important element in listening is patience. For many reasons, most people do not come straight to the point when they converse. They meander about until they get the confidence or find the right moment to say what they really want to. A good listener waits to see where the conversation is going before deciding whether and how to influence its course. It should be remembered that most people can work their way through a problem if they just have someone who is willing to listen to them.

When people do not understand what is being said, they usually stop listening rather than ask for clarification. A good listener seeks clarification of what is not understood. Though some managers would rather talk than listen, a good listener waits until the other person is finished before replying. Also, it is difficult to keep listening to someone when you do not agree with what he or she is saying. Even though disagreement exists, good listeners continue to listen so that they can properly evaluate both what has been said and how to react.

In counseling, creating a friendly, nonthreatening environment is important. Pay attention to seating arrangement, lighting, spatial distance, and timing.

When listening is absent, counseling becomes directive and one-sided. Even if it is decided that the employee should be directed to a solution, listening to the employee's reaction is necessary to know whether it is accepted. There is no point in wasting the effort if the employee has obviously rejected the advice and directions. The employee cannot be forced to change behavior. He or she has the choice and must recognize the potential benefits and costs associated with any decision.

With the basically responsible employee, the approach that appears best suited for most types of situations is the nondirective or client-centered method. The difficult employee or the employee who really needs advice will probably respond better to more directive approaches.

In nondirective counseling, the manager, when listening to the employee, must avoid showing anger, surprise, joy, sympathy, agreement, or disagreement with whatever the employee says. The manager must also accept or at least tolerate the employee's values and attitudes and try to avoid passing judgment on them. Acceptance should not be confused with agreement or approval. The manager must also feel that the employee really wants to do the right thing and can resolve the problems faced once interfering obstacles are removed. The manager must let the employee work out a solution that is consistent with or conforms to his or her values and beliefs. Of course, any solution must conform with the organization's accepted practices and standards of conduct. In this respect the employee cannot be allowed to carry out off-the-wall solutions. If the aforementioned conditions cannot be met, using the nondirective approach should be reconsidered. Also, if the employee is known to be untrustworthy, irresponsible, immature, or incompetent, nondirective counseling should be reconsidered.

In nondirective counseling the interviewing technique and phrasing of questions are critical. Questions that call for a yes or no answer tend to reduce the flow of conversation. Questions like "Would you like to discuss it with me?" and "Would you help me better understand your feelings?" are questions that encourage expression.

Many employees have difficulty verbalizing their problems. The manager must avoid putting words in the employee's mouth. The nondirective response of "I see" or "I understand" can help the employee express feelings. It is not unusual for gaps of silence to occur, particularly when the employee is thinking or anticipating a reaction from the listener. Though the manager may feel pressured to say something, it is usually best to let the employee restart the conversation. The manager should only initiate conversation if the meeting is in danger of collapsing because of the stress and tension built up during the period of silence. In general, when silence lasts longer than ten seconds, which to an inexperienced manager could seem like an eternity, it is time to say, "Tell me more."

Experienced managers recognize that what employees complain about is often not what is really bothering them. The same can be true in counseling. An employee may talk about a variety of things causing concern or frustration, and his or her remarks may even be contradictory. It may take some time before the real causes of the employee's problems can be identified and discussed.

As part of the nondirective technique, the manager should learn how to reflect upon what the employee says. Though some people believe that the nondirective approach to counseling means the manager remains passive throughout the meeting, this is incorrect. If it is to be productive, any discussion between two people requires a give-and-take environment. Though the employee should do most of the talking, the manager must contribute to the discussion. Instead of contributing by giving advice, the manager should reflect on what the employee has said in order to understand what he or she really means.

This method requires the manager to serve as a reflective mirror, restating each of the key things said by the employee. Key feelings must be reflected so they can be reviewed, discussed, and analyzed. In reflecting on key feelings, the manager allows nonessential information to fall by the wayside. For example, an employee may give all kinds of reasons for believing that he or she has been treated unfairly. The manager would reflect on the reasons by restating the key point, that is, the employee's belief that he or she has been treated unfairly. In reflecting, the manager should avoid using the employee's exact words, phrasing a question, or drawing a conclusion. If the employee believes that he or she has been unfairly denied a raise, the manager should state, "You feel that you have been treated unfairly." This is a statement of what the manager believes to be the employee's feeling, not a question or a judgment. In reflecting an employee's feelings, it is also important to be certain the feeling actually expressed is the one reflected. If the manager attempts to diagnose or anticipate the employee's feelings, the counseling relationship may be damaged.

In counseling it is not unusual for an employee to communicate mixed feelings or make contradictory statements. Rather than point out the inconsistencies, the manager should attempt to understand the reasons for them. Asking the employee to restate what has been said may help to clarify feelings and understandings.

If an employee becomes emotional during a counseling meeting, let him or her work through these emotions. Direct involvement is necessary only if the employee gets very depressed, hysterical, or enraged. After an emotional release, the employee may feel shame or guilt. If the employee wants to discuss the matter, he or she should be allowed to talk about it.

---

## Case   Sam Donaldson

Sam Donaldson has worked in your department for ten years. He is married and has two children. In all respects, he is an excellent worker. He is popular with nearly everyone and is active in church and civic groups. In addition, he participates in a number of company-sponsored activities.

In the past couple of months, you have noticed a change in Sam's behavior. He gives the appearance of being a man who is shouldering a heavy burden. Though his work has not been seriously affected, you have decided to see if you can find out what his problems are and help him to help himself resolve them.

You have called him into your office. After about fifteen minutes of conversation about family, children, the economy, and politics, you tell him a joke about two homosexuals. After you have finished telling the joke, you notice that Sam is not laughing. At this point, Sam tells you that a few months ago he realized he was a homosexual and has taken a male lover. He feels that his wife suspects he is a homosexual. He tells you he wants to leave his wife and move in with his lover, then asks for your advice.

### Questions

1. What will you tell him?
2. Should you inform higher-level management and/or the personnel department about the situation?
3. Can you discipline him?

When an employee displays feelings of confusion, hostility, insecurity, fear, or rejection, the manager can reflect on possible solutions or courses of action brought out by the employee during the conversation. Care should be exercised to avoid pushing the employee toward a course of action he or she may not be ready to accept. Remember, the objective of nondirective counseling is for the employee rather than the manager to develop a solution to the problem.

Except for the unusual types of situations mentioned earlier, confidences should be maintained. Because a manager is an authority figure, it is difficult under even the best of conditions for employees to express their true feelings. Considerable discretion should be used in handling sensitive or confidential information. Sometimes a problem or the solution to a problem may involve other employees. In this case the manager should discuss possible courses of action with the employee before taking action. By so doing the manager will avoid the possibility of betraying confidences.

## Giving Advice as an Approach to Counseling

Giving advice can sometimes be useful as an approach to counseling. Many problems employees face are relatively simple, and giving advice can save time and energy and enhance relationships. It is important that the employee know the advice comes from the manager's perspective and experience. But the advice may or may not fit the employee's situation and values, and the employee must understand that he or she alone must make the final decision on whether to accept it. If this precaution is not taken, the employee can easily misinterpret the manager's intentions or words. Many a manager has given advice with the best of intentions only to have it backfire. Managers should give advice only when they feel that the employee is genuinely seeking it and can properly assess how to act or react. The more serious and personal the employee's problem, the more cautiously advice should be given.

Managers who are asked for advice should preface it with statements like "From my experience . . . ," "The way I view the situation . . . ," or "If I were in your situation, I would consider. . . ." The use of such prefatory remarks helps the employee understand that the advice is being given from the manager's perspective.

In giving advice managers must avoid diagnosing an employee's problem and recommending a solution that from their perspective will resolve it. The risk is that the wrong problem may be identified and the solution may not fit the employee's value system. In addition, the employee may be unable to carry out the recommended course of action. Finally, the recommended course of action may turn out to be entirely wrong and produce disastrous results. In summary, managers can and should give advice to employees when it is sincerely requested. However, advice must always be given with caution.

## The Rewards of Counseling

When counseling is successful, everyone benefits—the organization, the manager, and especially the employee. Through counseling, particularly the nondirective approach, the employee can constructively vent frustrations and tensions. By expressing feelings, the employee can identify and address misunderstandings caused by differences in values, attitudes, and needs. The employee also learns more about him or herself. When people are frustrated and even worse, disillusioned, being able to express and work through these feelings can help to identify the true source of problems. Being able to squarely face the real issues and problems is the prerequisite to developing realistic, workable solutions. When people are preoccupied with tensions and frustrations, they cannot focus on the causes of their problems.

Once the veneers of feelings are stripped away and problems and their sources are identified, problem-solving behavior can emerge. Alternatives and courses of action can be identified, evaluated, and chosen. An employee who works out a solution acceptable to him or herself, the manager, and the organization learns to develop personal responsibility and self-discipline. Most people respond best to solutions they themselves develop as opposed to those imposed on them by others. Again, some people are unable or unwilling to exercise self-discipline. In those situations management must develop and impose solutions. Through conditioning, some people who must be directed will in time learn to develop personal responsibility.

# Handling Difficult Situations

Though most disciplinary interviews go smoothly, some do not. The manager's skill in conducting the interview will largely determine the degree of success. However, occasions do arise, for any number of reasons, where the employee is determined to be difficult. Obviously, the more that is known about an employee's personality, character, attitudes, beliefs, job, and personal situation, the better prepared the manager can be to conduct the interview. If the interview should get out of hand, the manager can always terminate it. But frequent use of this option implies that the manager cannot cope with stressful situations. An effective manager develops the skill to handle the majority of difficult cases without losing control of the situation. As a result, he or she gains the respect of the employee and others. Employees who know that a manager becomes easily frustrated and loses control of emotions will be quick to capitalize on these shortcomings to serve their own purposes.

In disciplinary interviews managers are expected to maintain the higher standard of professional and personal conduct. The disciplined employee should be given somewhat more latitude in displaying feelings than the manager conducting the interview, primarily because the employee is in an ego-diminishing situation and venting some feelings helps preserve one's sense of self-worth, relieve tension, and reduce anxiety. There are, of course, limits to what the manager must tolerate.

Emotions can and do run high in a disciplinary interview, and the employee may openly and candidly express frustrations and other feelings. For example, the employee may express frustration by talking down his or her job, the work of others, or the organization. The employee may threaten to cause problems by using political influence, filing a complaint with a government agency, suing in court, or even resorting to physical violence. In deciding whether and how to react, managers must weigh a number of factors, including the following:

- How serious does the employee appear to be?
- Can the employee actually make good on the threats?
- What is the likelihood of the threats being carried out?
- How potentially harmful could the effects be?
- Is the employee's outburst an isolated statement or part of a pattern?

An isolated statement made in the heat of the moment out of anger, frustration, or despair can usually be disregarded. However, if it appears the employee is quite serious and likely to carry out whatever was said, countersteps should be taken. For example, the employee who threatens to take the organization to court can be told that the organization is prepared and willing to defend the action. The employee can also be told that to take such action would be a waste of his or her time and money. The employee who verbally assaults the manager can be forewarned that continuance will result in further disciplinary action, although the manager must be careful to avoid overuse of authority. To help managers handle the difficult employee during an interview, the following character types and suggested ways of dealing with them are provided.

## The Discriminated Against or Persecuted Employee

This employee, regardless of what the discipline issue is, will try to make it one of illegal discrimination under law based on race, age, sex, religion, or national origin. It is a good defensive tactic and one that can easily cause the manager to get defensive and stray from the purpose of the interview. Once a manager becomes entrapped in an argument as to whether some form of discrimination under the law exists, it is difficult to extricate oneself. The manager must keep in mind and even remind the employee that the disparate treatment was based on his or her personal behavior and not under the alleged matters of law. Assuming there is no substantive evidence to indicate discrimination on the alleged basis or bases, it is best to stick to the issue and facts. Listen to the employee's allegation and ask what real evidence he or she has to support his or her views. If it appears that the evidence is groundless, either politely tell the employee so or simply return to the known facts of the issue. At all costs, avoid getting into an argument. Losing one's temper or saying things unrelated to the matter at hand will give the employee grounds to claim that the manager was out to get him or her, is a bigot, is sexist, is racist, or cannot control him- or herself.

## The Jailhouse Lawyer

This employee can be found in any type of organization and job setting, especially in a unionized organization. This employee knows the rules, contract language, organization policy, and something about the law. His or her strategy in a disciplinary interview is to intimidate and bluff the manager into believing (1) there is no case, (2) the case does not have enough merit to make discipline stick, or (3) if discipline is imposed, an Equal Employment Opportunity (EEO) or similar complaint will be filed. This employee will also try to find a breach of procedure, technical error, or omission in the due process procedure.

There are a number of ways to safeguard against this character type. First, make sure that all steps of the organization's due process procedure are followed. Second, be certain that the employee is aware of his or her rights as outlined in policies and procedures. Third, do not get into an argument with the employee. He or she will be quick to catch an error of fact or unsubstantiated opinion and use it against you. If the employee quotes chapter law or regulations, do not argue. Unless the employee has legal training or experience, whatever is said is likely to be wrong or only partially correct. Consult legal counsel and/or knowledgeable human resources specialists about the law and its impact on the case. If the employee is correct, thank him or her for the input. If the employee is wrong, politely and firmly say so. Should the employee threaten legal action, advise him or her of the right to do so. Again, stay with the issue(s) at hand.

## The Intimidator

This employee can present a real challenge. The intimidator's objective is to gain psychological control of the interview. The manager who cannot cope with this type of employee may precipitate a serious confrontation, be psychologically outmaneuvered and outflanked, or end the interview without having accomplished much. Typical tactics used by the intimidator include:

- Remaining standing while the manager is seated
- Turning from the manager so as to appear to be ignoring what is being said
- Whistling softly, looking around the room or at the ceiling, and avoiding eye contact
- Putting feet on the manager's desk
- Pointing a finger in the manager's face, glaring balefully, or raising his or her voice
- Moving around the room
- Staring intently at the manager and using facial expressions and movements to communicate fury, anger, or rage
- Overreacting with considerable display of emotion to whatever is said
- Interrupting
- Taking statements out of context and changing their intended meaning to suit other purposes
- Threatening to use influence with acquaintances or friends higher in the organization or community

Managers can use several techniques to successfully control this type of employee. The employee who likes to stand can be asked, not ordered, to have a seat. If asked why, the manager might reply, "I believe you will be more comfortable," "This meeting is going to last for some time," or "I prefer that you are seated." If the employee continues refusing to sit, the manager can either not make an issue of it or also stand while talking.

In response to the employee who turns his or her back, stares at the ceiling, or paces around the room, stop talking and wait until the employee is again listening. Silence is a very effective communication tool. Another useful approach is to speak softly and slowly. This usually gets the employee's attention because he or she needs to know what is being said in order to know what to say next. Raising one's voice should generally be avoided, as it usually indicates heightened emotions and a loss of control. The employee may later take advantage of it by accusing the manager of yelling and screaming. In some instances the manager's raising his or her voice could have a chilling effect on the employee, but for this approach to work, the manager must be in control of his or her emotions while displaying anger. If emotional control is lost, control over the situation is lost. With some employees this technique will bring instant results. The employee will recognize that he or she is in deeper trouble and behavior had better improve. However, with others, the opposite could happen. The employee will counter with a stronger display of emotions, which could quickly lead to an ugly confrontation. The manager could lose out because he or she was primarily responsible for controlling the situation. As with any of the approaches suggested, the manager must use his or her best judgment in choosing a course of action. If a chosen course is not working, direction should be changed.

Baleful glares and stares should be ignored. Once the employee sees they are not working, he or she will either stop and start paying attention or try something else.

The employee who places his or her feet on the manager's desk should be asked to remove them. If this does not work, the employee should be directed to remove them and forewarned that failure to do so will be cause for further discipline. The same approach would apply to the finger pointer. In response to the finger pointer or arm waver, the manager can also push his or her chair farther back from the desk, thereby putting more distance between him- or herself and the employee.

An overreactive employee should be asked to control him- or herself. The overreactive employee may behave this way for any of the following reasons:

1. It's part of his or her emotional makeup. Some people are very outgoing and display wide-ranging feelings, while others are much

more reticent and either keep feelings bottled up or actually do not feel wide ranges of emotions.

2. The employee knows the boss is easily intimidated and will back off a position.

3. The boss is a hothead and when angry is inclined to make remarks he or she later regrets. This boss usually ends up trying to make up to the employee.

4. The boss cannot control him- or herself and predictably makes derogatory remarks that can later be used against him or her.

Tell the employee who interrupts and takes things out of context that he or she will have a chance to speak after you have finished. If interruptions persist, tell the employee that if the interruptions do not stop, the meeting is over. Avoid arguing with the employee.

Most threats, whether stated or implied, do not have substance and can be disregarded. However, if the employee can use political influence as a countermeasure, some action should be taken. For example, the manager can:

1. Let the employee know that such threats are cause for further discipline

2. Take the offensive and counter with his or her own political influence

3. Build an airtight case so the employee's protectors will decide not to support a lost cause

4. Learn the source of the employee's influence with others and find a way to reduce or eliminate it

## The Baiter

This employee often resembles the intimidator but is more cunning and clever. The baiter's objective is to entrap the manager by causing him or her to say or do something that can be later used to discredit. For example, the baiter may:

• Challenge the validity and/or reliability of any damaging evidence based on opinion or judgment.

• Get the manager to make an off-the-cuff statement or derogatory remark about some religion, ethnic group, race, sex, and so on. This is often accomplished through reciprocal joke telling.

• Break down and start crying in the middle of the interview. The objective is to get the manager to physically touch him or her. This can later be used to allege that the manager made a sexual advance or assaulted him or her.

In handling the baiter it is best to stick to the issue and the facts. Avoid debating and arguing, and carefully choose words that are clear in intent and meaning. If the employee begins to cry, do nothing and wait until it's over before continuing. As appropriate, pass the tissues. Avoid physical contact.

## The Charmer

The charmer will use what is commonly referred to as charisma to manipulate and psychologically seduce the manager. The use of charisma may be purely psychological in nature or a combination of psychological and physical. The charmer will usually be subtle in "coming on" to the manager. A pretty face, a trim figure, and a captivating personality, whether male or female, can be a powerful potion for influencing the susceptible or unwary manager.

The most effective way to resist the charmer is to be prepared for the "come-ons" and ignore them. Most charmers will back off quickly when they recognize their tactics are not working.

## The Friend

It is not uncommon for close relationships and friendships to develop between people who work together. When a manager must discipline a close acquaintance or friend, it can be difficult for all involved. Some employees will draw on a friendship with the manager to get favored treatment. Human beings are social creatures and to varying degrees need to socialize. For some the costs associated with losing a friend can be significant.

The best way to handle such situations is to separate personal from professional feelings. This is easier said than done. It may be useful for the manager to tell the friend that playing on the relationship will only make the matter worse for all involved. The manager can also explain that he or she has responsibilities to carry out and, while not wanting to damage the friendship, must assume such risks in carrying out those responsibilities.

## The Chronic Excuse Finder

This employee always has an excuse to explain and/or justify whatever caused the need for discipline. No matter what has happened, either there were mitigating circumstances or someone else was at

---

## Case  Ellen Schmidt

Ellen Schmidt supervises the medical testing laboratory at a large metropolitan hospital. Roberta Jones is one of Ellen's technicians. Roberta, who is recently divorced and has four children, is technically competent and works hard. However, she has one problem—she is continually late for work. Ellen has spoken to her about it on a number of occasions. Roberta's lateness adversely affects the productivity of her coworkers. Her lateness holds everyone up from starting their work. The hospital's rules state that excessive, frequent, or chronic absence or lateness is just cause for disciplinary action up to dismissal.

When Ellen spoke to Roberta about her problem, she defended her lateness by going into considerable detail about her responsibilities to get the children up, bathed, dressed, and off to school. Roberta maintains that she works harder than anybody else and often stays over in the evening to make up the time that she has lost. Upon inves-

---

fault. The chronic excuse finder never seems to run out of creative reasons. He or she either cannot cope with life's obstacles or cannot accept responsibility for his or her behavior. Identifying this character type is fairly easy. For example, this employee can be counted on to say:

• I was absent or late because the car broke down, the children are sick, there were traffic jams, the alarm clock did not go off, or I ran out of gas.

• It was not my fault; if only the others had been on time, done their part, or not created unnecessary obstacles.

• I could have gotten it done if I had more time, money, people, supplies, or equipment.

Trying to outsmart, outtalk, or outmaneuver this employee is likely to prove futile. It deviates from the disciplinary issue and from efforts to identify the real cause of the problems. Staying with the matter at hand and avoiding being sidetracked is an effective way to handle this employee.

tigating this, Ellen finds that her claims are correct. Roberta does work harder than anybody else and has, in fact, stayed over on many evenings to make up for having been late.

It's Tuesday morning and, sure enough, Roberta is forty-five minutes late. Her lateness has kept three other technicians from starting their work. Ellen realizes that the situation requires action on her part and ponders what to do.

### Questions

1. What should Ellen do?
2. What alternative courses of action does Ellen have available to her?
3. What positive approaches to discipline can Ellen apply?
4. Is this a problem of changing behavior, or is it a problem of operating flexibility?

## Summary

If managers believe in the principle that the suspected or accused employee is innocent until proven guilty, then the disciplinary interview is a critical element in due process. Only after the employee has been heard and his or her testimony weighed can innocence or the degree of guilt be decided. The interview is a continuation of the fact-finding process.

The very nature of the interview itself makes it potentially a highly emotionally charged confrontation. The manager who is making accusations or presenting charges is primarily responsible for ensuring that the meeting goes smoothly and its purposes are fulfilled. This chapter has provided both general and specific information for managers to use in planning and conducting a successful interview.

As part of the discipline process, counseling should be used to reduce the likelihood of a recurrence of misconduct and to help the employee regain or keep control of his or her life. Unless the employee really wants to help him- or herself change behavior and be self-responsible, the potential success of counseling is low. Some counseling can be limited and some can be extensive and take years to achieve lasting results. For most employees a manager must simply be a good listener while the employee sorts it all out or uses a little advice to produce lasting results. For such counseling managers do not need extensive training or skills, but they should always refer what appear to be serious difficulties to professionals.

There is no one best approach to counseling. The interaction of many factors must be weighed in deciding how counseling should be conducted.

Most disciplinary interviews go well, though some can present real challenges. A manager's true skills are shown by the way he or she handles the difficult character types. It takes considerable skill and self-control to properly handle a difficult employee in the middle of an emotion-laden confrontation. This chapter has provided an array of guidelines to handle various character types.

In the next chapter I will focus on the various forms of discipline that can be used. I will also present information to show how the specific discipline should be determined.

## Key Points

- A suspected or accused employee is innocent until proven guilty. The disciplinary interview amounts to the employee's day in court.
- Conducting a disciplinary interview and weighing what the employee has to say in his or her defense before passing judgment is an essential element of due process.
- A badly handled disciplinary interview or worse, none at all, can permanently damage working relationships. It can also permanently emotionally scar the mistreated employee.
- As a preventive measure, executive-level management should establish clear guidelines on how disciplinary interviews should be conducted.
- A disciplinary interview should be thoroughly planned, which does not mean the meeting will always fully conform to the plan. However, the manager conducting the interview must never lose sight of its basic purpose and what he or she is trying to achieve.
- A disciplinary interview can be filled with strong feelings and related tensions. Considerable skill is needed to keep emotions from getting out of hand.
- The psychological climate for a meeting can be set in advance by how the employee is told about the scheduled meeting.

- There is no one best way to conduct all disciplinary interviews. There are general guides. Each manager must decide how to use these guides in planning each meeting.

- A disciplinary interview should be viewed as an opportunity and challenge as opposed to an unavoidable and unpleasant chore. This does not mean a manager should be overjoyed about having to conduct a meeting.

- In projecting thoughts and understanding others, nonverbal communication is just as, if not more, important than verbal communication.

- Counseling is an important tool for learning the underlying causes of misbehavior.

- The results of counseling should be documented to determine what progress has been made and what additional measures may be required.

- A manager's personality and preferred ways of dealing with employees will greatly influence his or her counseling style.

- Directive forms of counseling are characterized by giving advice, asking questions, making a diagnosis, and providing answers and solutions.

- Nondirective approaches focus on discovering the source of difficulties and the employee's working out the solution. The manager refrains from giving advice, making a diagnosis, and imposing solutions.

- Effective counseling is predicated on a manager's good listening skills and a desire to want to help the employee, as well as on the employee's desire to help him- or herself.

- Employees with apparent serious problems should be referred to professionals in mental health and social services.

- Though it is risky to stereotype people, some employees have distinct personalities that fit specific character types. Certain character types can be difficult to handle in disciplinary situations. However, useful guides exist to help handle various character types.

## Discussion Questions

1. Discuss the potential difficulties an employee may run into if he or she pursues due process outside the organization for perceived injustice.

2. What risks do employers run in having to settle differences with employees in the courts?
3. What can a well-planned and well-conducted disciplinary interview accomplish?
4. What steps should be taken in planning a disciplinary interview?
5. What factors affect the setting and climate of a disciplinary interview?
6. Discuss the various dimensions of nonverbal communication.
7. Should specific discipline be determined before the interview? Why?
8. Under what circumstances is it inadvisable to employ counseling as part of the interview process?
9. Why is counseling important?
10. Identify and discuss some of the job-related causes of misconduct.
11. Identify and discuss some of the job environment causes of misconduct.
12. Discuss the advantages and disadvantages of a nondirective approach to counseling.
13. Under what circumstances might it be best to use a directive approach to counseling?
14. How should an employee who claims discrimination and persecution be handled?
15. Identify some of the techniques an intimidative type of employee might use. How can these be controlled?

# 5 Determining the Appropriate Disciplinary Action

As emphasized in earlier chapters, an employee's guilt or innocence and the degree thereof should be decided after a disciplinary interview has been conducted. In some cases, after the employee has expressed his or her position, a determination can be made during the interview. In others, reinvestigation is indicated and a second interview will be necessary. And in still others, the manager will want to reflect on the interview and weigh many factors in deciding on the type and degree of discipline that should be given. This chapter focuses on the forms of discipline available and the evaluation of relevant and pertinent information for prescribing specific discipline. The objectives again are fair treatment of the employee and no recurrence of the problem.

The degree of flexibility inherent in the organization's disciplinary program establishes the parameters managers have to operate within. The scope of authority will also be influenced by the degree of independent authority managers have, as well as by traditions, customs, and present policies and practices. If a system exists like the one shown in Figure 5.1, determining specific discipline is a simple task. Managers need only review the status of the employee's disciplinary record, check which rule or rules have been violated, count the number of offenses that have occurred, and see what is the appropriate discipline. This system does provide for limited flexibility when a suspension from work without pay is indicated. Thus, to a limited degree, the merit principle can be applied. Most systems of this nature do not provide for any flexibility at all.

---

## Figure 5.1    Employee Responsibilities with Structured Progressive Discipline

Key to Symbols: W—Written Warning; 2–3, 3–4–5—Suspension Days;
D—Discharge

| | Offense | | | |
|---|---|---|---|---|
| | First | Second | Third | Fourth |
| 1. Smoking in unauthorized areas or near flammable materials | 3–5 | D | | |
| 2. Posting or removing notices, signs, and so on in any form from bulletin boards, on company property, without approval of management, distribution of hand bills or other literature, balloting, petitioning, and so on without management permission | W | 2–3 | 3–4–5 | D |
| 3. Leaving regularly assigned workplace without justifiable reason and/or informing supervisor, except for personal health needs | W | 2–3 | 3–4–5 | D |
| 4. Habitual tardiness or unauthorized absence | W | 2–3 | 3–4–5 | D |
| 5. Poor housekeeping surrounding immediate work area | W | 2–3 | 3–4–5 | D |
| 6. Improper use or care of company property, including production of scrap and/or material requiring rework | W | 2–3 | 3–4–5 | D |
| 7. Reading newspaper, periodicals, and so on on company time | W | 2–3 | 3–4–5 | D |
| 8. Selling tickets, soliciting contributions from other employees, and so on on company property without management approval | W | 2–3 | 3–4–5 | D |

| | Offense | | | |
|---|---|---|---|---|
| | First | Second | Third | Fourth |
| 9. Wasting time, loitering, loafing, or otherwise leaving work area during working hours | W | 2–3 | 3–4–5 | D |
| 10. a. Negligent or careless act that may result in personal injury or damage to company property | 3–4–5 | D | | |
| b. Negligent or careless act that may result in defective workmanship and failure to use specific tools and methods | W | 3–4–5 | D | |
| 11. a. Reporting to work under the influence of intoxicating liquor or beverage and/or narcotics or possession thereof | W | 3–4–5 | D | |
| b. Intoxicated on the job, being in possession of and/or use of intoxicating beverages or narcotics on plant premises | D | | | |
| 12. Insubordination, including refusal or failure to perform work assigned, use of profane or threatening language toward supervisors | 3–4–5 | D | | |
| 13. Sleeping on company time; the fact that an employee may be temporarily at leisure is not accepted as an excuse for violation of this rule | 3–4–5 | D | | |
| 14. Clocking in or out another employee's time card | 3–4–5 | D | | |
| 15. Theft of company property or property of another, or taking company property from the plant without an authorization pass from management | D | | | |
| 16. Horseplay, scuffling, running, or throwing things | 3–4–5 | D | | |

*(continued)*

## Figure 5.1   *continued*

| | Offense | | | |
|---|---|---|---|---|
| | First | Second | Third | Fourth |
| 17. Concealing, destroying, or failure to report defective work or damaged company tools, jigs, and so on | 3-4-5 | D | | |
| 18. Gambling on company premises. | 3-4-5 | D | | |
| 19. Falsifying work records, personnel or other records, including application form and so on | D | | | |
| 20. Immoral or indecent conduct, fighting, threatening, intimidating, or using obscene language toward fellow employees or supervisors | 3-4-5 | D | | |
| 21. Willful misuse, damage, or destruction of company property or property of others | D | | | |
| 22. Conviction of any felony offense or class A or B misdemeanor (parking or routine speeding violation not included) | D | | | |
| 23. Violation of or disregard for safety rules, including failure to wear safety equipment, such as safety glasses, foot protection, hard hats, hair snoods, ear plugs, earmuffs, rubber gloves, and so on | W | 2-3 | 3-4-5 | D |

|  | Offense | | | |
|---|---|---|---|---|
|  | First | Second | Third | Fourth |
| 24. Operating facilities in a manner that would directly or indirectly cause or allow contamination to pollute the atmosphere or disposal of waste or materials such as oil, paint, thinner, acids, and so on, in unauthorized places | 2–3 | 3–4–5 | D | |

An employee's immediate supervisor or any management representative has the authority to issue a notice to an employee for violating a company rule. *Separate violations of different rules shall incur penalties equal to separate violations of the same rule, except as the employee's record may be cleared as explained below.* All violations involving suspension or discharge will be issued by the employee's immediate supervisor or in his or her absence by any management representative, and a copy of such suspension or discharge notice shall be promptly furnished to the employee and such employee's grievance committeeman, where applicable.

An employee who violates a rule may clear his or her personnel record as follows:

1. If no further rule violation or warning notice is issued the employee within the three-month period following the date of issuance of a warning notice.

2. If no further rule violation is issued the employee within the six-month period following a two- or three-day suspension.

3. If no further rule violation is issued the employee within the twelve-month period following the date of issuance of a three- to five-day suspension.

4. An employee who is discharged under these rules shall not have his or her record cleared.

Within the system shown in Figure 5.1, management wisely included the following statement: "Separate violations of different rules shall incur penalties equal to separate violations of the same rule, except as the employee's record may be cleared as explained below." Had this statement not been included, an employee could conceivably break numerous rules only once without receiving anything more than a written notice. Many organizations have such systems of progressive discipline, and they usually do not work very well, principally because employees, particularly those prone to be discipline problems, carefully count how many times they can break certain rules within specified time periods and avoid getting into serious trouble. This occurs most often in attendance control programs that make allowances for a specified number of absences, late reports, and leaving work early before discipline is invoked. Under the system shown in Figure 5.1, an employee who concurrently broke rules 3 and 19 would receive the greater discipline, in this case discharge under rule 19. The principle governing this is that the greater discipline includes the lesser. However, the termination letter would note that two rules were violated.

The type of program shown in Figure 5.1 is more commonly found in unionized organizations. The degree of trust between employees and managers in unionized organizations tends to be less than what exists in well-managed nonunion organizations. Through the collective bargaining process, unions frequently work toward reducing management's flexibility in exercising authority. Unfortunately, managers often sow the seeds of their own problems by acting in ways that reinforce the mistrust. Prolonged adversarial labor-management relations have proved costly to many companies and even entire industries.

Out of economic necessity, as managers in unionized and nonunion organizations move toward more cooperative, participative relationships with employees, such structured punitive systems will be less commonplace. This will not happen overnight, and for sound reasons some organizations will retain such systems. However, the majority of nonunion and increasing numbers of unionized organizations will adopt or continue to use systems that provide for flexibility and application of the merit principle. Though such systems are more difficult to develop and incorporate into the organization's operating systems, they better serve the needs of managers and employees over the long term.

Whether a highly, semi-, or loosely structured system exists, some types of misconduct are so minor that formal discipline is unwarranted. For example: if a good employee sometimes takes a couple of minutes longer than is allowed or necessary for a work break, issuance of a formal charge of loitering or habitually wasting time would not be called for. Nor would a complete investigation. In this case the manager has noticed the behavior and should ask the employee if he or she was aware of it. If the employee is aware of it, the manager should find out the reason why he or she has been taking longer than normal. Should no plausible reason be given, it would then be necessary to tell the employee of the rule and why it exists. The employee should also be told that if the problem continues, formal discipline will be considered. This example assumes the situation is not widespread, the employee is not a general discipline problem, and he or she wants to and is capable of doing the right thing.

Should a record of this be made? As a general practice, some notation of the conversation should be entered on the employee's working personnel file—the one the manager uses as a data base for what eventually goes into the permanent record. The employee should also be advised that a notation is being made, and if there are no further occurrences, the matter will not tarnish his or her record. Conversely, similar action should be taken when an employee is commended for extraordinary service. Noting the bad without noting the good is an unsound management practice; it conveys an image of keeping records solely for the purpose of creating a file for disciplinary purposes. When commendable and detrimental behavior are balanced, a different image is communicated. Maintaining balanced records is a good human resources management practice. Employees should know what types of information are kept in their permanent records and, on request, should be allowed to review them. In recent years a number of states have enacted laws giving employees the right to see their records and challenge whatever they feel is unsubstantiated. The trend is for more states to pass similar laws.

Instances where a manager advises an employee to "cut it out," "knock it off," "stop it," or "do it differently" are so minor and infrequent that a formal discussion and a note in the employee's record are unwarranted. When no record is made, for all intents and purposes it will be considered not to have occurred at all. But if a pattern warrants a formal warning, a record should be made that contains reference to previous discussions. If the employee were to challenge reference to prior, undocumented discussions, management might have a difficult time proving they had taken place. If the case for discipline was damaged or even lost because no record had been made of previous discussions, management would be spurred to formalize the relationship and maintain stricter records. When a high level of mutual trust exists between managers and employees, few employees will challenge management's actions to ensure that all the *t*'s have been crossed and *i*'s dotted whenever discipline is involved unless they honestly believe that management has erred. Keep in mind that this situation involves minor discipline. For anything beyond very minor situations, records should be maintained.

# Negative-Punitive Forms of Discipline

In Chapter 1 reference was made to broad classifications of discipline. They were the negative-punitive forms, positive-constructive-rehabilitative forms, and other forms that would be considered either positive or negative according to how they were used.

Discipline programs that embody the merit principle usually have provision for using a wide variety of methods. Figure 5.2 lists the negative-punitive forms of discipline.

In the short term many of these approaches work rather well, but in the long term the costs associated with their use usually far outweigh the benefits. As stated in Chapter 1, under these forms of

---

**Figure 5.2    Negative-Punitive Forms of Discipline**

- Suspension from work without pay for a specific number of consecutive workdays
- Suspension from work without pay for a specific number of staggered scheduled workdays
- Ridicule, sarcasm, criticism, intimidation, and threats, used separately or in combination
- Assignment to unpleasant, undesirable, or dirty jobs
- Frequently informing employees at the last possible moment that they have been scheduled to work overtime
- Scheduling work seven days a week for extended periods
- Compulsory overtime—for example, scheduling ten- to twelve-hour days when seven to eight is the norm
- Requiring a public explanation or apology
- Purposely delaying disciplinary action
- Spontaneous or summary termination
- Eliminating the job
- Promotion or lateral transfer to obscurity
- Assigning no work

---

discipline, employees change behavior out of fear instead of an internalized desire to conform to reasonable standards of conduct and exercise self-discipline. Employees will conform as long as the fear of being caught and punished exists. But if the opportunity presents itself to misbehave or retaliate without getting caught, those employees who need to do so will take advantage of it.

Some people, as a result of conditioning from early childhood, have come to expect punishment when they misbehave. Though they may resent being punished, fear of it keeps them from misbehaving. Although children may be slow to respond to constructive forms of discipline, which emphasize personal responsibility and self-discipline, they will respond to punishment. For example, children who misbehave may be physically punished (spanked), psychologically punished (restricted from playing their video games), or socially punished (grounded). Punitive approaches generate much quicker results than lectures about right and wrong and personal responsibility. However, responsible parents recognize their obligation to help children grow into adulthood. As a child develops, discipline should shift from punitive forms and methods to ones that stimulate self-discipline and personal responsibility. The child who in all respects is maturing has a sense of self-worth, understands right from wrong, and is capable of exercising self-discipline. Unfortunately, many parents either do not provide the guidance for children to develop or continue to inhibit their development by perpetuating punitive forms of discipline in order to maintain control. As a result, these children physically become adults but lag behind psychologically.

Managers who have never learned to treat adults as adults because they never fully developed themselves or who have never learned to control their own children may show strong inclinations to rely on punitive approaches to discipline. Managers may also be supervising some employees who are unable or unwilling to behave as adults. They have little choice in the short term but to use punitive forms of discipline to control these types of employees when they misbehave. Though managers may well recognize the benefits of constructive forms of discipline, they know they will not work unless employees can and want to behave as adults. Helping employees grow, and shifting from punitive to rehabilitative forms of discipline as growth occurs, is a challenge for the best of managers. The results of success can be most gratifying. However, it must be recognized that in some cases the time, energy, and other resources required may not be available or justifiable.

As noted earlier, disciplinary situations can generate considerable tension. A parent can get very angry and frustrated with a child who misbehaves when he or she should have known better. Likewise, a manager can have the same feelings with respect to an employee's misbehavior. The parent who overreacts, yells, rants, and raves at the child may feel good for the moment because tension is released, but in the long term such behavior can do more harm than good for the child. It is not unusual for the parent who has overreacted to later feel guilty and in some way apologize to the child. The manager who overreacts, rants, and raves may also feel good for the moment, but the long-term damage to the relationship with the employee could far outweigh any short-term benefits. This is not to say that a manager should never raise his or her voice or overreact. Sometimes such action can have a positive effect. Further, it is unrealistic to assume that a manager will always be in full control of his or her emotions and never make a mistake.

When mutual trust, respect, and confidence exist between a manager and his or her employees, an occasional slipup will be excused. Frequent slipups will hurt the relationship. If trust, respect, and confidence are nonexistent, slipups will reinforce feelings of mistrust and suspicion. Once trust is lost, it is difficult to regain.

## Suspension from Work without Pay

In many instances, the traditional suspension without pay has outlived its usefulness, primarily because personal and social values have changed. A disciplinary suspension deprives the employee of compensation, as well as psychological and social benefits associated with the job. If an employee's economic, psychological, and social needs are largely fulfilled through work, then being barred from the job for a period of time is a high price to pay for misconduct. But if the employee's needs are only minimally satisfied through the job, a suspension will not be seen as being too costly. The same can be said if work is important but acceptable substitutes are readily available.

People's values influence how they think and act. Values are learned during the formative years and become ingrained as part of personality and character. By the time a child reaches adolescence, his or her value system is rather well developed. The shaping of values is a complex process that evolves from the influence of many factors, including parents and other family members, television, music, friends, teachers, heroes, and the society at large. Values can and do change, either quickly or gradually. For some people, values learned early may change little over their lifetime, while others may experience rapid and significant change, sometimes precipitated by traumatic events.

Value system differences help account for so-called generation gaps. People raised in different time periods and in different societal conditions are likely to have different value systems. Because our society has experienced and is currently experiencing significant economic and social changes, the values of people may vary considerably from one age group to another. The values of employees in their fifties and sixties may differ greatly from those of employees in their twenties and thirties. To be effective, discipline must be socially acceptable and fit with employees' values. This is an important reason to use varied approaches to discipline. Managers must deal not only with value differences but also with basic character differences. The result is that certain approaches work with some employees but not with others.

When young employees are compared with their older counterparts, the values and attitudes about obedience to authority, loyalty to one's employer, commitment to the job, dedication to tasks, job security, importance of leisure time, and the importance of a paycheck and raises may be quite different.

A suspension may well fit into the value systems of employees in their fifties and sixties but not into those of employees in their twenties and thirties. Older employees are often traumatized by a suspension, while younger employees may just shrug it off. The reason for this is that many employees under forty have, until recently, known nothing but relative prosperity their entire lives. They have not experienced the economic and emotional deprivation that usually comes with long-term unemployment, so the security of a steady paycheck may not be as important to them as it is to those who have experienced long-term unemployment. Younger employees may actually want the time off and even ask for days off that, when combined with the weekend, create a mini-vacation. If an employee views a suspension as a reward, it is not much of an incentive to change. Employees who think this way clearly understand that frequent suspensions will result in termination and, therefore, are careful to avoid getting too many of them.

The cost of an employee's absence is another disadvantage of suspensions. Benefits are still being paid, and work output will be adversely affected unless others fill in and pick up the slack. If this is not possible, then either work is held up or others have to work overtime. The worst possible case is that the suspended employee goes off fishing while work in process is either held up until the employee returns or others are assigned to perform it in order to maintain output.

Most organizations that use suspensions as a form of discipline

## Case    Robert Hartman

Robert Hartman has been employed by the company for five years. He is considered at best an average employee. On occasion, he has been disciplined for excessive absenteeism and lateness. He is known to sometimes loaf on the job by taking longer than the allowable time for coffee breaks and returning late from the lunch period. Over the past three months, Robert's supervisor, Sara Constable, has noticed that Robert goes to the bathroom frequently and spends a considerable amount of time there.

Company policy states that employees are expected to do a fair day's work for a fair day's pay. Company rules provide for progressive disciplinary action for loitering and wasting time. The minimum disciplinary action that can be imposed for a first violation is a verbal warning.

Two weeks ago, Sara began keeping track of how often Robert went to the bathroom. She observed that on the average, Robert went to the bathroom five times a day and stayed there from eight to twenty minutes. The record shows that this far exceeds the norm.

Three days ago, Sara asked Robert if he had any medical problem that necessitated his going to the bathroom so frequently and staying away from the job for such long times. Robert said, "No, I just have a small bladder and

suspend employees for a stated number of consecutive workdays. Others suspend employees on workdays when their absence will not hurt work requirements. In unionized organizations, when staggered suspensions are appealed to arbitration, arbitrators usually will not uphold such discipline unless it has been used as a matter of well-established practice. One reason is the belief that if discipline is at the convenience of employers and they incur no loss, they have little incentive to avoid disciplining employees; in fact, suspensions on slack days could be used to hold down costs. Another reason is that the suspension loses its association with the precipitating event. If discipline adversely affects both the employer and employee, a mutual need exists to avoid recurrence. This reasoning is sound. However, occasions could arise where a staggered suspension could

small bowels." Sara forewarned Robert that if he continued going to the bathroom so frequently, he would be subject to disciplinary action. Robert responded, "You can't stop me from going to the toilet."

Over the next few days, Robert used the bathroom more frequently than in the past. Sara decided that she had just cause for issuing a written warning. On receiving the warning, Robert filed a grievance against Sara contending that he was being harassed and discriminated against. In his grievance he stated, "You can't even take a crap around here without a supervisor bugging you."

### Questions

1. Did Sara handle the problem correctly? Why?
2. Could this incident have been avoided? Why?
3. Did Sara take the appropriate action when she disciplined Robert? Why?
4. As a higher-level manager, would you rescind the written warning or let it stand? Why?
5. What if Robert does have a small bladder and small bowels?

benefit management and the employee. In such uncommon instances a staggered suspension would be better than a consecutive one.

## Ridicule, Sarcasm, Criticism, Intimidation, and Threats

When asked, few managers would admit they ever use ridicule, sarcasm, and intimidation as forms of discipline. Though they have no legitimate place in the discipline process, they are nonetheless used. The moment of pleasure a manager may experience from ridiculing or being sarcastic with an employee will be at the expense of that employee's respect for him or her. An employee treated in this manner can be expected to either withdraw or find an opportunity to retaliate. If these forms of discipline are unsound, why do some managers use them? The answer has to do with personality and interpersonal factors, including the following:

- A strong need to dominate and control others
- Enjoyment in seeing others degraded and humiliated
- Frustration when other approaches have not worked
- Character disorder
- Deep-rooted prejudice
- Personality clash
- Personal insecurity
- Emulating behavior of a role model

It is one thing for executive-level managers to state that such treatment of employees is unacceptable and quite another to have managers behave as they should all the time. Training will certainly help. The best way to get managers at all levels to conduct themselves in a professional manner is for executive-level managers to set the right example. Setting the proper example, coupled with training, and refusing to support managers who resort to such tactics will be most effective.

Constructive criticism can be very effective. It can help the employee learn from mistakes, build self-confidence, and strengthen relationships. Intent, personal style, timing, the type of situation addressed, and the employee's perceptions will largely determine how such criticism is interpreted. Criticism is most often used in disciplining job performance problems. Before it is used, the following should be evaluated:

- Does the employee have proper training?
- Did the employee receive correct instruction?
- Did the employee have adequate resources to do the job?
- Does the employee have a sense of personal responsibility and the desire to do what is required or expected?
- Did the problem occur for reasons beyond the employee's control?

If it is decided the employee was at fault, criticism must be given with the intent of assistance and guidance, not degradation. Criticism when interpreted negatively, does not work very well.

Threats should be made with considerable caution and must never pertain to physical harm. They must be phrased in terms of forewarnings of consequences if behavior does not change. As with criticism, intent and perceptions shape how a threat will be perceived. On occasion an employee may threaten to physically harm a fellow employee or someone in management. If threatened with physical harm, a manager should avoid returning the threat. The manager should use his or her authority to discipline the employee under the organization's rules. The manager may also bring charges against the employee under civil law.

## Assignment to Unpleasant or Undesirable Jobs

This is a commonly used form of discipline. Every organization has its share of unpleasant tasks, and it is a questionable yet common practice for new employees to be assigned to them. The importance of initial impressions in shaping attitudes has been well documented. Assigning new employees to the least desirable work is an excellent way to facilitate shaping the wrong attitudes.

Assignment to unpleasant tasks as a form of discipline relies on fear. Employees behave because they do not want to be the ones assigned. But what happens if a dirty job must be done and no one deserves to be disciplined? Someone has to do the work. The hapless employee who is selected is likely to feel that he or she was singled out for discipline when none was deserved. Irrespective of the manager's explanation, the employee will probably feel persecuted.

## Compulsory Overtime

Though compulsory overtime is probably never given as an explicit form of discipline, it is often perceived as such by employees. If managers realized the true cost of overtime, they would seriously reconsider scheduling it as often as they do. Like many things, a little is okay, and too much is no good. Everyone recognizes and accepts that on occasion overtime situations can suddenly arise. But when they become frequent, something is obviously wrong. Managers sometimes fail to realize that employees have lives and interests outside their jobs. In today's pluralistic society, people may be involved in all sorts of activities outside of work that demand their time, energy, and talents. Whereas in the past, work was more a central part of people's lives, today this is no longer the case for most people. Last-minute notice of overtime does not give employees time to make adjustments regarding other commitments. An employee may have planned to have an anniversary dinner with a spouse, to attend an award ceremony for a child, or to play tennis with a friend. In any case, the employee is going to be somewhat upset by the situation. Again, if this happens infrequently, most employees will work the overtime and not feel any lingering resentment. But when in the employee's view it occurs excessively, he or she is apt to feel punished for what is seen as management's mistakes.

In unionized organizations a common feature of labor agreements is that employees can refuse scheduled overtime work, although the refused time will be charged against their overtime distribution record, as if they had worked them. Also, unless employees are given a minimum amount of advance notice of overtime, they can refuse the work and not have it charged against their record. Some agreements contain a clause requiring management to pay for a minimum number of hours if an employee is called back for work or given last minute notification of required overtime work. Last minute may be anywhere from four hours to three days. The purpose of such language is to penalize management for disrupting employees' personal lives.

Some managers, in their zeal to satisfy customers' needs, keep business from going to competitors, and maximize profits, schedule work seven days a week for extended periods. Many organizations have learned the hard way that pushing operating systems, as well as human and nonhuman resources, to their breaking points is a costly way to do business.

It can be argued that some employees will voluntarily accept seven-day schedules. Though this may be true, eventually they may resent working the hours or their associates may resent their earning so much more money. Even worse, managers who generally put in more than forty hours and do not get paid overtime will come to resent it. If the seven-day work schedule is required or is perceived as being required, managers can be assured that resentment will arise. Managers must remember that employees need time to be with their families and friends and to get away from work and enjoy a change of scenery. This also applies to managerial employees. The same reasoning applies to extended workdays over long time periods unless employees are working a four-day workweek.

### Requiring a Public Explanation or Apology

If employed with considerable discretion, this form of discipline can be useful. Sometimes an employee's explaining why something went wrong or misconduct occurred can be a therapeutic catharsis. When an employee's wrongdoing adversely affects the well-being of others, a public explanation or apology to them can be an act of courage and repentance. It can also set the record straight and clear up misunderstandings. People have a tremendous capacity to accept and forgive human fallibility if the wrongdoer is honest about it. (For example, had Mr. Nixon shown the good sense and courage to tell the American people he had used poor judgment and made a mistake regarding the Watergate break-in, he might have remained in office.) This does not mean that if one is honest about committing a crime, he or she is absolved of responsibility for it. But an open admission of guilt and genuine remorse is usually considered in the person's favor in civil and criminal cases. Coverups and lies only serve to arouse people's ire.

A person who voluntarily gives a public explanation or apology is not likely to feel that he or she is being humiliated or degraded. The feelings are likely to be ones of embarrassment and remorse. But when this form of discipline is required, its psychological effect on an employee can be devastating; it can also create long-lasting and deep-rooted resentment toward whoever required it.

## Purposely Delaying Disciplinary Action

As noted, our judicial system requires that justice be carried out in a timely manner. Purposeful or unintended delays will only raise the employee's level of anxiety. This is psychological punishment over and above whatever else may be given out by the system. Further, lengthy delay can cause memories to fade, and the employee might forget that he or she had done something wrong. Lastly, when a manager delays starting action, the misconduct is apt to grow proportionately in his or her mind. Unless legitimate reasons exist, the normal time from when management determined misconduct occurred through the investigation and interview to the actual awarding of discipline should not exceed five to seven scheduled workdays.

## Spontaneous or Summary Termination

No manager should have the sole authority to summarily terminate any employee. Termination is economic capital punishment. Spontaneous termination is accusation, trial, conviction, sentencing, and execution in one action. It completely ignores the principle that the accused is presumed innocent until proven guilty.

In some instances an immediate suspension from work may be required. This could be because the employee's being at work while an investigation is ongoing would cause serious problems with other employees, customers, or the public. For example, an employee's being accused or suspected of stealing confidential information, fighting, engaging in immoral conduct, or coming to work under the influence of drugs may warrant immediate suspension. However, innocence or guilt and the degree thereof can be decided only after an investigation has been conducted and an interview has been held with the employee.

## Eliminating the Job

To maintain efficient operations, management has the authority to eliminate unnecessary jobs. However, authority has been abused when a job is eliminated as a convenient way to get rid of a troublesome employee. This form of discipline is often used when discharge cannot be substantiated or the employee can be expected to fight a discharge. When an employee's job is abolished and he or she is permanently laid off, it is not easy to prove the action was for discipline purposes and not for economic reasons.

In some instances a variant of abolishing the job is used. It involves offering the employee a substantially lower-paying, less responsible job than the one he or she formerly held. Management does this believing the employee will resign immediately or shortly thereafter. If this does not happen, other methods are used to drive the employee out.

## Promotion or Lateral Transfer to Obscurity

The objective of this approach is to get a troublesome employee out of the mainstream and into a stagnant channel where he or she is emasculated and politically neutralized. It involves promoting or laterally transferring the problem employee from a visible, responsible job to one that may carry a loftier title but has little if any real power and no meaningful responsibilities.

When used to silence an employee who is legitimately questioning but who at the same time is raising eyebrows and reddening faces, this method is highly punitive.

## Assigning No Work

With this approach, instead of firing the employee or abolishing the job, the employee is kept in the job but stripped of responsibilities. The result is that the employee sits around all day with nothing to do. This approach is more likely to be used in the public sector organizations where long-tenured employees are protected by a civil service system. This technique is highly punitive because the employee may suffer a loss of self-respect and the respect of associates. In addition, coworkers may ostracize or turn against the disciplined employee.

A variant of this is to give the employee meaningless make-work tasks. The employee becomes something of a joke as he or she tries to work on assignments that everyone else knows are meaningless. When the employee finally figures out what is going on, he or she usually resigns. Sometimes the employee stays around and literally just takes up space.

## Punitive-Rehabilitative Forms of Discipline

Beyond the strictly punitive forms are various ones that can be either punitive or constructive, depending on how they are applied and perceived. If applied or perceived in a negative way, they serve no better purpose than those already discussed. This is not to say they will not work. If applied and viewed constructively, they can provide all the benefits associated with rehabilitative discipline. It is important to remember that no matter what management's intent is or how the type of discipline is administered, employees' perceptions about the organization's employee relations philosophy are based on what they have seen or heard. These perceptions, which may or may not be consistent with what management claims, define the real framework managers have to operate within. No matter what management believes, if employees believe a form of discipline is punitive, it is punitive. If an organization has a history of adversarial employee relations and has consistently used punitive forms of discipline, employees' perceptions of the intent of discipline will not change until executive-level management's philosophy changes. This will mean a change in policies, practices, procedures, and even personnel. Patience will be required because deep-rooted attitudes of suspicion and mistrust do not change overnight. Figure 5.3 lists the approaches to be discussed in this section.

If management has long nurtured a trusting, cooperative working relationship with the majority of employees, the approaches discussed in this section will prove useful and effective. These techniques can work if less than optimal conditions prevail, but they should be used with caution. When adversarial conditions prevail, individual managers must persuade disciplined employees that the organization is not out to get them and make their lives miserable. As with all methods discussed, the objective is to get a permanent and positive change in behavior.

---

**Figure 5.3   Punitive-Rehabilitative Forms of Discipline**

- Verbal and written warnings
- Permanent transfer to another job
- Permanent transfer to another shift
- Frequent checks on an employee's job performance
- Demotion
- Discrimination in raises and promotions
- Denial of privileges
- The silent treatment
- Changing work assignments
- Peer pressure

---

## Verbal and Written Warnings

Verbal and written warnings can be either punitive or constructive forms of discipline. Intent, application, and interpretation determine their true meaning. Verbal warnings can range from a passing remark to a lengthy sit-down meeting. Such a warning is intended to let the employee know that some type of behavior is unacceptable and must change or further discipline will be necessary. Obviously, before any overtures about further discipline are made, an inquiry as to the reasons for the misbehavior should first take place. In some cases no record of the verbal warning will be made. In others a summary of the discussion will be placed in the employee's working personnel file, not the permanent file, which should be retained in the human resources function's office. The working file should only contain information relating to the employee's performance and conduct for the current year, which may be a calendar or service date year. If the employee heeds the verbal warning, no further discipline will be necessary and no mention of the matter need be made part of the employee's permanent record.

If the problem persists, more severe discipline will be necessary. In a structured discipline program the typical next step is the written warning. In the semistructured or unstructured system various options are available. Some types of misconduct are serious enough that a verbal reprimand would be insufficient. Enter the written warning. Though any form of disciplinary action above the level of a verbal warning should be communicated to the employee both verbally and in writing, the written warning stands by itself as a form of discipline, although the form and content of the warning can vary widely.

Some organizations use a standard form letter where the rule(s) violated are typed in along with the employee's name. Figure 5.4 illustrates a punitively worded standard form letter. Because this format tends to be impersonal and broadly worded, its use is not recommended.

A written warning should be constructively worded, have a personal touch, and be tailored to the situation. Figure 5.5 is an example of such a letter.

Both letters serve the same purpose, but the one in Figure 5.5 contains more thorough documentation. It also emphasizes confidence in the employee's desire and ability to change and the manager's availability to help.

## Permanent Transfer to Another Job

Sometimes a discipline problem can be traced to how an employee relates to his or her job and other employees. Though there is considerable room for improvement in the recruitment, selection, orientation, and placement process, mismatches between employees and jobs are not entirely unavoidable. Nor can the relationships between people always be smooth. Because change is always occurring, it is

---

**Figure 5.4   Punitive Warning Letter**

Written Warning

Date: May 24, 1985

From:   J. Lawrence

To:   P. Wyman

Rule(s) Violated:   No. 15

Date(s) of Violation:   May 20, 1985

Explanation:   On the referenced date you failed to follow the correct billing procedure in invoicing the MNO Company. Your action violated Company Rule no. 15, Careless Workmanship. This is not the first time this has happened. If it happens again you will be subject to a three-day suspension. A copy of this warning will be kept in your personnel file for one year.

---

---

**Figure 5.5   Constructive Warning Letter**

Date:   May 24, 1985

From: J. Lawrence

To: P. Wyman

Subject: Professional Conduct

Over the past few months I have discussed your job performance with you on three occasions. The dates were March 27, April 3, and April 11. We agreed that the problem was due to your lack of attentiveness to detail. Each time we met, you assured me that such mistakes would not occur again. In recent weeks things appeared to be improving. However, on May 20 you made a series of mistakes that resulted in incorrect invoices being sent to the MNO Company.

We discussed the matter in my office on May 21. I had concluded that you were solely responsible for the errors. Your mistakes were identical to ones that have occurred in the past. They have caused embarrassment to the company, our department, your coworkers, and most of all yourself. In light of this, I am prompted to formally reprimand you by this letter of warning. This letter will be retained in your permanent records for one year as per company policy. If the problem persists, further corrective action will be necessary.

I know you want to do what is right and I am confident in your ability to follow procedure. If I can help you in any way to correct this problem, please see me.

---

obvious that people and jobs will change. Career pathing, employee development counseling, and especially flexible job bidding or transfer procedures can be quite useful in reducing mismatch problems and, when they do occur, reducing the likelihood of their becoming serious enough to be the cause of misconduct. Employee-job mismatch problems can occur because of:

- *Technological changes.* Changes in technology cause specific job duties and the functional role of the job itself to change. New technology may simplify a job requiring highly developed skills. Technology in the form of automation, robotics, microprocessors, or computers may replace skills formerly required of the employee.

With the new technology, the skilled employee no longer needs to make judgments; the equipment makes them instead. The employee may suddenly feel underutilized, unnecessary, or expendable. On the other hand, changes in technology can require that new knowledge and skills be learned, and the employee may be unsure of his or her abilities to learn the new knowledge and skills. Employees may express these fears in ways that could bring about the need for discipline. Some manifestations are increased absence, depression, or resistance to change.

It would be incorrect to conclude that technological changes are always detrimental to employees' welfare. Changes in technology may allow employees to have more control over their work, be relieved of the boring aspect of job activities, have more opportunity to grow professionally, and enjoy increased job security.

▪ *Non-technical changes.* A person's work provides some measure of psychological and social gratification. These rewards can be intrinsic to the job itself (interesting, challenging work that makes a useful contribution) or to the job environment (its importance as viewed by others, its prestige and status, and the employee's political power). Obviously, changes in technology can affect these dimensions of a job. Less obvious is that reorganizations, changes in product or service mix, and the politics of human interaction can and do affect jobs and their incumbents. An important job may suddenly be relegated to obscurity, and the emotional cost to the affected employee can be devastating. Or a relatively obscure job can suddenly become highly visible and important, and the employee who enjoyed being in the background may find him- or herself in a highly visible and vulnerable position. This could generate all sorts of psychological problems, which may underlie a discipline problem.

Like changes in technology, non-technical changes are not always detrimental to employees' welfare; they can present all kinds of opportunities for professional growth and development.

▪ *Changes in people's needs, desires, expectations, and aspirations.* To the degree these kinds of changes increase or decrease, a job may provide more or less satisfaction. An employee's dissatisfaction with his or her job can show itself in many constructive or destructive ways. Destructive ways may well become cause for discipline.

▪ *Job burnout.* In recent years much has been said and written about job burnout. No matter what kind of work a person does, he or she can emotionally tire of doing it. In burnout situations the employee can become apathetic, indifferent, or resentful and hostile. Job performance and interpersonal relations are likely to be adversely affected. In severe burnout cases a vacation and change of scenery will no longer help.

▪ *Personality clashes.* Personality clashes between people who work together can affect job performance and interpersonal relationships. For many reasons some personality types tend not to relate very well to one another. Because people differ does not mean they cannot adjust to one another so that they can work well together. But when differences are enormous and people are unwilling to compromise, adapt, or adjust to one another, problems occur. This can be a real problem when a supervisor and an employee are unable to get along or when associates who are dependent on one another cannot get along.

When misconduct can be traced to an employee's job and/or interpersonal relationships on the job, a permanent transfer can be an effective form of constructive discipline. When an employee is told to look for or take a permanent transfer, he or she is likely to view it as punishment. If the employee either requests a transfer or, after discussing it with management, sees the wisdom of it, he or she is likely to view the transfer as a constructive solution to a problem.

## Permanent Transfer to Another Shift

A permanent transfer to another shift can be used to avoid or resolve many of the problems illustrated in the preceding pages. However, there are other conditions that can make a shift transfer an appropriate form of discipline. Many organizations no longer adhere to the traditional 9:00 A.M. to 5:00 P.M. work schedule. Today, work schedules for daytime (first shift) employees start anywhere from 6:00 A.M. to 9:00 A.M. Some people are slow to get started in the morning, while others come out of bed ready to work. Consequently, some people have no trouble getting to work on time, while others have considerable difficulty. The ones who have difficulty are likely to have lateness problems.

I recall the case of an employee who just could not get to work on time—he was always fifteen to twenty minutes late. His problem started shortly after he joined the company. He was an outstanding worker and management did not want to fire him, but verbal and written warnings failed to produce a change in behavior. During a counseling meeting it was learned that the employee had always started work at a much later time than was required by his present employer. Management suggested he transfer to the second shift, which started at 2:30 P.M. The employee agreed and the problem disappeared.

Another reason for considering a shift transfer is that lifestyles change, and working on a second or third shift may better fit the needs of employees who are on first shift and vice versa. More than 55 percent of the women in this country work outside the home, and this number is projected to increase. With two breadwinners in the family, such necessities as transporting children to their various extracurricular activities, shopping for groceries, and getting the car repaired can become problems. If these problems are not sorted out between spouses, they will increase in severity and spill over into the workplace. Allowing employees to change work shifts can be an effective method to deal with this cause of absence, lateness, and leaving work early.

For example, when one employee was transferred to the second shift, a significant deterioration in attitude and performance was observed within a few weeks. On investigation it was learned that he had recently married a woman who worked on the first shift at another company. Because they worked on different shifts, their sex life had all but disappeared. This was causing problems at home. After studying the matter, management transferred the employee back to the first shift, and his performance and attitude improved considerably. Word of this, of course, got around, and there was some concern that others might contend they had similar problems in order to get a shift transfer. To everyone's surprise, no one took such action. In employees' eyes, management's action was seen as being sensitive to the employee's situation. Although this may not always be the case, this example serves to illustrate the point.

Requiring a permanent transfer to another shift becomes punitive when the intent is to assign an employee to the least desirable shift as punishment. Again, irrespective of management's motive, what is important is how the affected employee and possibly others perceive it. Requiring a transfer from a desirable shift to one viewed as undesirable as a punishment is akin to assigning an employee to the least desirable job.

## Frequent Checks on an Employee's Job Performance

This approach can be quite effective with employees who have performance problems. In a positive sense, managers can make frequent checks to see how an employee is progressing. In this way they can identify potential problems before they become actual ones. Also, the employee can ask questions or seek the supervisor's advice and counsel.

With a troublesome employee, managers can use frequent checks to keep him or her in line. The checks can be used in conjunction with frequent discussions about attitude and personal responsibility. Though the employee may see this as harassment, it is quite proper for a manager to initiate prudent actions to ensure that an employee is working properly. If the employee's performance improves, the frequency of checks should decrease.

## Demotion

If used properly, a demotion is an excellent form of corrective action. When used to punish, it can be more punitive than termination. First, let's look at some of the conditions that could lead a manager to consider demoting an employee.

Some people are promoted into positions they cannot handle. This is not so much promotion to one's level of incompetence as it is promotion to where developed skills are not the ones needed to do the job well. Different jobs require different skills and abilities. Because an employee is a good technician does not mean that he or she will be a good supervisor, and because an employee is a good supervisor does not necessarily mean that he or she will be a good middle-level manager. The point is that some people end up in jobs they cannot perform competently. This has nothing to do with their overall competence. Too often managers who fill positions do not know what capabilities are needed to be successful in specific jobs. Or they make promotions based on criteria that were correct in the past without properly considering how the job and its environment have changed or will change.

In other instances job requirements grow beyond the ability of the incumbent. This is a common occurrence in two types of situations. The first is where a company has grown very rapidly, resulting in large increases in responsibilities within jobs. It takes one level of skill to manage operations in a company with one facility employing 75 people and quite a different level of skill to manage operations in a company with multiple facilities employing 750 people. Though the person in the job may be developing professionally, he or she is not growing fast enough to handle the increased responsibilities. The second situation is one in which traditional ways of doing things have quickly and dramatically changed. Examples include the automobile, steel, and air transportation industries.

Managers should consider demotion only when it is well documented that the employee cannot satisfactorily meet the job requirements and the employee is primarily to blame. It would be unfair to demote an employee for reasons not related to job performance, including the lack of proper training.

Although most people know when they are in a job they cannot do well, few people will admit it. The employee who requests a demotion risks losing face, being labeled a quitter or a loser, and suffering reduced income. Consequently, in nearly all instances, management and not the employee will initiate a demotion action.

With proper counseling the employee may learn to cope with a demotion and even see that it was in his or her as well as the organization's best interests. Because the employee has failed in a particular job does not mean that he or she is a failure. One important thing a manager can do for a demoted employee is to help him or her retain dignity and self-respect. This means emphasizing the positive side of the action.

Most employees want to feel they are doing something worthwhile, and it is important to show a demoted employee how he or she is still making a contribution to the organization's total effort. Managers should also consider the possible reactions of the employee's associates to the demotion. It may be useful to ask them to help the employee make necessary emotional and technical adjustments to the new position. Discussing such matters with other employees should be done with caution and even with the demoted employee's advance approval. It should never be done if it will adversely affect the demoted employee.

Managers should never demote an employee with the hope that he or she will resign. If termination is warranted, the employee should be fired, not demoted. Successively demoting an employee and giving him or her meaningless job assignments and minimal raises while hoping for a resignation is more severe discipline than termination is. It is also a form of cowardice. Further, what if a demoted employee who is expected to resign does not? Should management then harass the employee for contrived reasons until he or she resigns, or look for an excuse to invoke a discharge? What if the employee accepts the demotion and then looks for ways to get even? When so motivated, employees can be quite clever in causing trouble without getting caught.

A demotion becomes a punitive form of discipline when its intent is to punish the employee. This occasionally occurs when an employee has politically fallen out of favor. The perceived troublemaker is demoted to some obscure job as an example to others who may be tempted to misbehave. In some instances an employee may even be promoted as a form of "demotion." Sounds rather strange, does it

## Case   Larry Nolan and George Roman

Larry Nolan and George Roman work in the company's forge department. Larry has been employed by the company for five years. He is a highly productive worker but has often violated company rules and received appropriate discipline. George has worked for the company for three years and is considered an average employee. The only discipline he has received is for occasional absences and lateness.

For some time it has been evident that friction between the men has been steadily increasing. Their differences came to a head one evening in the lunch room, when Larry allegedly threw some food that George was about to eat onto the floor. George, being justifiably upset, hit Larry in the face. Larry did not strike back but instead dared George to hit him again. As testified to by various witnesses, Larry moved closer to George and dared him again. George obliged Larry and hit him a second time. Before a full-scale fight erupted, a number of employees intervened and separated the two men.

The matter came to management's attention only after Larry requested another pair of safety glasses. His supervisor asked how the pair he had been issued broke. Larry then stated his version of the incident. George was called to the supervisor's office and in the presence of Larry questioned as to what took place in the lunch room. George became quite upset and said that no one would take food from him without a beating and that the next time he would kick Larry's ass all over the lunch room. The supervisor immediately suspended George from work until further notice.

not? However, it is done. For example, an employee who is in a very influential position may be given a lofty title, new but meaningless responsibilities, and even a pay increase as a promotion to obscurity. The objective is to get the employee out of the mainstream of power by moving him or her up and off into a corner. Instead of being a lateral transfer to obscurity, it is a promotion to obscurity.

A demotion is punitive if it is handled in such a way that the

In assessing the entire matter, management questioned various employees who were in the lunch room when the incident occurred. Their stories varied considerably, but there was consistent agreement that George did indeed strike Larry. George, in defending his actions, contended that Larry had no right to throw his food on the floor. Larry's version of the incident differed considerably. He said that the food was wrapped in some paper he thought was garbage, and in the course of cleaning the table, he accidentally pushed the food on the floor. He meant to put it in the trash container at the end of the table.

Management concluded that George's suspension for his outburst in the supervisor's office and the fact that he struck Larry justified a two-week suspension without pay. Larry was issued a written warning for having harassed George.

## Questions

1. Did management handle the disciplinary interview and investigation properly?
2. After assessing the matter, did management take the appropriate action in the disciplining of both employees?
3. In what ways would you have handled this matter differently?
4. Can such incidents be avoided or the likelihood of their occurring be minimized?

---

employee feels humiliated and experiences a sustained loss of self-respect. Where, when, how, and why an employee is told of a demotion all influence how it will be received. No matter how sensitive a manager tries to be, some employees will negatively interpret the action. The employee needs to understand that irrespective of how he or she feels, a responsibility exists to perform adequately in the new position. The employee must also understand that further discipline will be necessary if performance continues to deteriorate. This usually means termination.

## Discrimination in Raises and Promotions

If they are to be effective, managers must differentiate in the ways they treat employees. They should always assess employees' job performance based on a variety of factors, not just the quantity and quality of work performed. They should consider work habits, interpersonal relations, judgment, adaptability, attendance, and other factors, although specific factors and their relative weight will vary among jobs. The job performance of an employee who is a discipline problem must be reflected in downgrading the performance appraisal. Though one minor instance of misconduct will likely have little if any effect on an annual performance review, serious or recurring misconduct will certainly have an adverse effect. When such is the case, the employee's merit raise should be proportionately reduced. Also, it would be foolish to consider promoting or in other ways rewarding an employee who is a discipline problem.

When a raise is reduced or withheld and promotion denied because of documented, downgraded job performance, the action is constructive. When performance is downgraded for contrived reasons, the action becomes punitive. As with the other forms of discipline listed in Figure 5.3, how the action is handled by management and perceived by employees will ultimately define whether the discipline is punitive or rehabilitative.

## Denial of Privileges

An employee who is unwilling to live by the organization's standards of conduct can and should be denied privileges normally accorded those who perform adequately and conform to the standards. For example, I once developed an attendance-monitoring and control program that, among other things, provided for reserved and named parking spaces for those who maintained a specified minimum level of attendance. When for unexcused reasons an employee's cumulative absence and/or lateness exceeded the standard, he or she lost the reserved parking space and had to park in a general parking area some distance from the facilities. The space was left vacant or assigned to another employee. In this organization a reserved parking space was a valued status symbol, the loss of which was quite effective in giving employees an incentive to shape up. It should be mentioned that this approach to employee absence will seldom work with employees who have a chronic attendance problem. Disciplining the chronically absent employee will be addressed in Chapter 7.

## The Silent Treatment

All people have needs to be accepted and recognized for their contributions. For some these needs can be quite strong. As a form of discipline, the silent treatment can be quite useful with those who have strong needs for affiliation and affirmation. Managers know they must frequently interact with some employees, make them feel they are important to the group, and let them know how well they are doing in their work. When these forms of social and psychological reward or income are withheld, the affected employee will feel hurt and rejected. If not told the reason for this, he or she may become paranoid and exacerbate the discipline problem. Without suitable explanation, this form of corrective action will be viewed as highly punitive. But when an explanation is given and is accepted as valid, the action takes on a positive tone.

In practice the manager simply minimizes interaction with the employee and excludes him or her from all but required activities. Further, the manager stops giving recognition and praise for performance. In retaliation the employee may start withholding cooperation and reduce job performance to what is minimally acceptable. To reduce the likelihood of this occurring, the employee should be told the purpose of the discipline and be forewarned that if a positive change in behavior is not forthcoming, further action will be contemplated.

## Changing Work Assignments

Sometimes an employee's discipline problem can be traced to job boredom or burnout. Some jobs are highly structured, providing no latitude for changing work assignments within them, while others are relatively or highly unstructured, allowing for assignment to many different tasks. Changing work assignments as a form of corrective action is most applicable to unstructured jobs. This approach should be considered when transfer to another shift or job is neither desirable nor feasible.

In a constructive sense, assignment to different work is like a change of scenery. Though the new work may be no more challenging than the former work, it is nonetheless different. Assigning the employee to different and more challenging work can provide an excellent opportunity for the employee to show his or her talents and capabilities.

When an employee is assigned to the least desirable work more often than others working in the same classification, this clearly becomes a punitive form of discipline.

## Peer Pressure

As with the silent treatment, this approach is most effective with employees who have a strong need for acceptance and whose success or failure on the job largely depends on close interdependent working relationships. In any organization two major kinds of influences compel employees to behave certain ways: first, there are the expressed codes of conduct and prescribed ways of doing things; second, there are the unwritten, unsaid, implicit ways. The formal organization, with its standard operating procedures, exerts direct and subtle pressures on employees to behave certain ways. Likewise, one's associates, coworkers, and contemporaries also exert pressures. When formal and informal influences complement one another, the organization can derive substantial benefits. When formal and informal influences contradict each other, the problems can be serious and numerous.

The influences of employees' coworkers can be considerably stronger than those of the formal organization. Coworkers can say or do things for or against an employee that managers at any level could never say or do. For employees with a strong need for acceptance, peer pressure can bring about major changes in behavior. The most effective way a manager can utilize peer pressure is to take steps to show the employee's peers that his or her misconduct is harmful to the group's welfare. The more threatened the group feels itself to be, particularly the informal leaders, the higher the probability that they will take steps to bring the employee back into line. The following example illustrates how an aberrant employee's associates can be persuaded to exert pressure:

> The data-processing department can barely stay ahead of the work. Even with full attendance, employees occasionally have to stay late on Friday to meet weekly schedules. In recent weeks employee Dresner has been returning late from lunch and taking off Friday afternoons. His lateness and partial absence have necessitated that his coworkers stay late on many days in order to meet deadlines. No one likes to stay late, but

everyone except Dresner has a strong sense of commitment and team-work. The manager has spoken to Dresner about his attendance. The results have been negative. He does not believe that Dresner has good reason for either his lateness or his absence. In this past week the manager has noticed that a number of people have started complaining about having to stay late. While at lunch with some of the department's informal leaders, he mentions that if Dresner would stop being late and leaving early, others would not have to stay late to do the work he should have done. He mentions that he has spoken to Dresner but has gotten nowhere. He also mentions that Dresner appears to be taking advantage of things and making it difficult for everyone else. Within a few days the manager notices that Dresner is on time and once again doing his share of the work.

Again, as with other approaches listed in Figure 5.3, motive and perceptions determine whether the action is constructive or punitive. With this approach it is most important that the manager have credibility with employees and that he or she be convincing in show-ing how the employee's behavior is a problem for both the group and the organization. When approaching the group's most influential members, the manager should emphasize his or her desire to help the employee change, protect the group's interests, and avoid using for-mal, punitive types of discipline.

Peer pressure is usually quite effective with employees who are recent immigrants to this country. Immigrants typically have a strong need to be accepted in their new homeland, a willingness to do the least desirable work, an unfamiliarity with our language and culture, and a closely knit social structure with a well-defined social hierarchy. Because of these factors, especially the desire to be ac-cepted and the cohesiveness of the social structure, when one mem-ber misbehaves, it negatively reflects on the entire group. Discipline by the group usually far exceeds anything the manager would or could impose.

## Positive-Rehabilitative-Constructive Forms of Discipline

The forms of discipline to be discussed in this section are best used with employees who are reasonably mature, want to live by the rules, are willing to exercise personal responsibility, and respond well to nondirective counseling. With discretion these approaches can be used to get irresponsible employees to behave responsibly. Figure 5.6 lists these forms of discipline.

---

**Figure 5.6   Positive-Rehabilitative-Constructive Forms of Discipline**

- Counseling
- Probation
- Decision leave—suspension from work with pay
- Flextime
- Temporary reduction in scheduled work time
- Training or retraining programs
- Periodic reorientation for employees
- Participation in recommending discipline
- Shock reduction in suspension
- Leave of absence with or without required assistance by professionals

---

To effectively compete in dynamic business environments, managers must balance the needs of customers with those of employees. With respect to employees, the oft-quoted phrase "People are our most valuable resource/important asset" is not just a hollow slogan; it is a way of thinking and operating. Examples of companies that operate this way are Motorola, Delta Airlines, and IBM. Managers in organizations that operate on this philosophy work hard at creating and maintaining a high level of mutual respect, trust, and confidence, as reflected in policies and actual practices. Sound management practices minimize the occurrence of discipline problems. Although there is nothing new or magical about these practices, they work quite well. Most managers know they exist and know how to use them, but some managers are unwilling to implement and administer them. A few noteworthy practices are:

- *High selectivity in hiring new employees.* Within the spirit and letter of the law, the more selective an organization is about who is hired, the less likelihood there is of hiring people who are inclined to be discipline problems.

- *Comprehensive formal orientation of new employees to help them develop the right attitudes about responsibility to their work, other employees, and the organization.*

- *Proper placement of new employees in jobs that stimulate rather than bore them.* It is best to place people in jobs they can grow into, unless being fully competent before starting work is an essential requirement.

- *Competitive compensation, recognition for service and performance, opportunity for advancement, job transfer availability, due process, upward communications, and employee involvement in decision making.* These are just a few of the human resources management practices that should exist. Though much can be said about these practices, this book is not intended to be a general management practices text.

It must be pointed out that many of the constructive approaches to discipline are positive approaches to managing. They can be used to prevent disciplinary situations as well as to resolve them.

## Counseling

Counseling was discussed in Chapter 4. It can be used by itself or in conjunction with other forms of discipline. Either way, counseling should be part of the discipline process. In addition to the counseling managers can routinely give, specialized employee assistance programs should be available for the employee who has a very serious problem and who cannot or will not talk with his or her manager. The employer who helps an employee overcome a problem will gain in the eyes of the employee and others who become aware of the organization's commitment to its members.

Providing specialized assistance for troubled employees should be the province of human resources specialists. In small organizations, where the human resources function is limited, liaisons should be developed with accessible social services and mental health professionals and organizations. A large organization can often justify the cost of having such professionals on the staff.

## Probation

When an employee is suspended from work, everyone loses for the following reasons:

- The employee loses pay and the social/psychological benefits associated with work.
- The organization loses the employee's services.
- To maintain work flows, other employees may have to work harder or put in extra time. This could result in hardships for employees and/or increased costs for the employer.
- The work will be delayed until the suspended employee returns. This could hold up others' work and even result in cost overruns and missed deadlines.

• Customers or customer goodwill may be lost because of late or missed deliveries due to the suspended employee's absence.

• Time and paperwork costs are incurred in temporarily transferring another employee to fill the job of the suspended employee.

• Productivity may be lowered because an inexperienced employee had to be assigned to the work normally done by the experienced, suspended employee.

A much better, more economical, and far more effective approach is to place the employee on probation for a period of time. The employee is placed on probation from his or her job with the understanding that any misconduct during the probation period will mean possible termination. Managers who use probation instead of suspension treat the employee like an adult and support the philosophy of constructive discipline. Though most suspensions are for less than five days, probation should be for a minimum of one month. If the employee can change behavior for a month, then perhaps the new habits will permanently replace the old ones.

An employee on probation does not suffer loss of income and the opportunity to work. The employee cannot take a vacation while the work awaits his or her return or others have to do it. Quite the contrary, the employee is expected to report to work, perform regular work assignments, and continue earning a paycheck. This approach can be especially useful with the employee who views suspension as a form of vacation.

Probation is more commonly used in nonunion than in unionized organizations. Some unions argue that probation does not work because the employee must suffer a loss of something in order to understand the seriousness of the situation. This argument is without merit because employees can readily be made to understand just how serious being placed on probation is. The more progressive unions clearly see the merits of probation over suspension.

## Decision Leave—Suspension from Work with Pay

Imagine suspending an employee and paying him or her for the time off. It is like giving the employee a paid vacation. Decision leaves do not work quite that way. Those who have used it have found it to be most effective. Managers who have relied on the more traditional methods are either outright resistant to using it or are highly skeptical.

A decision leave should be limited to one day and used when either the employee's cumulative record of misconduct has brought him or her to the brink of termination or the employee has broken a major rule that warrants possible termination. When a decision leave is given, the employee should be told to consider whether he or she wants to stay employed with the organization. The employee is given a choice: return fully committed to living up to the standards, or return and resign. The employee must fully understand that he or she is on the edge of being terminated and has a way to go to clear up his or her record. Any further misconduct would likely mean termination.

The idea of paying the employee for the day is based on:

- Management's belief in not punishing employees
- Treating employees as adults
- Reaffirming management's commitment to trying to retain employees and being as fair as possible with them
- Making the employee feel guilty because the organization is willing to pay for him or her to sit home, sort things out, and choose a course of action.

The point about the employee's feeling guilty for being paid cannot be taken lightly. Organizations that use the decision leave (sometimes called the "Think It Over" or "Sorting It Out" Day) often find that employees receiving one will ask for the day without pay. They feel that a suspension without pay is less serious than a decision leave and they are not as close to being fired. Also, guilt for wrongdoing is at least partially removed because the employee feels he or she is paying for the misconduct.

The decision leave is usually quite effective. Some employees return and resign, which allows them to leave on a positive note and avoid the disgrace of being fired. It also saves the organization from the further expense of keeping the employee on the payroll. The majority who decide to stay make enough of a change in behavior to keep their jobs. But those who do not change quickly get into trouble and are terminated. They leave knowing that they were given every reasonable chance, and they are not likely to find sympathy from their peers. Respect for the system is strengthened because management is perceived as being fair and compassionate.

## Flextime

Changes in social values, lifestyles, technology, and family situations have made the traditional 9:00 A.M. to 5:00 P.M. workday about as out of place as the traditional definition of the American family—a working father, a mother who stays home, and two children. Today more than 55 percent of the women work outside the home, and about 17

## Case   Arnold Sims and Taylor Jones

Arnold Sims and Taylor Jones have worked in the company's inspection department for two years. Both are highly skilled and have good work records. Arnold and Taylor are popular and are known to be practical jokers. They enjoy playing tricks on one another and often socialize after hours. The work area contains a lot of electronic equipment and is potentially dangerous. Although the company has a good safety record, management has been relatively lax in enforcing its rule against horseplay. Horseplay has been something of a problem, though no one has been injured.

Arnold and Taylor's supervisor, Allen King, recently decided that the horseplay was getting out of hand. He informally told the entire department a couple of times that it had to stop, and he specifically told Arnold and Taylor that they must stop the horseplay. The company has a rule

percent of the children are living with a single parent. With transportation to and from day-care centers and schools, medical appointments outside of work hours, social, athletic, and educational obligations, people often find it difficult to balance all their activities and obligations and still come to work on time and do a full day's work.

For example, a working parent may suddenly have to leave work to tend to a child who has become ill at school and needs to be taken home. An employee undergoing long-term medical care has to take regular treatments three times a week during working hours. A parent has to drop a child off at a day-care center and rush across town hoping to get to work on time. In each of these cases, absence or lateness could warrant discipline. But, would warnings and suspensions be the best way to handle such situations? Not likely. Adjusting the employee's scheduled work hours, allowing for missed work to be made up, and even allowing for work to be done at home are better than warnings and suspensions. Not all work environments can accommodate a flextime work schedule. The integrated factory or office where work flows in a continuous process cannot accommodate flextime; nor can a work environment where employees must be available during certain hours to provide services.

against horseplay. A first offense warrants either a verbal or a written warning. This morning Arnold and Taylor were horseplaying and Allen issued both of them a written warning. It is the first warning for horseplay he has issued in three years.

Arnold and Taylor are upset and have complained that they are being singled out and discriminated against. They also contend that in the past, supervisors engaged in horseplay and were not disciplined.

### Questions

1. Did Allen handle the situation correctly? Why?
2. As a higher-level manager, would you support Allen and uphold the warning or would you rescind the warning? Why?

## Temporary Reduction in Scheduled Work Time

It seems that when we least expect it, a serious problem arises. It may happen to us or to someone close to us. It may be a serious accident or illness, the death of a loved one, the loss of property or a bad investment, an unexpected divorce, or the denial of an expected promotion. When tragedies and even disappointments occur, behavior will be affected. When work is adversely affected, a discipline problem exists.

Take for example an employee who is going through a divorce that he or she does not want. The trauma of the divorce process is causing problems at work. Though a written warning, along with a threat of further discipline should the problem persist, could shock the employee into changing, it likely will only add to the employee's problems. What the employee needs is understanding and assistance, not insensitivity. Allowing the troubled employee to continue, with the hope that he or she will eventually self-correct, would not be fair to those who are coping with their own problems and doing their jobs well. It would be more practical to temporarily reduce the employee's workday or workweek. Having the employee work only half the normal workday for the week or three full days out of five while recovering, with or without the assistance of specialized counsel, could benefit all concerned. Whether pay is given for lost time should be a matter of policy. Typically, employees are allowed to draw on accrued sick days, personal leave, or vacation so they can continue to receive full pay. In some instances short-term medical insurance will cover salary lost for the time not worked.

It is useful to point out that reduced work hours or workdays are routinely used for employees who are recovering from physical illness and are not quite ready to work full time. There is no sound reason why this practice cannot be extended to cover emotional illness and other personal difficulties.

## Training or Retraining Programs

This approach to discipline can be especially useful for employees who lack proper training, those who have been unwilling to change methods that have become obsolete, and those whose problems can be traced to the misuse of skills and abilities. The traffic courts have used this approach to discipline for many years. Drivers who accrue numerous minor traffic citations or who are found guilty of driving while intoxicated are frequently required, as part of the corrective action process, to attend safe-driver–training programs. Judges long ago recognized that punitive approaches such as suspension of license, fines, and even jail sentences did not always work. This is not to say that compulsory attendance at a driver-training program will necessarily work either. Sometimes effective discipline must involve a combination of punitive and rehabilitative approaches.

If an employee's problem is solely due to lack of proper training, providing training is the best approach. When to some degree the problem involves attitude, training or retraining should be used with other approaches.

## Periodic Reorientation

Over the years the benefits and services made available to employees by employers have significantly increased, and employees have now come to take such things for granted. Dental insurance, paid legal fees, employee assistance programs, day-care centers, longer paid vacations, more paid holidays, paid sick days, even paid personal leave days, paid maternity and now paternity time off are examples of benefits and services only relatively recently provided to many employees.

Employees in general, but especially those who are discipline problems, tend to neglect their responsibility to show appreciation for what has been done for them by living up to the standards and doing a fair day's work for a day's pay. Those who have never experienced long-term unemployment, those who have never worked in a poorly managed organization, and those who have never worked for an organization that provided few if any benefits seldom fully appreciate the benefit of having a steady job and working for a generous and well-managed organization.

As part of constructive discipline, it can be quite useful to give a disciplined employee a thorough reorientation about what the organization provides for him or her and what is expected in return.

## Employee Participation in Recommending Discipline

Employee participation in recommending discipline can occur in one of two ways. First, the disciplined employee can be asked to sit in the manager's shoes and consider what he or she would do if the roles were reversed. This can be very effective in teaching personal responsibility. Employees who are asked to do this often tend to be harder on themselves than management is likely to be on them. The employee's role in such circumstances should be to suggest or recommend, not to determine.

Second, an elected group, never a group selected by management, can function as an advisory committee on discipline to management. Group members should be elected rather than appointed so they will not be viewed by others as owing their allegiance to management. When employees have input into the discipline process, a number of beneficial things can happen. Some are as follows:

- Employees are more inclined to support the discipline program if they are involved in its administration.

- Through participation employees learn to see things through management's eyes, which can promote understanding between employees and managers.

- Disciplined employees know their peers are not likely to support their misconduct when they are the ones who are recommending corrective action.

- Because employees generally do not like to see each other lose income because of a suspension or termination, they may be more inclined than managers to look for approaches that address the causes of misconduct. This usually leads to constructive discipline.

Employees should not be given either the responsibility for final determination of specific corrective action or the authority to actually impose discipline. Those should remain with management because managers are ultimately responsible for the treatment of employees and because employees given such authority could be exposed to unnecessary peer pressure. The risk of such is reduced when their role is limited to making recommendations. Also, if employees were to impose discipline that from management's perspective was either too lenient or severe, managers would then find themselves in the uncomfortable position of having to overrule the employees. This action would destroy the credibility of the employee committee and make managers appear as dictators. Again, the role of employees should be limited to advising and recommending.

## Shock Reduction in Suspensions

For some time the courts have used shock probation, with mixed results. Shock probation is the release of a person who is serving time in jail before he or she is eligible for parole. The action is taken without advance notice and is based on the belief that the person serving time has been a model of good behavior, has learned his or her lesson, and will gain nothing more by serving the remainder of the prison term. The technique is controversial, and results of its use as a rehabilitative tool are not entirely clear.

As applied to employees, an employee who is given a lengthy suspension or probation would have the discipline lifted. Managers taking such action would have to do so infrequently and for well-documented reasons. Otherwise, the credibility of management's ability to initially take the correct action would be called into question in employees' minds. Also, frequent use of this technique could establish precedent and practice that, if not applied to all instances of misconduct, could undermine a discipline program's effectiveness because of indefensible inconsistencies.

## Leave of Absence

In some cases an employee's difficulties are debilitating to the point where he or she cannot meet minimum performance requirements. The problem may be related to the employee's physical and/or emotional health or to the health of a loved one. The last thing the employee needs is additional pressure brought on by punitive discipline. Where a temporary reduction in scheduled work time is not feasible, a leave of absence should be considered.

Policy provisions exist in most organizations for giving a leave of absence. During the leave period, compensation is maintained in whole or in part by use of sick days, vacation, short-term and long-term disability insurance, and workers' compensation.

An employee who requests or is requested to take a leave of absence is expected to recover and return to work in a reasonable time period. When physical illness is involved, it is relatively easy to determine when the employee is able to return to work. Emotional illness, however, can involve long-term treatment, and progress toward recovery can be difficult to measure. Some employees may be reluctant to seek treatment when emotional illness is involved.

Managers frequently ask if employees can be required to go for medical treatment as a condition of a leave of absence. Though an employee may feel that management is attempting to exercise control over his or her personal life, clearly management has the right to impose such a requirement. The employer is paying the bill through salary maintenance and benefits and has a right to see that the money is spent wisely. Further, the employer has an investment in the employee, and it is sound management practice to protect investments in human assets. The employee always has a choice: refuse the leave or accept the offered terms.

Another commonly asked question is: Can progress reports be required from mental health care professionals who are called on for services? Yes, they can and should be required. The information should be limited to the amount of progress being made, and unless extraordinary reasons exist, the information should be treated in a confidential manner. An exception would occur where the employee is a danger to him- or herself or to others. Comprehensive medical information should be made available to the employer's qualified medical personnel. Large organizations frequently employ full-time medical specialists, while medium- and smaller-sized ones either employ them on a part-time basis or use them on a referral basis. There is no precise dividing line as to what information should be requested and what will be provided. Generally, requested information should be limited to what is essential for determining the employee's fitness for work. Some specific guidelines to consider are:

- How serious is the illness?
- What is the expected or projected time period for recovery?
- Are any special accommodations recommended or required?
- Will the employee be able to resume a normal work schedule when he or she returns?
- What can management do to facilitate recovery?
- If the employee will not fully recover, to what extent will he or she be incapacitated?

- What is the likelihood of a recurrence in a year, in three years, in five years?

# Applying Merit to Discipline:
# The Bank Account Concept

All employees must be judged by the same standards, and rules must apply equally to all working under the same policies and similar work environments. This does not mean that the same disciplinary action must be taken with all employees who are guilty of the same or similar misconduct. Disciplinary action should be consistent, but it must be given according to the individual situation. This is one of the most difficult ideas for managers to properly apply in practice.

Under normal circumstances, people do not always want to be treated the same. They want equal rights, but they want treatment according to merit. It is inherent to the management process that managers from the supervisory through the executive level differentiate among employees. However, the burden of proving that discrimination among employees is valid and justifiable is always management's responsibility. An example of this important concept should prove helpful.

Company X has a rule against stealing. If an employee is caught stealing, the discipline can range from a written warning to termination. Manager A knows a number of employees are taking pencils, pads, pens, and other supplies home with them but has decided not to do anything about it because she does not view it as serious. Anyway, employees do not see it as stealing.

Manager B has the same problem but views it as being serious and takes corrective action under the appropriate rule. Manager B's employees become upset because of the inconsistent application of the rule against stealing. From the information in the example, there is no apparent justification for Manager A's not enforcing the rule. The employees who are disciplined could charge discrimination because other employees are known to be stealing and are not being disciplined.

The same example can be changed to illustrate the problem of inconsistent treatment of employees within a group. Manager B catches two employees taking pencils, pens, and writing pads home with them. Both employees have been in the organization the same number of years and have nearly identical service records. Neither employee denies having stolen and separately each gives similar reasons for stealing. Manager B gives the first employee a written warning and the second employee a one-week suspension. The second employee files a grievance alleging discrimination. Would the aggrieved employee win the case? Probably, because there appears to be no valid reason for differentiating the discipline given the two employees.

To determine the appropriate action when employees break rules, the bank account concept should be used. It is the mainstay of any discipline given on merit, and it is the basis for giving different discipline to employees who are guilty of the same misconduct.

The bank account concept can be explained in the following way. Most people have checking and savings accounts. When they deposit money into an account, the bank puts it to use to earn additional money. Banks pay interest to customers who put their money on deposit. This interest compounds over time. If withdrawals are not taken and deposits continue to flow in, a sizable account balance can accrue. Now, what does this have to do with determining discipline? Every employee, irrespective of his or her position and responsibilities, has a banking relationship with the employer. Employees make deposits, earn interest, and take withdrawals. All employees are eligible to make deposits, just as banks will accept the deposits of anyone who opens an account. Bank customers can take withdrawals from their accounts as long as they have sufficient funds on deposit to cover the withdrawals. Money can be withdrawn in small amounts, or the entire account can be drawn out at one time. When the account balance is zero, the account is closed. When an employee's organizational bank account is zero, the account is closed and the employment relationship ends. How do employees make deposits and take withdrawals from their organizational bank accounts? Figure 5.7 lists the forms of deposits and withdrawals.

By virtue of continued employment, employees make deposits to their accounts. If they do their jobs well and do not get into trouble, account balances continue to build over time. The longer an employee has been with his or her employer, the more both employee and employer have invested in each other. A long-term employee with a good record of service is owed more by his or her employer than one with limited service. Pension benefits, service awards, raises, and promotions are usually tied in part to length of service. Though raises and promotions should not be based exclusively on length of service, time on the job with experience gained can correlate with higher performance. Because of the deposits built over time, long-term employees can draw on their accounts longer than short-term employees before depleting them.

Judges, arbitrators, and government administrators are generally

---

**Figure 5.7   The Organizational Bank Account**

Forms of Deposits

- Years of service
- Quantity and quality of service
- Record of attendance
- History of raises
- History of promotions
- Special recognition and awards
- Record of meritorious written performance appraisals
- Documented meritorious performance in critical or emergency situations

Forms of Withdrawals

- Documented frequency of misconduct
- Substantiated seriousness of misconduct
- Overall poor attendance
- Absence on important workdays
- Marginal or unacceptable written performance appraisals
- Documented interpersonal relations problems
- Proven incidents of initiating or instigating trouble

---

reluctant to uphold the discharge of a long-term employee unless the misconduct was so serious that one offense warranted termination or behavior had deteriorated over an extended period and rehabilitative efforts had failed. The following example illustrates this point:

> Employees Lakowski and Ballard have worked for the LMN Company for twenty-five and three years, respectively. Lakowski has an excellent service record, while Ballard's is marginal. Lakowski and Ballard got into a serious fist-fight. Fighting is a serious form of misconduct and a major withdrawal. The investigation and interview yield nothing conclusive about who started it. Both traded punches and tell different stories. Should they get equal discipline? The answer is no. Both must be disciplined, but Ballard's bank account will likely be at zero balance or even overdrawn. Lakowski's will be substantially reduced, but he likely will have a positive balance. Ballard would face termination and Lakowski discipline short of termination.

Not all readers will accept the decision rendered in the example. Those who do not may be persuaded by the following. Suppose two citizens separately rob banks. In both robberies no one was injured, and each robber employed a similar method. A jail sentence for a minimum of two years to a maximum of ten years is mandatory for robbery. Robber A has been a model citizen all his life and robbed the bank because he needed the money to support his family. A number, of character witnesses testify about his good character. Robber B is a habitual offender and has been in and out of jail most of his life. His record and evidence of bad character are brought out at his trial over the objections of his attorney. His attorney maintains that past crimes have no bearing on the matter at hand because his client has paid his dues to society. Juries find both guilty. Should the judge give equal prison terms? The answer is no. To do so would be unfair, because the felons' records are substantially different. Robber A would likely be given a sentence closer to the minimum and Robber B one closer to the maximum.

The same reasoning can be applied to cases where an employee's misconduct has been a persistent problem over many years and management has condoned it. Countless cases exist where long-term employees known to be poor performers are either abruptly fired or are progressively punished over a short time span and then fired. Their inadequate performance was condoned for years until it suddenly became unacceptable. Either it got substantially worse than it had been or management decided something had to be done. What makes discharge wrong under these conditions is that management tried no meaningful rehabilitative efforts. Instead, management operated under the doctrine that employees are subject to being fired at will. This is akin to the "divine right of kings" or sovereignty doctrine. Such is out of place with contemporary social values.

If a terminated employee has been receiving normal raises, average or better performance reviews, and timely promotions, then irrespective of what the employee's actual performance is, the official record shows that it has been adequate. This is how across-the-board "merit" raises, inflated performance reviews, and promotions based on seniority get employers into trouble. An employee whose personnel file is filled with exaggerated performance reviews has built up a substantial bank account. One year's documented poor performance does not wipe out twenty years of good reviews, even if it is generally known that the reviews are inflated. What if no formal reviews were ever conducted? In spite of all that has been said and written about performance appraisals, many organizations, particularly those with fewer that one hundred employees and those that are unionized, still do not use them. Even if there are no reviews or records are periodically thrown away, the mere fact that an employee has retained employment over many years means the employer has accepted his or her performance as being adequate.

What if the employee's file contains many poor reviews? A poor review in and of itself means little unless some action is taken to affect the employee's status. Giving normal raises despite poor reviews contradicts the review, makes it somewhat meaningless, and reinforces poor performance. Managers must show that meaningful corrective action has been applied. If corrective action is taken and progress does not result in a timely manner, then at some point the employee should be removed from the job and possibly terminated. The amount of effort management is obligated to put forth to try to help an employee is determined primarily by:

- Prevailing social values and attitudes
- The degree to which management is responsible for the situation's having reached the point of intolerability
- The size of the employee's net balance in his or her organizational bank account

Generally, the longer an employee's length of service, the more obligated management is to apply constructive-rehabilitative corrective action. Such approaches may be used in conjunction with punitive approaches, but it is better if punitive approaches can be avoided altogether. The subject of terminating long-term employees will be discussed in Chapters 6 and 7.

## Deciding Specific Discipline

As stated, the bank account concept provides a useful conceptual framework for applying merit to discipline. When deciding how much of a withdrawal an employee is making for specific misconduct and what specific corrective action is appropriate, managers need to consider a number of factors. To achieve consistency in a program that provides for merit, the same factors must be evaluated in all cases.

### The Seriousness of the Misconduct

Misconduct falls into two categories: (1) major offenses, for which an employee can be fired, and (2) minor offenses, usually requiring something less than termination. The minimum and maximum discipline that can be imposed for each type of misconduct should be spelled out as part of program policy. By establishing minimums and maximums, management sets necessary parameters that help achieve a high level of consistency. For some types of misconduct the parameters may be broad, while for others they may be narrow.

An example of a major offense would be use, possession, or being under the influence of an intoxicant. For such misconduct the range of discipline is likely to be narrow. It would be illogical to give a verbal warning as minimum discipline. Instead, the minimum might be a lengthy suspension or probation, while the maximum would be termination. In this example flexibility is limited.

An example of a minor offense would be failing to follow the proper procedure for requisitioning material from stock. The minimum discipline would likely be a verbal reprimand, while the maximum might be a written warning and possibly some time off without pay. This wider range of choice for discipline provides for more flexibility. Unless the employee was a repeat offender or had a cumulative record of misconduct, discharging someone for such misconduct would be far too severe.

The discharge of an employee who continually violates the minor rules is handled by a policy statement to the effect that "frequent, cumulative, or excessive violation of any one or a combination of the rules will be cause for possible termination." An employee approaching this point must be clearly forewarned that he or she is close to being fired.

If no parameters exist or if they range from a verbal warning to termination for each written employee responsibility, individual managers' evaluations of specific situations will likely vary so widely that they will be indefensibly inconsistent. Parameters and written criteria with guidelines for their evaluation will help to ensure consistency while retaining flexibility for applying merit.

## The Employee's Record of Conduct

The employee with a record of little or no misconduct, other things being equal, is likely to receive minimum discipline for a first offense. If there is a record of misconduct, the length of time since the last occurrence must be considered. As a rule of thumb, prior minor misconduct should not be considered if more than twelve months have passed since it last occurred. Serious misconduct should be considered if it occurred within the past eighteen to twenty-four months. Time periods should be based not on a calendar year, where on December 31 all discipline during the past year is erased, but on an anniversary year. Organizations that use the calendar year often must clear the record of employees who by December 31 are on the verge of discharge. Frequently, these employees continue misbehaving and again come close to discharge by December. But on January 1 they again start with clean records.

For those readers who are caught in this dilemma, the following suggestion is offered. Though most policy statements and negotiated labor agreements state that specific reference to instances of previous misconduct cannot be used if they are more than a year old, management can refer to general patterned misbehavior without citing specifics. For example, employee Ballard has continually gotten himself to the edge of being fired by December 31. The labor agreement says that all records must be wiped clean on January 1. As usual, Ballard starts misbehaving in January. This time his discipline should not be minimal; it should be closer to the maximum. Without referencing any specific previous misbehavior, he should be told verbally and in writing that because of his well-established pattern of misconduct and failure to respond positively to continuing efforts to rehabilitate him, severe action is warranted. Figure 5.8 illustrates how a written letter could be worded.

When files are purged annually, discipline records are normally thrown away. This is fine if all managers conscientiously apply discipline when necessary. When such occurs, disciplined employees must shape up, resign, or be fired within a year's time. When managers are not as conscientious as they should be, problem employees are retained and misbehavior persists. If an employee's file shows no evidence of misconduct and failure to respond to discipline, then for all intents and purposes the employee's record is clean. Thus there is no justification for imposing severe discipline for current minor types of misconduct. However, if the employee had been properly forewarned that he or she faced serious action because of recurring misconduct, and the forewarning was not contested at the time it was given, management could defensibly impose strong discipline without the existence of past records. The uncontested forewarning established that a problem existed.

If records are permanently retained, a manager should not be allowed to search through an employee's file for something from the past to support disciplinary action that is too severe for current misconduct. Information beyond one year for minor misconduct and possibly up to two years for major misconduct should not be considered for current discipline purposes unless (1) a clear cyclical pattern of misconduct exists, and (2) corrective action was taken and the employee was forewarned that if permanent changes did not result,

---

**Figure 5.8   Employee Probation Notification**

February 4, 1985

Dear Mr. Ballard:

On January 3 you reported late for work. On January 7 you were absent for an unexcused reason. On January 15 you left work early. Your actions were in violation of the company's attendance policies and rules. Your supervisor spoke with you about your continual attendance problems. You were forewarned that such behavior could no longer be tolerated.

On January 29 you were absent for an unexcused reason. In light of your failure to positively respond to management's previous attempts to help you maintain acceptable attendance and your continuing pattern of absence, lateness, and leaving work early, you are being placed on probation for the next thirty calendar days.

As stated in Company Policy no. 17, probation means that your job security is endangered. Any breach of company policies or rules during this period will subject you to possible termination. You are being given the maximum discipline under the company's progressive discipline program because your situation is serious. If you wish to remain employed with the company, your attendance will have to meet the standards.

Sincerely,

Frank J. Edwards
Manager, Adm. Services

---

the past would be neither forgotten nor forgiven. Employees should know if records are retained, and current information (up to two years) should be separated from old records.

What about recurrences of misconduct within a single year? Time between occurrences of misbehavior must be considered in prescribing discipline. Some organizations use stated fixed periods in deciding whether to increase the level of discipline. For example, a repeat of misconduct within ninety days of the first occurrence would warrant the next step in discipline. With this approach, however, the employee who repeats within eighty-nine days gets the next level of discipline, while the one who repeats in ninety-one days receives the same discipline as given for the first occurrence. Generally, the longer an employee goes without getting into trouble, the more it should be counted in his or her favor. Therefore, approximate time periods are recommended. This gives managers flexibility and effectively deals with the employee who waits until the proverbial ninety-first day before repeating misconduct.

## The Employee's Length and Quality of Service

A long-term employee with a good service record would certainly receive lesser discipline for the same misconduct than a short-term employee with a poor service record. Most organizations have fixed probation periods during which a new employee can be dismissed if he or she fails in any way to perform and/or behave as required. In unionized organizations bargaining unit employees are usually denied seniority rights, that is, union protection, until after probation is successfully completed. Once it is completed the employee starts accruing job rights; that is, he or she begins accumulating deposits in the bank account. The same applies to employees in nonunion organizations. Once probation is successfully completed, an implied contract for continued employment exists between the employer and employee. Most personnel policy manuals and employee handbooks contain language to the effect that once probation is completed, the employee enjoys permanent status, participates in benefits, accrues certain rights based on seniority, and, most important, can only be dismissed for cause. Managers now have to live by these written words. The longer this implied contractual relationship exists, the stronger it becomes. Management must take this into account when determining discipline.

For all intents and purposes, a short-term employee's investment in the organization and the organization's investment in him or her is minimal. Because a strong bond does not exist, the employee has few deposits in his or her bank account, the bank account can be more readily depleted, and the ties can be easily severed. Management is not obligated to spend considerable time, energy, and money attempting to rehabilitate a short-term employee.

## The Employee's Position in the Organization

Generally, higher-level employees should be held to higher standards of conduct because these employees are highly visible and their behavior impacts heavily on the organization. This is particularly true with respect to managers.

If people in highly responsible jobs, especially those involved in exercising authority and leadership, do not set and maintain the standards for proper conduct, who will? When standard-bearers who misbehave are not disciplined, respect for management and authority will erode. Because of their roles and responsibilities, employees in higher-level positions can be subject to more severe discipline than those in less visible and responsible jobs who are guilty of the same misconduct.

## Changes in Behavior as a Result of Previous Discipline

Changes in behavior must be evaluated in light of the seriousness of the problem and what has been done to deal with it. A longstanding problem is usually more difficult to correct than one of recent origin. If no progress has been made, the approach to handling it should be changed. If progress is impossible, say, because of physical or mental impairment, management should consider transfer to a more suitable position. Disability retirement or medical termination may also have to be considered. If some progress has occurred, but the employee has relapsed to old ways, the time span and degree of change will have to be weighed against what effort has been spent and what has been gained. A major relapse in a short period after extensive rehabilitative efforts have been put forth could justify serious consideration of demotion or separation.

## The Employee's Physical and Mental Health

An employee's problem may be caused by physical or mental impairment. If the problem is temporary, a probable recovery rate can be projected by qualified medical personnel. If recovery is impossible or only partially achievable and the employee cannot meet the standards required of others in similar jobs, removal will have to be considered. In a competitive world it is unrealistic to guarantee employees lifetime employment. Others capable of performing the work must eventually assume the job duties of the incapacitated employee. Partial and sometimes full lifetime income is guaranteed by the array of disability insurance provided by the employer, private insurance, and the government.

## Motives for Misconduct

As discussed in previous chapters, motive is important. Though ignorance cannot totally excuse misconduct, whether the employee knew right from wrong should be considered. Ignorance based on inadequate or faulty training should not be counted against the employee.

### Case   John Smith

John Smith works as a laborer in the company's assembly department. The position is an entry-level one. Laborers, on an as-needed basis, are assigned various unskilled jobs. John has been with the company for ten months and is not a disciplinary problem. However, his attendance barely meets the company's minimum standard, and he has been told that he risks getting into trouble if he does not improve.

In the production process a number of long, wide, shallow tanks filled with oil and other chemicals are used. Periodically, the tanks must be drained and the accumulated sludge cleaned out. Although the sludge is foul smelling, it is nontoxic. Laborers are usually assigned to clean the tanks. It is one of the most unpleasant job assignments in the plant.

One evening, John's supervisor, Tom Edwards, assigned John to clean the sludge out of tank number six. For various reasons, employees consider number six to be the hardest tank to clean. John said that it was not his turn and that he had been assigned to clean the tank the last time. Tom replied that there was no such thing as turns in cleaning the tank and that he had to do the job. John then told Tom to get another laborer to do the job. Tom said that the other laborers were busy and proceeded to give John a direct order, forewarning him that if he refused, he would be given a written warning for insubordination.

John climbed into the tank and started cleaning it. About

---

Nor should situations beyond the employee's control. But where the employee clearly understood or reasonably should have understood right from wrong, such can be counted against the employee. The same applies when misconduct is intentional. Willful neglect is most serious, whereas justifiable ignorance can be viewed as least serious. Incompetence falls somewhere between the two. Incompetence because of faulty training is one thing, but incompetence because of faulty learning is quite another.

In considering motives for misconduct, managers must carefully

ten minutes later he emerged and told Tom that the fumes had made him sick. Tom said that he did not look sick and ordered him back into the tank. John complained that he was sick to his stomach and he was going to throw up. Tom told him to get a drink of water, rest for a few minutes, and then get back to work.

At that point, John said he was too sick to work and was going home. Tom told him that if he left he would be leaving without permission. Leaving work during scheduled work hours without permission is in violation of a written company rule. Under the company's progressive discipline program, the minimum discipline that can be given is a written warning.

John left work without Tom's permission. Tom issued a written warning. After receiving the warning, John filed a grievance, which said in part that the warning was unfair and he was being discriminated against by Tom.

### Questions

1. Did Tom handle the situation correctly? Why?
2. Did Tom take the appropriate action when John said he was going home? Why?
3. As a higher-level manager, would you rescind the written warning or let it stand? Why?
4. What should be done to avoid this type of problem?

document the particulars and have sound reasons to support the weighting given to such factors.

## The Organization's Past and Present Disciplinary Policies and Practices

Circumstances can result in management's changing disciplinary policies and practices. Leniency in discipline, even condoning such misconduct as absence and lateness, can be reversed and vice versa.

The reasons for changing policies and practices should be communicated to employees so they will have sufficient time to adapt to changing requirements. Generally, sudden crackdowns are unfair, and expectations of instant change are unrealistic. It is important that whatever action is taken conform to current policies and practices. If management is tightening up heretofore loose practices, what was formerly seen as minor and given minimal discipline will now be seen as more serious and warranting moderate discipline. If management has been lax in enforcing a rule, inconsistency can render the rule unenforceable. To remedy this, management could (1) inform all employees that beginning on a certain date the rule will be vigorously enforced, or (2) deactivate the existing rule and replace it with a revised rule that actually means the same as the old rule.

## Similar Cases

In Chapter 2 guidelines were given to show how consistency in handling similar cases could be achieved under a merit program. Written guidelines, training, follow-up, monitoring, record keeping, and dissemination of information about how specific cases were handled are all necessary.

## Mitigating or Aggravating Circumstances

It would be an injustice not to consider how mitigating or aggravating circumstances may have directly caused or contributed to the disciplinary situation. The degree to which such circumstances can influence the determination of discipline must be weighed in proportion to all other relevant factors. When such circumstances are considered, documentation must be part of the record. Consideration of extenuating factors, however, cannot be allowed to become a permanent psychological crutch for an employee. At some point the chronically troubled employee must overcome or control whatever difficulties are contributing to behavior and/or performance problems.

## The Employee's Replaceability

An organization should not permit any employee, however valuable, to become irreplaceable. Sometimes, however, it does occur. It would be an injustice to all other employees to allow any individual or group to "act beyond the law" because of their value to the organization. In the short term management may feel compelled to give an irreplaceable employee less discipline than others for the same misconduct. This is a very dangerous course of action. If an "irreplaceable" employee continues to misbehave, a suitable replacement should be sought. If one cannot be found, then management must show the good sense and courage to treat the employee no differently than anyone else, even though the employee may either leave or retaliate.

## The Employee's Popularity

In most organizations problem employees are usually the least popular, but this is not always the case. Severely disciplining a very popular employee can bring about a negative reaction from other employees. In theory, popularity, like irreplaceability, should not be considered. However, not considering popularity can be very expensive. In the short term management may feel compelled to give a popular employee more latitude and be more lenient in imposing discipline. However, to do so would send the wrong message to other employees and would erode the respect good employees have for management. The reasons why a troublesome employee is considered popular should be quickly identified and ways to change perceptions implemented. On the other hand, a popular employee may risk losing status if others perceive him or her to be a discipline problem. Advising the employee of this should not be overlooked, nor should the use of peer pressure be ignored.

## Can the Case against the Employee Survive Review?

Possible review should be the last factor considered. If all is done correctly, the case should survive reviews. All too often, however, managers ask this question first. This is wrong. Government administrators, judges, and arbitrators do not manage organizations; managers do. But managers must manage in ways that are in consonance with the law and prevailing social values. It is recognized that outsiders will occasionally yield to political pressures, make honest mistakes, and modify or even rescind proper discipline. When this occurs, managers should seriously consider exercising appeal rights.

Based on all the aforementioned, the specific type and degree of discipline should be decided. Once the decision is made, it should be communicated verbally and in writing to the employee by the employee's immediate supervisor. Though others may have participated in assessing the situation, the employee's immediate supervisor should play a major role in the process. The same applies to recommending raises and promotions. The closest possible working relationship should develop between employees and their immediate supervisors. Immediate supervisors, regardless of their specific job titles, should have the most influence in determining rewards and discipline for the employees under them.

## Communicating the Decision

Once the decision is made, a meeting should be scheduled with the employee. The employee should be told of the decision and the basis for it. If the employee becomes argumentative, he or she should be advised of rights of appeal and the meeting should be ended. If, as in most cases, the employee accepts the news in a mature manner, discussion should ensue as to how recurrences can be avoided. The employee must clearly understand what the organization will or will not do to minimize the likelihood of a repetition. The employee must also understand the full extent of the withdrawal and how his or her status has been affected in the short and long term.

Management should try to show the employee that the discipline being imposed is in both the organization's and his or her best interests. Though the employee may not always see it this way, management should endeavor to work toward that end.

Confidence should be expressed in the employee's ability to exercise personal responsibility and, to the extent necessary, take the appropriate steps to change behavior. The employee should be advised that if the problem persists or others requiring discipline arise, further action will result and present misconduct will be considered as part of the total record. Summary notes of the meeting should be made and kept on file. As necessary, a follow-up meeting should be scheduled.

A formal letter of discipline should be given to the employee. It can be given during the meeting, at the end, or shortly thereafter. The letter should be similar to those shown in Figures 5.4 and 5.5. It is essential that the letter contain the following:

- Basis for cause to discipline
- Specific violations of rules/employee responsibilities, acts of misconduct
- The extent to which previous misconduct is being considered in the present situation
- The results of the investigation of the matter
- The specific form and degree of corrective action being imposed or taken
- Expectations for changes in behavior

- Period for which discipline will be retained as part of the employee's permanent record
- Forewarning that if the need for discipline persists, it will be viewed in a more serious manner and require further corrective action
- The employee's right to appeal if dissatisfied with the action

In some instances the decision should be communicated either to other managers or to all employees. In either case the employee should not be named. The following are a couple of the reasons why this might be done:

- Other employees need to see that management is intent on enforcing the rules.
- The discipline given for particular misconduct can serve as a guide for other managers faced with similar misconduct. This can help bring more consistency to the disciplinary process.

Even if the specific case will not be publicly disseminated, centralized records and periodic summary reports on how discipline situations are being handled should be distributed to managers. Otherwise, managers in different functional areas may have no idea as to how others are evaluating cases and deciding on appropriate action. Policy and procedure guidance constricts the framework for thinking and acting, while information on how cases are being handled gives additional structure and shows application.

## Summary

Although there are many forms of discipline, no particular form is always best suited for specific misconduct. Many questions must be answered and factors considered in deciding just what is the appropriate discipline. The action must be consistent with current practices and with how others with similar misconduct and records have been treated, but it must be given on the basis of merit. To accomplish all this requires considerable competence. The convenient way, one that requires little skill, is to use a highly structured, progressive discipline system. However, unless flexibility (judgment) is engineered into a discipline system, it will ultimately fail because it will be perceived as being unfair.

This book's main theme has been discipline according to merit, which implies the use of varied forms of discipline. In this chapter I have outlined a wide variety of disciplinary techniques, each with potential advantages and disadvantages. Some are far riskier to use because they can produce more harm than good. In general, the punitive forms are easier to use. The constructive forms often require considerable thought in their application. Over time, however, they often produce more lasting positive results. Regardless of what approach to discipline is taken, the intent should be to get a lasting improvement in behavior. Misintent by either the manager or the employee will reduce the chances of success.

This chapter has also focused on the factors that should be considered in deciding what corrective action to take. Such factors as the nature of the misconduct, the employee's past and present behavior patterns, the employee's length and quality of service, motive, seriousness, and mitigating circumstances have been discussed. They purposely have not been weighted. Each organization must establish its own system of weighting factors. In different work environments different weightings may exist for the same factors.

Readers have also been introduced to the bank account concept. This logical and easily understood concept lucidly shows how and why discipline must be given according to merit. The concept should be explained to employees and embraced in the basic framework of all organizations' disciplinary policies, practices, procedures, and programs.

The next chapter will focus on how to handle those cases where the decision is made to fire the employee. Although the thrust of all discipline programs should be to correct and not terminate, termination must always remain an available choice. No employer should have to retain any employee who is unwilling or unable to consistently conform to reasonable standards of conduct. Sometimes employees must be fired. For many reasons, most organizations do not handle terminations well. This usually results in bitter feelings and, with increasing frequency, challenges to the action. Terminations must be handled in a humane, dignified way. They must also be done in such a way that, if challenged, the action will be upheld, irrespective of who reviews the matter.

## Key Points

- Employees' personnel records should contain documentation of contributions as well as problems.
- When punitive forms of discipline work, they usually do so for the wrong reasons.

- Though positive approaches may be more desirable to use, punitive forms are the only ones that work with some employees.
- Suspension from work can result in more hardship for the employer than for the disciplined employee.
- Some punitive forms of discipline, such as requiring a public apology, summarily terminating, transferring to obscurity, and not allowing the employee to do any work, can cause long-term emotional damage.
- Some managers have a stong preference to use punishment because it allows them to dominate and control.
- To be effective, approaches to discipline must fit employees' values.
- Too much overtime, last-minute overtime, and a seven-day workweek can make employees feel that they are being punished.
- To summarily terminate an employee is to accuse, try, convict, sentence, and execute in one action.
- When considering various forms of discipline, how employees will perceive the discipline (as punitive or constructive) should be taken into account.
- To avoid the potential problems associated with outright termination, some managers take the less risky approach and just eliminate the employee's job. Employees quickly recognize the motive for such action. Claiming economic necessity, while in truth the action was taken for other reasons, can damage management's credibility.
- People are not always able to grow or change with their jobs. Mismatches between employees' skills and job requirements can result in performance and attitude problems. Lateral transfers and demotions can be positive forms of corrective action.
- Management has the right and responsibility to single out troublesome employees for frequent checks on their work and discussions about their attitudes.
- A punitively directed demotion can be more humiliating to an employee than being fired.
- Employees have a strong incentive to change behavior when they are denied meaningful rewards because of misconduct.
- In any work environment where employees are close knit, peer pressure is one of the most effective forms of discipline.
- Many positive forms of discipline are preventive in nature.
- Counseling should always be part of the corrective action process.

- Placing employees on probation is more constructive than issuing suspensions, and it is more likely to work.
- A decision leave gives employees one of two choices: permanently stay out of trouble or resign. Any continuance of misbehavior will result in termination.
- Flextime is a management tool that can help prevent discipline problems primarily due to absence and lateness.
- To varying degrees, job life and home life affect each other. Giving employees with personal problems reduced work time can be effective in helping them resolve personal difficulties. Sometimes, it may be better to do the opposite and keep employees busy with work. It takes their minds off personal problems.
- Ensuring that employees are properly trained and have adequate resources can prevent certain types of discipline problems. Sometimes employees forget what they have been taught. Refresher training can be most effective in getting employees back on track.
- Employees must occasionally be reminded of what their employer has done and is doing for them in the way of rewards. Employees should understand that cooperation, loyalty, and good job performance are expected of them.
- Allowing employees a voice in shaping work-related policies and practices increases the likelihood that they will abide by them.
- Any organization's most valuable resource is its employees. This investment must be properly maintained and protected. Whether employees' difficulties are physical or emotional, job related or personal, a leave of absence with or without required assistance by professionals can help safeguard management's investment in employees.
- The bank account concept is a simple, easily understood way to explain to employees how and why merit is used in deciding specific corrective action.
- Specific discipline must be proportional to the seriousness of the misconduct.
- Corrective action must conform to prevailing policies and practices. Management can change policies and practices but should advise employees of such before they become effective.
- An employee's record—that is, the status of his or her bank account—should always be considered in deciding discipline. Recent behavior—behavior that has occurred in the past one and possibly two years—should be more heavily weighted than what happened long ago.

- Behavior patterns are important to consider in deciding specific discipline. The employee who has been steadily improving behavior but has a minor relapse deserves different consideration than one whose behavior has been steadily deteriorating.
- How and why misconduct occurred must be considered. Willful intent is one thing, while carelessness, ignorance, or negligence are others. Willful intent and gross negligence are very serious, whereas something unintended caused by lack of awareness can be seen as less serious.
- Mitigating, extenuating, and aggravating circumstances should be evaluated. These factors do not necessarily excuse misconduct, but they can help place matters in the proper perspective.
- In deciding specific discipline management must consider how, under current policies and practices, other employees have been treated for similar misconduct.
- A positive approach should be used in communicating disciplinary action decisions. Confidence that behavior can and will change should be indicated. At the same time, it may be necessary to forewarn the employee that if problems persist, stronger action will be taken.

## Discussion Questions

1. Should a record be made of all verbal reprimands, no matter how minor? Why?
2. Why do some employees only respond to punitive forms of discipline?
3. Why are managers more inclined to use punitive forms of discipline rather than constructive ones?
4. Why is a suspension without pay ineffective with many younger employees?
5. What are the potential dangers associated with assigning problem employees to do unpleasant tasks as a form of discipline?
6. Explain why employees may view compulsory overtime as a form of discipline.
7. Explain the meaning of transferring to obscurity.
8. Identify and discuss what should be included in a written warning.
9. Identify and discuss how technical and nontechnical change can underlie discipline problems.

10. Discuss how to tell an employee he or she is being demoted.

11. Explain why a demotion can be more emotionally crippling than termination.

12. Why do some managers demote employees who really deserve to be fired?

13. Why is it essential that troublesome employees not receive the same rewards (raises, privileges, promotions) as good employees?

14. How can a manager use peer pressure to influence a problem employee's behavior?

15. Discuss the benefits and risks of using a decision leave for discipline.

16. What are the advantages and disadvantages of having some form of employee input in prescribing discipline?

17. Identify five preventive approaches to discipline and explain how they should be used.

18. Explain the bank account concept. How does it work in practice?

19. To what degree should an employee's past record be considered in deciding on specific discipline for recent misbehavior?

20. How would you weigh the various factors considered in determining what specific disciplinary action to take?

21. How can current practices about deciding specific discipline for particular forms of misconduct be communicated to managers in small, medium, and large organizations?

22. Should an employee's replaceability or popularity be considered in deciding specific discipline? Why?

23. What is the best procedure to use in evaluating whether a disciplinary action will be upheld if it is appealed within the organization? Outside the organization?

# 6 When Termination Is Necessary

Each year millions of people are let go from their jobs. While some are terminated for one serious wrongdoing or an accumulation of many minor acts of misconduct, others lose their jobs because of organizational politics. Many are terminated for reasons related to economic and business conditions beyond management's control. Sometimes discharged employees are given explicit reasons for their ouster. More often, they are not. Figure 6.1 lists many of the reasons why people are separated from their jobs.

No one could rationally argue that managers should not have the authority to terminate employees. When business conditions deteriorate, management must be able to reduce the workforce in order to bring costs in line with revenues. When employees are disruptive, incompetent, or for any other reasons unable to do their jobs, managers must be able to take corrective action. If managers could or would not take steps to ensure that the organization continues to exist in a healthy state, chaos and disaster would eventually result.

Managers must continually adapt to change, discarding outdated practices for ones that fit contemporary social attitudes and values. Both David Ewing in *Do It My Way or You're Fired* and Robert Coulson in *The Termination Handbook* said that traditional approaches to discipline taken by managers, particularly termination, are undergoing profound changes.

---

**Figure 6.1   Reasons Why Employees Are Terminated**

- Temporary or permanent business shutdown
- Changes in products, processes, or technology
- Reorganization and elimination or reduction of certain jobs
- Mergers, consolidations, takeovers
- Business transfer or relocation
- Breach of major written rule or practice, such as theft or fighting
- Breach of major unwritten rule or practice, such as whistle-blowing
- Cumulative violation of minor rules or practices, such as absence, lateness, uncooperativeness
- Organizational housecleaning or purge for economic and/or political reasons
- Prejudice and bias with respect to race, age, sex, religion, handicap status, or ethnic origin
- Off-the-job lifestyle and/or activities
- Union organizing activities
- Physical and/or emotional problems, such as heart condition, alcoholism, and nervous breakdown
- Inability to meet job performance requirements

---

# Erosion of the Employment- or Termination-at-Will Doctrine

Some estimates claim that more than one million people are wrongfully fired every year. How can managers get away with this all too common practice of literal termination at will? The reason is rooted deep in American common law and the character of business organizations. No national law requires that employers show just cause for termination, nor are we likely to see one enacted in the near future.

But the historically unencumbered freedom of managers to terminate employees at will has been eroding for the past fifty years. At first this erosion was barely noticeable, but recently it has been rapid and significant. Many events and trends have interplayed to bring us to where we are today. Some of these are shown in Figure 6.2.

The employment- or termination-at-will doctrine is outdated and is being subjected to increased challenge. The protection of individuals from arbitrary action by authority is deeply rooted in our legal and social fabric. Our Constitution, Bill of Rights, and court system

**Figure 6.2 Reasons for the Erosion of the Employment- or Termination-at-Will Doctrine**

- The enactment of laws in the 1930s protecting employees' rights to form and join unions
- The growth of unions in the 1930s
- The passage of civil rights–related laws in the 1960s
- Federal executive orders and state laws in the 1960s and 1970s pertaining to government employees' rights to form and join unions, collectively bargain, and even strike
- The civil rights movement of the 1960s and 1970s
- The growth of unions in government in the 1960s and 1970s
- Arbitrators' decisions over the past forty years
- The women's movement of the 1970s and 1980s
- The increased numbers of successful lawsuits for abusive discharge and discriminatory practices in the 1960s, 1970s, and 1980s
- State laws enacted in the 1980s protecting whistle-blowers
- Social and legal acceptance of employees' rights to dissent in the 1970s and 1980s
- Federal and state privacy laws passed in the 1970s and 1980s
- Fear of white-collar employees forming or joining unions
- Increasing shortages of certain skilled employees in the 1960s, 1970s, and 1980s
- Increased exposure by the media to abuse and misuse of power in organizations during the 1970s and 1980s
- Increased social awareness and concern about the effects of organizational products, services, and practices
- The passage of laws pertaining to health and safety and pension reform in the 1960s and 1970s
- Employee involvement in decision making in the 1970s and 1980s through the quality circle concept
- Court decisions in the 1980s upholding the notion of an implied employment contract when company policy states that employees become permanent after completing a probation period and can only be terminated for cause

## Case   Chuck Brooks

Chuck Brooks is currently classified as a systems analyst. He has worked in various data-processing–related jobs during the eleven years he has been with the company. He held a supervisory position for two years but, by mutual agreement, vacated it. He is considered to be an average to above average employee by the supervisor he worked with. He is quite popular with his associates.

A year ago Chuck went through a divorce that left him emotionally devastated. His job performance deteriorated. Management let it slide for a while, believing the situation would improve after he got over the divorce. Unfortunately, it did not, and he was first verbally counseled and then placed on employment probation.

Last week it was learned that Chuck has been making many personal long-distance telephone calls and charging them to the company, which is in violation of company policy. Confronted with the evidence, Chuck admitted to the wrongdoing. Management has decided to ask for his resignation. If it is not given, he is to be fired.

As his supervisor, you are responsible for directing the course of the termination meeting.

focus on the protection of rights, including the right to be heard and the right to due process. A collision between the employment- or termination-at-will doctrine and protection of individual rights from arbitrary and unwarranted use of authority was inevitable. It was only a matter of time until the civil rights movement spilled over into the workplace and emerged as the employee rights movement.

Drawing on the events and trends listed in Figure 6.2, the following points can be made:

• With increasing frequency, employees are showing a willingness to challenge abusive terminations. In the past the courts did not favor employees' arguments about such discharges, consistently reaffirming the common law practice of employers' rights to terminate at will. But today the courts are hearing more and more of these cases. Ever so slowly at first but now with increasing frequency, judges are ruling against employers who terminate at will.

## Questions

1. Who do you want to attend the meeting with you? You can have any or even all of the following: the director of human resources, Chuck's former supervisors, your boss, the director of security, the company's internal lawyer, and your boss' boss. On what basis did you make your choices?

2. If Chuck offers to resign and asks for recommendations, what will you tell him?

3. If Chuck resigns or is fired, how long should he be allowed to stay on the premises?

4. Chuck says he will resign if he is given two months severance pay. The company rarely gives severance pay under such circumstances. You know that if he is not given the pay, he will not resign and is likely to challenge a discharge in court. Litigation is expensive and time-consuming. What will you do?

5. Chuck agrees to resign and asks to clean out his office. You fear he may take some proprietary information with him. What will you say?

- In more and more states legislators are introducing just cause legislation to protect unorganized workers. Eventually a law will be enacted and other states will follow suit.

- The Railway Labor Act, the National Labor Relations Act, the Norris–La Guardia Act, the Civil Rights Act of 1964, the First Amendment to the Constitution, the Safe Water Drinking Act, the Clean Air Act, the Age Discrimination Act, the Water Pollution Control Act, the Solid Waste Disposal Act, and many others protect employees from discharge for reasons covered by these laws. Most states have complementary or companion legislation to the federal laws.

- Various professional societies have advanced the view that members must be protected from arbitrary action by authority and are entitled to due process to resolve disputes they have with employers.

- Declining productivity and threats to survival by foreign competition have compelled American managers to reexamine traditional employer-employee relations and management practices. Managers are learning and more important accepting that fair treatment is a requisite to establishing and maintaining employee cooperation. Increased cooperation is an essential ingredient in the formula for increased productivity.

All this is bringing about a reshaping of managers' roles and their relationships with employees. Managers steeped in traditions, past practices, and what they believe are unalterable prerogatives of authority will find it difficult if not impossible to adapt to changes they find alien and threatening. Nevertheless, changes are taking place. Though the workplace is unlikely to become a pure or even a representative democracy, it is becoming more psychologically habitable. The often claimed but less believed and practiced phrase that "People are our most valuable resource" is earning credibility as proactive managers seek to manage better. It is interesting that some of the most progressive management practices are found in the newer, developing organizations that do business in very competitive environments. A notable example is Intel. Some of the most outdated, anachronistic practices are found in established organizations that have stagnated and are experiencing great difficulty in the marketplace. Some companies in the steel, rubber, and rail transport industries are good examples. Further, these organizations are finding it difficult to attract and retain the most capable people. With those whom they do employ, relationships are often adversarial or ones of benign neglect. There is hope for some of these managers and their organizations; for others it is already too late. They will not survive the current economic shakeout in their present form. They will either be taken over by a better-managed organization, diminish in size, or go out of business. In the long term society will benefit from this economic Darwinism. However, in the short term the costs will be high, and many innocent people will experience serious economic and emotional hardship. The effects of this process are currently most apparent in the Midwest.

In light of the events and trends outlined in Figure 6.2, some managers will maintain that the government, unions, dissident employees, judges, arbitrators, and anyone else they can think of are all trying to take away their authority to fire employees. Astute managers will understand the true meaning of what is happening. They will recognize that their authority is being reshaped, not taken away, and that management will still retain the right to terminate for cause. They will also recognize their increased responsibility to use discipline as a constructive management tool.

# Management's Responsibility to Terminate for Cause

Fewer than 20 percent of American workers are protected by collective bargaining agreements. For those who are protected, nearly all agreements contain statements that discipline will occur only for just cause. Further, these agreements almost always contain provision under the grievance procedure for internal due process and final determination by a mutually agreed on arbitrator. A growing number of employees have a degree of protection under federal and state equal employment laws, and government employees are covered by civil service laws. The effectiveness of these various forms of protection is a matter of debate. Overall, they work reasonably well to protect employees from unjust, capricious, or arbitrary actions by management. However, the wheels of justice can turn ever so slowly, and employees who turn to the courts often experience considerable financial and emotional hardship before justice is served. Consequently, many employees are unwilling to use the law to protect themselves. Still, the employee protected by various laws and systems is obviously better off than one with no form of protection, and most American workers stand relatively unprotected from management's potential misuse of authority. Society will ultimately decide whether authority is being properly used, and if managers abuse their authority, society will assume their responsibilities and their authority over employee relations. In order to retain authority, managers must not misuse it.

As Ewing pointed out in *Do It My Way or You're Fired*, in some areas management's authority is still strong, in others it is in an uneasy balance with employees' rights, and in still others authority is weak and rights are strong. Management can apply corrective measures without serious hindrance when an employee violates a clearly stated, legally enforceable, socially acceptable standard of conduct. Obviously, procedure and process must approximate what has been spelled out in the preceding chapters of this book. Management is on less certain ground where its standards of conduct are unreasonable or conflict with employees' social and professional obligations or personal convictions. Public exposure of questionable business practices, expression of personal views in the media that conflict with organizational views, and the placing of loyalties to a profession ahead of the organization represent gray areas. Whether cause for discipline exists in these cases is a matter of individual interpretation and prevailing values, and opinions may vary widely.

---

## Case  Cindy O'Donoghue

Cindy O'Donoghue is your administrative assistant. You hired her two years ago as a clerk typist, but when your previous assistant left six months ago, you offered the position to Cindy. When she took the job, you told her that loyalty and keeping information confidential were critical components of her job.

For the past year you have been having an affair with a woman who works in one of the branch offices. You have been discreet, and no one except Cindy knows about it. Cindy put two and two together after screening a number of telephone calls from this woman and inadvertently opening a very personal letter she sent.

Recently, news about your extramarital involvement leaked out, which certainly proved embarrassing. You fear that if your wife finds out, she will ask for a divorce, which you neither want nor can afford. You suspected that the leak came from Cindy and confronted her, but she neither confirmed nor denied your allegation. You decide to fire her and attempt to give her notice, but she says that she

---

Enlightened managers recognize the need to use discipline constructively, encourage self-discipline, and attempt to salvage rather than dump employees, although every line has an end point. As stated earlier, an employee's misconduct can be so serious that one proven offense warrants termination. However, in most instances where discharge is considered, the employee has been something of an irritant for a period of time. Usually the employee has failed to heed the expressed and/or implied warnings, and someone or some group has decided that the employee has to go.

Most managers find it difficult to fire an employee. Though they may find a certain amount of satisfaction in getting rid of a troublemaker, the experience of telling someone face to face that he or she is fired can be unsettling. Some managers can do it with emotional detachment. Many, for reasons ranging from cowardice to the availability of human resources specialists to do such tasks, will do everything possible to avoid a face-to-face meeting. Still others accept it as

will go to higher authority and possibly even your wife if you attempt to force her out. You know she is capable of doing it. Except for this problem, she has been a very capable assistant. Rather than submit to her blackmail, you decide to get rid of her.

### Questions

1. Do you have the right to fire her? After all, disloyalty and breaking confidences are serious.
2. What are the ethical, moral, and legal issues involved in this case? How should you deal with them?
3. Should you consult your boss and the employee relations manager before taking action? If you decide to, what will you say?
4. Assuming that you go ahead and fire Cindy, how will you deal with her threats?

part of their responsibilities and do it with a sense of professional empathy and compassion.

Generally, the more questionable the grounds for termination, the more reluctant the person who gave the order will be to do it face to face. The person who gave the order will probably not want to be asked to substantiate the decision before an employee who may be angry or despairing. Even when the grounds for firing clearly exist, most managers would prefer to avoid a face-to-face meeting. They also want to get the fired employee off the premises and have him or her processed out of the organization as quickly as possible. As will be discussed, many factors should be considered before a discharge decision is finalized, but once the decision is made, it should be carried out in a systematic, orderly, and timely manner. For all involved considerable effort should go into making the process as painless as is realistically possible. If badly handled, firings can have costly, even devastating economic, social, and emotional effects on individuals, organizations, and even society itself. Considerable research from many disciplines has generated a wealth of information about the adverse effects of being terminated. Though termination can be an expensive, exasperating, time-consuming process, keeping employees who should be let go can be far worse.

## Should the Employee Be Given One Last Chance?

Why should managers consider giving an about-to-be fired employee one last chance? After all, the employee has either committed one grievous act of misconduct or has accumulated a record of numerous minor infractions and has not responded to rehabilitative efforts.

Terminating an employee should never be taken lightly. The possible effects of such action on the organization, its employees, and the affected employee must be considered. As part of the evaluation process, the risks and benefits of giving one more chance should be considered.

Referring to the bank account concept presented in Chapter 5, when an employee reaches the discharge point, his or her organizational account balance is zero. Giving the employee another chance is the same as making him or her a loan. Taking such action is not without its attentive risks, and prudent managers may readily conclude that the potential risks far outweigh the benefits. In deciding whether to give an employee another chance, managers should address the following questions:

- Why should such an action be considered at all? After all, the employee is an adult who knew the likely consequences for misbehavior.

- What about the precedent-setting aspects of giving the employee another chance? If we do it for one employee, will we have to do it for all others who face being fired?

- How would such action be interpreted by other employees and even by outsiders who may learn about it? Will this be viewed as an inability on the part of management to take a firm stand?

- Will leniency serve as an incentive for other employees to misbehave because they know management will not carry out threats of discharge?

There are no easy answers to these questions. However, though each situation and organizational environment is unique, common threads often exist, and the following is offered to provide a framework for managers to use in deciding cases.

As discussed earlier, employees should know the required standards of conduct as a condition of employment. Not all standards can be reduced to a nicely packaged set of written employee responsibilities. Some standards are implied, germane to the nature of the business, or part of the organization's culture. Whether written or implied, these standards should fit in with society's values and be reasonable, legal, ethical, moral, and consistently enforced. When misconduct occurs to the point where termination is warranted, management should be prepared to take such action. If managers fail to take action, respect can erode and control can eventually be lost. On the other hand, managers must temper intellectual judgment with human feelings of compassion, kindness, generosity, and sensitivity. They must make decisions in terms of human values. This requires the courage to take risk, as well as an awareness of and a willingness to accept the consequences of being wrong.

The employee given another chance when one is not intellectually justified may continue to misbehave to the point where termination is again warranted. He or she may even have the audacity to ask for yet another chance and, if denied, appeal the matter to outside authority. A few instances of such audacity and ingratitude would stiffen the resolve of most managers to "show no mercy" in all discharge situations. However, an organization is a very human environment, and if managers are seen as being inflexible, cold, hard, detached, and lacking the human qualities of sensitivity, empathy, and compassion, management's esteem in employees' eyes will suffer. Managers must be willing to show the courage to take risks with people. Those who dishonor themselves by continuing to misbehave should be fired. The employee who is given a second chance and gets him- or herself fired again is unlikely to find sympathy or support among former associates or even outsiders.

If the deliberations about giving about-to-be fired employees another chance are thorough and another chance is offered, most who take it will shape up. For some the positive change can be dramatic, though others may not improve much beyond minimum standards. As stated, giving employees another chance is the same as making a loan to their organizational bank account. Those who change will repay the loan, perhaps with considerable interest. For example, the alcoholic employee frequently must hit bottom before a turnaround is possible. Bottom is not the same for all alcoholics. For some it is the loss of family, friends, job, career, wealth, and confidence. Others hit emotional bottom much more quickly. The alcoholic employee who faces losing a meaningful job may see the handwriting on the wall and take the initiative to change behavior. Regardless of what external pressures are applied, changes in behavior must ultimately come from within. The reformed alcoholic whose employer "went the extra mile" in giving assistance and not firing him or her may be quite generous in praising management's efforts. Others will learn of what has happened, and relationships will benefit. The reformed employee may even become a model employee.

Not every employee who is offered another chance will accept, but the opportunity to accept or refuse an offer can serve to reduce feelings of bitterness and resentment associated with possible and actual terminations. A refused offer can reduce the fired employee's desire to make claims to outsiders for damages or say disparaging things about the former employer.

Giving one employee another chance does not set a precedent. Were such actions to be considered precedent setting there might be no end to employees being given additional chances. However, some employees, arbitrators, lawyers, judges, and juries are sensitive to possible precedents, as well as to prevailing and past practices. As a negotiating tactic, union representatives frequently cite one past occurrence as having applicability to all other similar instances. In settling grievances managers must often include in their written responses: "The settlement of this grievance is not to be interpreted as a precedent for future cases." Managers in nonunion organizations historically have not had to be as concerned about possible precedents. However, all this is changing, and in the future these managers will have to be more aware of the precedent-setting implications of their decisions. To avoid setting precedents, some managers will decide to treat everyone the same all the time, which is unrealistic.

## What to Consider

Unless the environment has changed, similar cases should be handled in similar but not necessarily exactly the same ways. Documentation of all relevant facts and related information is essential. For permanent record purposes, the reasons for any action should be made in writing. Documentation, including the reasons for whatever action is decided on, should be sufficient so that anyone reviewing the record can readily see and understand the basis for the decision. Though cases for employees may be similar, the facts, circumstances, records of service, policies, and business conditions will vary from case to case. These differences reduce the precedent-setting aspects of cases. It can hardly be argued that a practice is established when one case is handled in a particular way. But if many similar cases are treated in the same way over time, a clear practice exists. Past practices can be changed if management has valid reasons for doing so and informs employees that the change is effective on a specified date.

Employees' reactions to managers giving some people second chances will vary. Some will see it as a sign of weakness, but if it is done discriminately, most will see it in a positive light. Good employee relations are fostered when employees perceive managers as being fair, sensitive, and compassionate. In view of the attitudes and behavior exhibited by many managers toward employees, it cannot be overstated that the mind and the heart must be used in managing people. Technical competence is important in today's complex society; understanding and being able to relate to people is essential. Michael Maccoby, in his classic book *The Gamesman,* presented compelling arguments to show how the head and the heart must complement each other in managing people.

Because management is willing to bend for some employees, a few may feel they can misbehave without fear of being fired. Again, giving one employee a second chance does not mean others must be treated the same. The employee who takes advantage of management's compassion should find rigidity where his or her case is concerned. Firing those few who seek to take advantage of the system's flexibility should keep others from seriously considering such action.

Just as determining appropriate discipline requires consideration of numerous factors and answers to specific questions, deciding whether or not to offer another chance involves similar considerations. These considerations are shown in Figure 6.3.

If managers use a set of established criteria to help them decide if one more chance should be offered, consistency in decisions is likely to result. Additionally, the amount of emotionalism and subjectivity will be reduced. No matter how refined the process or how capable managers are, feelings and subjectivity will be part of the process. And if not used to excess, they humanize the process. However, it is important that the process be rational and managers be able to honestly defend whatever decision is made.

If an employee takes a sudden and dramatic change for the worse, something significant caused it to happen. If the source of the employee's difficulty can be uncovered, perhaps it also can be treated and a quick turnaround might occur. Traumatic events such as loss of a loved one, sudden divorce, or failure to get an expected promotion can induce an employee to vent his or her hurt, frustration, and anger in negative ways. Honesty, firmness tempered with compassion, and offers of assistance—all with the understanding that if misbehavior

## Figure 6.3   Suggested Factors to Be Considered in Deciding Whether to Give an Employee Another Chance

- How long has the problem with the employee existed?
- Did the employee break many minor rules over a long period of time or a major rule(s) in a short period?
- What corrective actions have been taken to influence the employee's behavior?
- What results have been demonstrated by the employee?
- How important is the employee to the organization?
- How popular or influential is the employee?
- How remorseful or repentant is the employee?
- How have other employees in similar circumstances been treated in the past?
- What are the organization's prevailing policies and practices?
- Are there mitigating or extenuating circumstances pertaining to the employee's job or personal life?
- What are the employee's employment opportunities?
- What is the employee's age?
- What is the likelihood that the employee will make a permanent positive change in behavior?

persists, termination will be the next step—could bring about the desired change in behavior.

If the employee's behavior has been deteriorating over time and various remedies have been applied without success, the question of whether the employee can be salvaged must be asked. At some point it is time to throw in the towel. As with all decisions, judgment must be used and probable outcomes assessed. If punitive forms of discipline have been used without success, giving one more chance should be considered. If the problem has existed for a long time and management is now suddenly cracking down, it is unfair to ask the employee to shoulder the full responsibility for changing behavior. It is also unrealistic to expect the employee to make an immediate, dramatic change in behavior. Management must accept some of the responsibility for having condoned the employee's misbehavior for so long. In effect the employee has been allowed to develop a bad habit, and this habit may have become part of his or her character.

In some cases newly appointed managers inherit the problems of predecessors. These managers run high risks in demanding instant changes in behavior, although sometimes such demands may be necessary and fully justified. The manager who inherits an unproductive, inefficient work unit may have been given the position with orders to quickly turn it around. In such cases, if intolerable work practices are allowed to continue, it is the new manager who will face removal.

As has often been pointed out, concerns with output must be balanced with obligations to employees. But in reality these two concerns are rarely if ever equally balanced. Historically, concerns for output have generally far exceeded concerns for employees, but current social changes require that a better balance exist. Generally, new managers should be required by their bosses to make an effort to turn around problem employees before deciding to replace them.

As discussed earlier, actions taken by management for previous misconduct, results demonstrated by the employee, and the employee's record of service must all be considered in deciding specific discipline. The employee whose conduct has been steadily improving and then abruptly backslides should be looked at differently than the employee whose behavior has not been improving. Likewise, the employee's importance to the organization, political influence, the organization's present and past practices, and any mitigating and extenuating circumstances should be considered.

The employee's attitude is an important factor. One would normally expect that an employee who is about to be fired will be sorry for having gotten into so much difficulty. In evaluating this factor, the underlying reason(s) for remorse should be assessed. The people who best know the employee are usually in a good position to identify his or her motives and attitudes. Also, people with well-developed interviewing and counseling skills can be effective in identifying motives. However, some people are very adept at expressing seemingly sincere remorse when they are actually feeling something else. Though it is difficult to accurately pinpoint an employee's real motives for saying or doing something, the effort should be made nonetheless.

Leniency should be considered if an employee is sincerely repentant for his or her misbehavior. The employee who is sorry because he or she got caught or because he or she may be unable to find a comparable job should not be offered another chance. Consideration must be reserved for those who understand why they have reached this stage of discipline and want to change because it is the right thing to do.

Some consideration should be given to the employee's age, employment opportunities, and ability to maintain a reasonable lifestyle.

Though the law forbids discrimination in employment because of age, age discrimination both in favor of and against employees is deeply engrained in our society. Older employees who are fired often find it quite difficult to get another job. The exceptions are those older employees who have unique skills in high demand or have connections with people in other organizations. Most people have neither; for them termination is an emotionally devastating experience and sometimes an economic death sentence.

It is a well-established practice for arbitrators to consider an employee's prospects for reemployment when deciding the appropriateness of a discharge action. Arbitrators know that a fired employee who is fifty-seven years old will have a far more difficult time finding another job than one who is twenty-nine years old. This does not mean arbitrators will overturn the discharge of older employees. But the action will get close scrutiny, and alternatives to firing will be seriously considered before a discharge is upheld. Though probably less than 5 percent of the firings in America will be reviewed by arbitrators, managers should learn how and why arbitrators think the way they do. The views of arbitrators largely reflect prevailing social values. Also, where discharge is concerned, attorneys, government administrators, judges, and juries are increasingly sharing the views expressed by arbitrators and vice versa.

Early retirement is one option available for the older, long-term employee who can or soon will receive pension benefits. Managers have used early retirement in lieu of outright firing quite successfully for many years. Encouraged (or forced) retirement is a more humane way of severing a relationship than termination. The end result is the same—the employee is out of the organization. However, managers will find it more difficult to move long-term employees out of their jobs as the mandatory retirement age moves upward and people continue to live longer in relatively good health. The difficulty will be compounded by changing attitudes about abusive discharge, job rights, and lifetime employment.

Perhaps the most important question that must be answered is: What is the likelihood that the employee will make a permanent, positive change in behavior? If management believes the employee is likely to change, the risk should be taken. If an offer is made, the conditions should be clearly stated verbally and in writing, and the employee's acceptance of the terms should be a matter of formal record. If the employee successfully meets the conditions of the agreement, everyone has gained. But, if the employee fails, he or she should be fired. The reasons should be stated in writing and placed in the employee's official personnel file.

# The Termination Process

Once the decision is made, the process should be set in motion, although firing an employee should never be done emotionally. When emotions overtake logic, mistakes occur. Though emotions are heightened when firings occur they must be kept in perspective. This does not mean the process should be devoid of compassion. Though management may be overjoyed at finally getting rid of a troublesome employee, effort should be made to avoid gloating about it.

Managers often feel some guilt about having to fire an employee. The reasons for this can be varied and complex, ranging from a sense of failure at being unable to turn the employee around to knowledge that the employee is being "railroaded" out. It is also more usual for those who made the decision to assign to others the responsibility for carrying it out. Though sound reasons occasionally exist for having others carry out the decision, the person(s) who made the decision should usually do it face to face with the employee. If a manager believes the decision is correct, he or she should show the courage, maturity, and professionalism to say so to the employee. Unwillingness or inability to do so could be interpreted as a sign of weakness, a lack of conviction, and even cowardice.

With few exceptions, no one manager should have the authority to act alone in firing an employee. A discharge action should be reviewed and planned before being implemented. The longer the employee has been with the organization and/or the more serious the reason for the intended action, the more the matter should be thought out. If an employee is to be fired for reasons such as immoral conduct, embezzlement, gross dereliction of duty, or misappropriation of assets, it will be very difficult for the person to find another job. These reasons are far more serious than being fired for poor job performance, fighting, or excessive absenteeism. Those cases where it is believed the employee will have great difficulty continuing his or her career should be given the fullest possible consideration.

Though the employee's immediate supervisor should play a major role in determining and carrying out a termination decision, others should give input. The thoughts of human resources specialists and even legal counsel are not only useful but perhaps essential. This is especially true if the employee is likely to contest the firing. Too often those closest to the situation lose their perspective and allow emotions to override good judgment.

It has become increasingly common for all discharge cases except those of probationary employees to be reviewed by more than one level of management in consort with human resources specialists. It

## Case   Ginger Norbert

Ginger Norbert has worked at the company for the past twelve years. She has worked in various positions and not proved very competent in any of them. Repeated efforts have been made over the years to get her to improve performance. The company has been very lenient with employees; very rarely is anyone fired or asked to resign. Ginger can best be described as "deadwood."

Ginger has never broken any written rules, nor has she ever been given a poor performance appraisal. The performance appraisal process, however, is something of a joke: only if someone is about to be fired does he or she get an unsatisfactory review.

Management has decided to crack down on incompetence and inefficiency, and the president has ordered a purge of all deadwood employees. You have been told to get rid of Ginger. She cannot be transferred and must be terminated. Incidentally, Ginger is a member of a minority, over forty years old, and handicapped.

is not unusual for the chief executive officer to personally review the cases of long-term employees—those with ten or more years of service—facing termination.

## The Goal

The primary goal of termination is to get the employee out of the organization and off the payroll. Historically, employers have attempted to minimize discomfort and inconvenience for themselves, often with the result of maximizing hardship for the employee. Innumerable horror stories of inhumanely handled discharges have been read, heard, observed, and experienced by people. Although such stories tend to get distorted as the word spreads, there is usually more truth than fiction in them. For example, from time to time we hear about the employee who after twenty-five years of loyal service is suddenly fired without apparent cause on a Friday afternoon with about five minutes' notice. His or her work records are now under armed guard and the employee is given fifteen minutes to clear out.

## Questions

1. How will you handle the matter?
2. Should you try to get her to resign? Should you go to higher authority and get permission to offer monetary incentives to get a resignation?
3. If Ginger is fired and tries to collect unemployment compensation, how will you defend the action?
4. To what extent if any should Ginger's status under equal employment opportunity and companion laws be a factor in handling the matter?
5. How will you defend the action if Ginger files various complaints under the law?

The employee is humiliated and made to feel like a thief or worse. The news media can have a field day with such a story. Badly handled firings serve to:

- Make other employees anxious that it could happen to them
- Damage the organization's public image
- Damage the public image of employers in general
- Evoke sympathy for the fired employee
- Induce legislators to propose legislation to protect employees from abusive discharge by employers
- Give employees an incentive to unionize
- Give the fired employee a reason to retaliate
- Make juries sympathetic to employees and punish employers by making exorbitant awards for damages

To adapt to society's changing attitudes and values, minimize possible adverse effects, and act in a way that enhances the organization's image, management must assume a larger share of inconvenience and discomfort associated with terminations. This does not mean employers should assume all or even most of the discomfort. After all, if attempts at constructive discipline have been made prior to termination, management has already incurred much expense and inconvenience. If a single act of misbehavior justified a discharge action, management has also suffered a loss—perhaps one of major proportion. For example, the employee may have irreparably damaged expensive equipment, caused the loss of important records, or caused the loss of customers. But whatever the loss the organization has sustained as a result of an employee's improprieties, care must be taken not to discharge the employee in a way that looks as if the rich, powerful employer has stepped all over the poor, defenseless employee. This does not mean management should bend over backward to accommodate a fired employee. The aim must be to take a reasonably balanced approach.

Managers should take reasonable and prudent steps to safeguard proprietary information. Most employees who are fired will not steal such information. But for those few who may be so inclined, actions as drastic as locking up files may be necessary. Questions may arise as to just what information in an employee's possession is proprietary, and management must be prepared to tell the employee what records and other information he or she is not entitled to take away. This could require supervision of record removal. If disagreement cannot be satisfactorily resolved, the employee should be barred from access to proprietary information.

Management should also find out the status of work in progress so that others can maintain work flows by picking up where the terminated employee has left off. For this the employee's cooperation may be essential. Most fired employees will cooperate if they believe it will serve their interests and they are not too angry about what has happened. Managers may have to engage in some negotiations over the conditions of separation to get a fired employee's full cooperation in handing work over to others.

Most managers understand the importance of a good public image. The more an organization must conduct its business in public view and the more its products and/or services impact on the public welfare, the more sensitive managers have to be about their image. No matter how fair management tries to be, some fired employees will make disparaging statements about their former employers and take legal action to correct perceived injustices. If the organization has built and maintained a good public image, disgruntled ex-employees will be less likely to get public support. However, the organization with a poor public image may find that some people, including those called on to judge the merits of management's actions, may be consciously or unconsciously sympathetic to the employee's plight.

## Preparing for the Termination Meeting

The importance of thorough documentation cannot be overstressed. Terminations, more than any other form of discipline, are most likely to be challenged. No discharge action should be hastily carried out. In some instances the employee may have been under suspension, and in others the employee's behavior may have progressively deteriorated, but no final decision should be made until after all available relevant information has been reviewed and the employee has been given an opportunity to be heard.

In any disciplinary situation but especially when termination is involved, managers should communicate the action in private. Disciplining an employee in front of his or her coworkers only serves to humiliate the employee, create a climate of fear and intimidation, evoke sympathy for the disciplined employee from associates, and cause respect for management to erode. It can also be an incentive for the disciplined employee to take retaliatory action in order to save face.

As stated, the person who moved to fire the employee should be the one to face the employee, although there are some reasons to have a neutral person such as the human resources or employee relations manager communicate the decision. The action should be communicated in person, not in a letter, telephone call, or telegram, unless there is no other way to contact the employee. An employee's immediate supervisor should not face the employee when:

- Emotions about the firing are running high and a face-to-face meeting could precipitate an ugly confrontation
- The employee is expected to become argumentative, belligerent, and possibly even violent
- The employee is perceived as being one who probably will look for ways to challenge the action in a number of forums
- The supervisor is new to the organization or the job
- The supervisor does not handle such matters very well

To ensure that the meeting goes smoothly and to have witnesses to what is said, more than one other person from management should act as a witness in a termination meeting. Remember that in a disciplinary interview a witness for management should not be present because it could damage future relationships. However, in a

---

## Case    Janet Hauck

Janet Hauck is the director of new product development and has been with the company for ten years. She and her staff have been responsible for developing and launching a number of very successful new products; one of which saved the company when it was perilously close to going bankrupt.

Earlier this year, Janet was passed over for the executive vice-president's position. The consensus of opinion was that she lacked sufficient seasoning. An externally recruited person ten years her senior and with a strong track record was hired. Janet was extremely disappointed in not having been selected. She reports to the executive vice-president, and their working relationship is less than harmonious.

Janet has been deeply involved in developing a new minicomputer that is far more advanced than anything available. The project is very hush-hush, and elaborate precautions have been taken to ensure that nothing leaks to competitors. Everyone connected with the project believes that the new computer, dubbed the X7, will be the most successful product ever introduced by the company and that it will sweep the market.

Through an undercover agent, it was learned that Janet has offered to sell her knowledge about the product to a competitor who first approached Janet through a third party. Janet pursued the offer and aggressively negotiated a high fee for her information.

Before any information was given, Janet was confronted. She claimed to have known from the beginning that it was

---

termination meeting there is no concern for the potential damage to working relations because the relationship is over. When more than two people represent management and the employee is alone, the psychological climate is highly imbalanced and the employee is apt to feel threatened. This could cause the employee to be very submissive or defensively hostile. Judgment should be used in deciding who and how many should participate in the meeting. In unionized organizations the employee will surely have representation. In a

a setup and that someone or some group wanted to damage her reputation and hurt the company. She further claimed to be on the verge of going to the chairman of the board and making everything known. Some believe she is telling the truth; others believe she is lying. Those who believe her think she should have said something right away. Those who think she is lying want her fired and blackballed from the industry.

## Questions

1. To what extent should Janet's position and service record be factors in deciding what action to take?
2. Should Janet be terminated? Why?
3. If she is fired, what should her staff be told?
4. If the media makes inquiries, what should be said?
5. Management fears that if she is fired, she will immediately go to work for the competition. When she was hired, she signed a proprietary information agreement; however, they have been difficult to fully enforce. What can be done to safeguard proprietary information?
6. Should Janet be given another chance? If so, under what conditions?
7. Someone has suggested that Janet be offered another chance and be made to sign a very tightly written proprietary information agreement; then, after the X7 is launched, an excuse should be found to fire her. What do you think of this suggestion?

union situation management representation should usually equal or exceed in number employee representation.

Before the actual meeting takes place, certain paperwork should be in process, including all the paperwork normally associated with an employee's leaving for any reason.

The actual meeting should be scheduled from a day to a week after the firing decision has received necessary approval. If the employee knows that the firing is imminent, it is best to get it over with rather than allow anxieties to rise. For the employee a delay could be worse than the action itself. For management a delay could serve to generate problems, particularly if the employee is a known troublemaker.

The meeting should be conducted in a polite but formal manner. The employee's record in summary form should be presented. If the record has been considered as part of the discharge decision, previous meetings and actions taken with results achieved should be discussed. The reasons for the decision should be stated honestly but with tact and diplomacy, and the employee must clearly understand the bases for the decision. Being less than honest can result in problems. For example, the employee may see the given reason(s) are contrived and have a strong incentive to challenge the action. Furthermore, reasons that lack substance may not hold up under review from outside authorities.

Unlike a fact-finding interview or a meeting where discipline less than termination is the action to be taken, the employee's input should not be asked for or encouraged except to ascertain understanding of what is being said. As far as management is concerned, the termination decision is final and the relationship is over. Though a discharge action may be rescinded through due process appeal, at the time of the meeting the intent is to make it final. If terminations are frequently rescinded by either internal or external authority, something is seriously wrong with the organization's disciplinary process and managers' judgment.

If the employee will not be offered an opportunity to resign, a discharge letter should be given to the employee at the end of the meeting. If it is given at the beginning, the employee is not apt to listen to whatever else is said after it is read. The letter should be a matter of formal record. Even if resignation is going to be offered, a prepared discharge letter should exist. It can induce the employee to accept or request a resignation in lieu of being fired.

Though the termination meeting should occur shortly after the decision is made, the timing of the employee's actual departure may vary from immediately after the meeting to weeks later. A flexible policy is recommended because the circumstances surrounding each discharge action can vary widely. In determining the proper timing of physical separation, the following should be considered:

- The need for the employee's services to facilitate an orderly transfer of information and responsibilities to others
- The employee's need to clean up loose ends of work in progress
- The employee's need to save face

- Allowing the employee sufficient time to remove personal property
- Allowing sufficient time to secure return of organizational property assigned to the employee
- Allowing time for debriefing of information known only to the employee about work in progress
- Management's attitude toward the fired employee

In general, when lower-level employees are fired, the terms of separation are not open to discussion. Entitlements to vacation, continuance of insurance, pension vesting, severance pay, and so on are fixed by policy. But it is common for negotiations to occur when higher-level employees are fired. Higher-level employees, especially executives, often have unique compensation packages that include written contracts, performance bonuses, profit sharing, and stock options. Also, higher-level employees may be in a position to do considerable damage to a former employer. A smooth separation will certainly reduce the likelihood of this happening.

As social attitudes toward termination continue to change and litigation proliferates, managers increasingly will have to be flexible in the ways all employee firings are handled. In the future, the lower-level employee may be able to cause just as much and maybe even more trouble than a higher-level employee. For example, think of how many different legal actions could be taken by a female employee who is a member of a racial minority, is physically handicapped and over forty-five years old, has twenty years of service, is represented by a union, and is being terminated for publicly claiming sexual harassment.

## Conducting the Meeting

**Location.** The meeting should always be held in an environment where management has the psychological advantage, usually a manager's office or a conference room. The climate should be formal, polite, and professional. The employee should be told of the decision and the reasons for it. The official letter of termination should be prepared.

It is important to reemphasize that emotions should be kept under control. It is not unusual for a fired employee to ask or even plead for another chance, but the time for second chances has passed, and the employee should be told the decision is final. If the employee attempts to debate the decision, the spokesperson for management should avoid a debate. If the employee becomes threatening, abusive, or worse, he or she should be reminded about the matter of recommendations and referrals. If the employee continues to act belligerently, the meeting should be ended and the employee processed out as quickly as possible.

**Resignation.** The employee may be offered the option of resigning, or it may be requested. Resignation in lieu of discharge has a number of advantages:

- The employee is allowed to save face.
- The employee is less likely to initiate claims of injustice.
- If charges are filed, they are not likely to be favorably ruled on by a court or government agency.
- The employee will be unable to collect unemployment insurance.
- The employee will find it easier to get another job.
- The employee may be eligible to receive certain benefits, such as prorated profit sharing, bonuses, contributory stock, and savings plans.

Though resignation in lieu of outright firing is tempting to both employers and employees, it should not be offered or granted in all instances. Resignation should not be available where very serious wrongdoing with costly results has occurred. It is not uncommon for employers to ask for a resignation in lieu of firing when the case against the employee lacks substance. The perceptive employee may recognize this and refuse the offer, even when a generous amount of severance pay is offered with it. In this case management must either back down or take its chances and fire the employee. The employee who knows that the case against him or her is weak has a strong reason to file action for damages.

Though a terminated employee may have grounds for taking legal action, it will not automatically happen. Legal action can be emotionally and financially costly. The costs and time delays may outweigh the potential gains, especially in the case of an older employee who is eligible for retirement.

**Resignation and Early Retirement.** Requesting that an employee take early retirement in lieu of being fired can be a humane and sensible way of moving an employee out. Most long-term employees who get fired are not fired for misconduct such as fighting, misappropriation of assets, moral turpitude, and so on. They are fired because they are unable to successfully adapt to changing job requirements and performance standards.

It can be very difficult to tell a loyal, long-term employee who has given many years of good service to the organization that he or she cannot cut it anymore and must leave. Assignment to other duties is a possible option, but it may be neither feasible nor practical. In such cases early retirement is a practical solution. The option can be made more attractive to the employee by attaching some form of retirement bonus to the offer.

**References and Referrals.** Depending on the reasons for termination, the employee may be offered a letter of recommendation and even referrals to other employers. A fired employee will probably ask what is going to be said when prospective employers or their agents make verbal and written inquiries. It is best to forthrightly tell the employee what will be said and to whom inquiries should be directed. Generally, unless an employee has been fired for very serious misconduct, employers will give a neutral or favorable recommendation. Even when an employee has been fired for serious wrongdoing, former employers frequently do not answer written inquiries and verbally say only that the person is not eligible to be rehired. Most employers are reluctant to seriously impair a former employee's chances of finding another job.

If the employee is not to be given a neutral or favorable recommendation, discretion should be used in saying anything damaging about an ex-employee. Anything that cannot be substantiated could lead to serious problems. Anything negative that is said or written must be substantiated.

**Personnel Records.** The employee may request copies of certain documents in his or her personnel file. Some employers still refuse to give employees copies of anything. Again, given the changing social and legal climate about accessibility to records, it behooves management to be more flexible. The employee should be asked why copies of records are being requested. If the reasons seem plausible, copies should be given.

**Benefits Eligibility.** During the course of the meeting, the employee's right to proportional shares of certain benefits should be explained. Some of these will be fixed by policy, while others will be open to negotiation. Those likely to be discussed are:

- Accrued vacation time
- Accrued holiday pay
- Accrued sick pay
- Pay for compensatory time
- Continuance of medical and life insurance
- Bonus and profit-sharing accrual
- Pension-vesting rights
- Stock option rights
- Savings plan rights
- Severance pay
- Final paycheck

**Return of Assigned Property.** Before the employee actually leaves, all assigned property should be accounted for or returned. A partial list would include:

- Automobile
- Manuals, data files, reports, and confidential documents
- Specialized equipment such as personal computer and tools
- Keys and credit cards
- Parking sticker or permit
- Expense account advances

**Severance Pay, Outplacement Services, Use of Facilities.** Providing severance pay, outplacement services, and use of organizational facilities should be based on the reason why the employee is being fired.

Severance pay for lower-level employees is usually fixed by policy and based on length of service. For higher-level employees with employment contracts, the written terms of the contract typically specify what amount of severance is to be paid. In these instances the subject is usually nonnegotiable. For all other employees, room for discussion exists.

In some cases generous severance pay is given as a form of conscience money because it is an unsaid fact that the employee does not deserve to be fired. This is wrong but likely will continue to exist. In cases where discharge is warranted, generous severance is given to reduce the employee's inclination to take legal action. This is understandable and defensible. However, there is the risk that if word gets around, employers who do this could be subjected to a type of blackmail. In most cases reasonable severance, usually based on length of service and position, is given to help ease the financial hardship the employee may endure while searching for reemployment.

In recent years employees have been offered use of an outplacement service, though it is often only available to higher-level employees. The employee often shares the expense of the service by accepting reduced severance pay. A carefully chosen, reputable service with a good track record can benefit both the employee and the employer. The outplacement consultant can help a bruised ego recover, dissipate feelings of anger, build self-confidence, and get the employee on the right track to finding another job.

Depending on the reason for termination, the employee may be offered use of an office, as well as telephone, duplicating, and even typing services, to facilitate finding another job. (Some employees may refuse such an offer because they do not want to be around those who are still employed.) The terms and conditions of such an offer if made should be outlined. The risk of offering such services is that the former employee is still around, which could embarrass and irritate some, particularly those who initiated the firing action. If such services are offered, the location of the office should be in an area away from the mainstream of work activities.

## Summary

At least once in his or her career, every manager will likely be involved in firing an employee. Some will go through this experience dozens and conceivably even hundreds of times. Few will ever come to enjoy it. Nor should they. However, firing an employee who is unwilling or unable to conform to reasonable standards is an inherent responsibility in managing people. No matter how distasteful, it has to be done.

For numerous reasons, including lack of knowledge and wrong attitudes, too many managers do a less than credible job in handling terminations. Ignorance is readily corrected by training, but attitudes are not easily changed. Irrespective of how much information is known, if the wrong attitudes persist, knowledge will be either disregarded or applied improperly. The focus of this chapter has been to shape the right attitudes about termination and to provide a foundation of knowledge so that terminations can be handled well.

There are no defensible reasons for stripping a fired employee of his or her pride, dignity, and sense of self-worth. For most people being fired is a humiliating experience, and the employer does not need to add more stress and strain to the process by mishandling it. Even though termination is final, this form of discipline can be constructively applied. It is hoped that the employee will learn from his or her mistakes and not repeat them with the next employer. When a termination is handled correctly, everyone benefits. If handled badly, everyone can lose.

The next chapter will address typically encountered types of discipline situations, and it will provide guidelines and suggestions about how managers should handle these various forms of misconduct.

## Key Points

- It is estimated that more than one million people are wrongfully discharged every year.
- The employment- or termination-at-will doctrine has been eroding for the past fifty years. At first the erosion was barely noticeable, but recently it has gathered considerable momentum.
- With increasing frequency through this decade, employers will find themselves in litigation with terminated employees.
- Managers have the right and responsibility to terminate for just cause. However, terminations must be handled in ways that conform to the letter and spirit of the law and prevailing social values.
- Most managers find it discomforting to fire an employee face to face.
- Before any contemplated termination is acted on, management should seriously consider offering the employee one last chance.
- Many questions must be answered in deciding if an about-to-be fired employee should be given another chance. Perhaps the most important is: What is the likelihood that the employee will make a permanent, positive change of behavior?
- Any time an employee is given one last chance, the reasons and terms for it should be fully documented.
- The more damaging the reasons for an employee's discharge, the more thought should be given in deciding whether to terminate.
- Offering early retirement in lieu of termination can be a dignified way of ending a working relationship.
- To minimize the possibility of wrongfully discharging an em-

ployee, someone other than the manager who initiated the action should review it before the decision is carried out.

- It is important to handle any discharge action in such a way that the employee's dignity and self-respect are not seriously damaged.
- Before a discharge is carried out, proprietary information should be safeguarded.
- In discharging higher-level employees, management should be prepared to negotiate on the terms and conditions of separation.
- Except in unusual cases, the manager who initiated the action to terminate should be the one who communicates the decision.
- The employee subject to discharge should be told the real reason for the action, assuming, of course, that a bona fide reason exists.
- If the terms of separation are nonnegotiable, the employee should be told the terms and informed that they are nonnegotiable.

## Discussion Questions

1. Identify and discuss six reasons why employees are terminated.
2. Discuss why the termination-at-will doctrine is eroding.
3. Why do some managers and/or their designees still terminate employees in ways that humiliate them?
4. Why are some managers reluctant to tell an employee face to face that he or she is fired?
5. What factors should be considered in deciding whether an employee should be given one more chance?
6. How can the factors be ranked?
7. What kinds of terms and conditions should be part of a one last chance offer?
8. How does the bank account concept relate to giving one last chance?
9. How can management minimize the risk of setting a precedent when an employee who could be fired is given one last chance?
10. When might it be better for someone other than the manager who initiated the discharge action to conduct the termination meeting?
11. How does a termination meeting differ from a disciplinary interview?

12. When could an employer benefit if a terminated employee's departure was delayed for a few days or longer?

13. How could allowing an employee to voluntarily resign in lieu of being fired benefit both the employer and the employee?

14. What forms of persuasion can a manager use to get an uncooperative terminated employee to cooperate in processing his or her separation?

# 7 Handling Typical Disciplinary Situations

Organizations and the people who manage them are essential in our complex, continually changing, highly interrelated society. Without all types of organizations, we could not sustain our way of life. Whether we are fully cognizant of it, we place great faith in organizations and the people who manage them. The more we expect from organizations, the more faith we put in them. As a result of our rising expectations, the responsibilities of organizations and those who manage them increase proportionally.

Managers, especially those whose decisions impact heavily on the way organizations function, must remain continually alert to the need to change. Business organizations exist essentially to serve the needs of others; and they must remain sensitive to the changing needs of those they serve, their employees, and society as a whole.

The continuing cooperation of employees is essential to any organization's ability to function well. Over the long term, it is essential that good relations exist between the organization and its employees. When the employer-employee relationship fails, employee cooperation deteriorates and adversely affects organization performance.

Considerable attention has recently been focused on employee relations. Attention is one thing, but action that generates lasting positive results is quite another. The failure of managers to develop and maintain productive employee relations is a principle reason for unions, laws pertaining to fair employment practices, labor relations, civil rights, employee welfare and safety, and the employee rights movement. As long as managers merely speak of developing productive employee relations but do not take actions, unions and government will intervene and, in the process, reduce management's authority and flexibility. If managers do not choose to develop productive employee relations, someone else will do it for them.

As the employee rights movement continues to gain momentum, organizations will have to change their management practices. They need not curtail or abdicate authority, but they must change the ways in which they use it. As long as organizations exist, managers will have to manage. But they will have to carefully balance the rights of individual employees with the rights and interests of management, organizations, and society.

The need for this book evolved from the changing nature of the employer-employee relationship. The "good ole" days of the all-powerful organization, with its docile, obedient, loyal employees are gone. One hopes they are gone forever. Some managers will long for those "good ole" days, attempting to live in the past. Although few will openly embrace ongoing changes, most will effectively adapt to what is being thrust on them. In adapting, managers must be careful not to abandon their authority or abdicate their responsibility to manage, for organizations must continue to operate effectively and efficiently while serving society. Discipline situations will continue to occur and managers must use their authority to keep control.

This chapter focuses on the specific types of discipline situations that managers are most likely to encounter. It offers managers general guidelines on how to address these situations and take the right action. It is impossible to spell out the precise type and degree of discipline for every situation. Each organization is culturally unique, and the particulars surrounding each discipline situation are often quite different. However, because disciplinary action must conform to social values and perceptions of what is fair and proper, the ways managers use authority to discipline employees must fit within the social and legal framework. Further, even though no two employees' situations are likely to be exactly the same, common factors must be evaluated in similar ways. For each discipline situation presented in this chapter, a conceptual framework has been provided to guide managers toward consistency in handling cases where these types of misconduct have occurred. These frameworks do not provide the answers; they help users develop them.

## Habitual or Patterned Misconduct

In most organizations a small percentage of employees cause most of the problems. They habitually get into trouble, and more often than not their misbehavior is even predictable. The shrewdest and most capable never get into enough trouble to get themselves fired. If they accumulate enough progressive discipline to bring them close to dismissal, they will shape up long enough to improve their record so that if they again misbehave, discipline short of discharge is called for. They seem to sense just how much and how often they can misbehave without losing their jobs. They are a continuing source of irritation and frustration to even the most capable and tolerant of managers, and they make fools of managers who are unable to control them. Managers often become entrapped in a psychological cat-and-mouse game with these employees. All too often time and energy that could be put to productive use must be spent in trying to cope with a seemingly impossible situation.

The following suggestions and guidelines are offered to get these employees to either permanently improve or cause their own discharge:

- Accurate, up-to-date records of their conduct and job performance must be maintained. It may be possible to identify patterns and even underlying causes from this information. Even if clear patterns cannot be identified, records of misconduct and evidence of action taken and results achieved are essential. Without such documentation, managers will be unable to substantiate why these employees must be treated differently from nonhabitual offenders.

- These employees must be forewarned verbally and in writing that their misbehavior has been tolerated for too long and that failure to permanently change will result in discharge.

- These employees should be more closely supervised than others. Though some may allege harassment, management has a legitimate right to treat them differently from other employees because of their recurring misconduct. They cannot be trusted like other employees.

- Expired disciplinary actions should be kept on file. The employees should know this and be told that it is because of their habitual misbehavior. It is important for records to show that problems have been ongoing and previous corrective action has failed to achieve lasting results.

- There should be less progressiveness to the discipline given to these employees when they again misbehave. Instead of being given minimum discipline for an offense, they should be given a higher degree, even the maximum, because of their habitual misbehavior and the failure of lesser discipline to work. Though expired discipline perhaps cannot be specifically referenced, the existence of past records can and should be mentioned. It would be referenced in a general sense, not by a chronological listing of specific misconduct.

---

## Case  Hal Shaw

Hal Shaw is a maintenance technician assigned to the company's facilities department. He is a skilled tradesman with fifteen years of service. Though at times he has been known to be obstinate, stubborn, and hard-headed, Hal is a good worker. But Hal is one of those people you have to ask and not tell. If you leave him alone and tell him what you want done, he works well; if you hassle him and order him around, he becomes difficult. Hal and his supervisor, Sam Morgan, do not get along. Sam is a hard-driving autocrat.

The plant has a lot of large machinery that is dangerous to work around. Safety is continually stressed, and the company's accident record is excellent by industry and insurance standards.

Two days ago there was a major breakdown of a major piece of equipment that has many high-voltage lines running through it. The breakdown appeared to have been caused by an electrical malfunction, which in turn caused mechanical damage. When Sam was informed of the breakdown, he and Hal went to the site and made a visual inspection.

Sam decided the repairs could be made and ordered Hal to make them. Hal asked if he could have another mechanic assist him because of the potential danger involved. He thought that four eyes and hands would make for far safer working conditions than his working alone. Sam said no one else was available and the repairs had to be started

---

Misconduct that is considered current should be specifically referenced, as was discussed in Chapter 5.

• Management should not hesitate to terminate those who fail to make significant improvements and continue to misbehave.

# Absenteeism and Lateness

Absenteeism and lateness are problems in any society where the benefits of leisure time activity are extolled to the highest levels. The more employees are rewarded with paid time off and the more they

right away. He did say that if someone became available later in the shift, he would send that person over to assist. Hal continued to press his request for assistance and repeatedly made the point about safety. Sam rapidly grew tired of Hal's persistence and finally gave him a direct order. Hal refused to comply. Sam ordered him a second time and forewarned him that if he refused, he would be charged with insubordination. Hal again refused and was charged with being insubordinate. Sam suspended him for the remainder of the shift.

## Questions

1. Did Sam handle the matter correctly? What could he have done differently?
2. Whose opinion regarding the safety of work should be given more credit, Sam's or Hal's? Why?
3. Can Sam make the charge of insubordination stick? Why?
4. Did Hal behave properly in this incident?
5. Did either have hidden motives that may have affected their behavior? If so, how should they be considered in deciding who to support?
6. If Hal gets away with this, is there a danger of setting a bad precedent for similar cases in the future?

enjoy leisure activities, the more inclined they will be to take time off. Factors ranging from management's apparent condoning of excessive absence, to a "use them or lose them" sick pay policy, to employees' putting in too much overtime, contribute to attendance problems.

Absence and lateness often cycle with the economy. When jobs are scarce and many are out of work, employees are seldom inclined to misbehave and risk losing their jobs. When jobs are plentiful, however, employees who can readily find work can afford to be more independent. The possible loss of a job is not too costly because another job is readily available.

With proper conditioning and encouragement, most employees

will not become absence and lateness problems. Excessive absence and/or lateness is symptomatic of something, and before severe discipline becomes necessary, management should attempt to identify and treat underlying causes. However, causes cannot always be treated, even if identified. In addressing employee absence and lateness problems, the following should be considered:

• Every employer has a right to expect employees to conform to reasonable standards of attendance and promptness in reporting for work.

• Whatever the reasons for attendance or lateness problems, there is a point where an employee's continued absence and/or lateness becomes intolerable.

• General and/or specific standards for attendance must exist and be communicated to employees. Without reference points, comparisons and determinations of what is unacceptable are impossible. An example of a general standard would be: good attendance is the norm and not an exception in our organization. Our customers and your fellow employees count on you to be here every day work is scheduled. Management expects that only on rare occasions will some employees find it necessary to be off from work. A specific standard would be: any combination of three late reports, absence, or leaving early during a three-month period will be considered excessive and cause for discipline.

• Different standards for different types of work and work environments are proper. Employees who put in a lot of unpaid overtime may be allowed to take an occasional day off without it counting against them, whereas employees who put in a lot of paid overtime may not be accorded the same privilege.

• Standards should be relatively and even totally uniform for employees doing similar work in similar environments under the same system of compensation.

• Whenever employees are absent, reasons and explanations should be sought and a record kept.

• The records of employees whose absence and/or lateness is moving toward unacceptability should be discussed with them.

• From their first day on the job, employees should understand and accept that good attendance is the norm, not an exception.

• Standards should reflect consideration of frequency, duration, and criticalness of absence and lateness. Thirty days of continuous absence for bona fide illness or injury should not be viewed in the same way as a thirty-day total of Monday and Friday absences. Absence on an important workday should be viewed differently than one where work was ahead of schedule. For example, an accountant's absence on the day the fiscal year ends because of minor illness would be viewed differently from absence for the same reason on any other day of the year.

- In assessing employees' attendance, evidence of patterns and underlying motives should be sought. Absence to avoid doing unpleasant tasks is quite different from absence due to hospitalization.

- Employees with attendance problems should be told how their absence affects others, and they should be reminded of their obligations and responsibilities.

## Dress and Grooming

In our culture, where individuality and freedom of expression are highly regarded, employees' tastes and preferences sometimes conflict with employers' legitimate business interests. The following thoughts and guidelines are offered to help managers maintain the proper balance between employee needs and business interests:

- Employers have a right and responsibility to establish dress and grooming standards.

- These standards must fit the organization's business, its operational environment, and the expectations of those whom it serves. For example, for safety reasons management could forbid employees from wearing long hair, beards, excessive perfume, loose-fitting clothing, or fashion shoes. To maintain a certain image, employees could be forbidden from wearing certain types of clothing and grooming themselves in ways that would alienate customers.

- Different standards may exist for different types of work in the same organization. For example, employees working in an office where client contact occurs could be forbidden to wear blue jeans, whereas employees of the same organization working in a plant could be allowed to wear blue jeans.

- With few exceptions, standards should be broadly worded. Because dress and grooming standards are subject to frequent change, it is a waste of time to develop rigid, precise standards. Exceptions would occur where safety is concerned or where a uniform image must be maintained. For example, police officers can be required to wear a certain type of uniform while on duty.

- Whenever possible, standards should be flexible enough to accommodate individual employee tastes and preferences as well as changing fashions.
- Where relatively specific standards exist, they should be reevaluated periodically to see if they are still necessary and appropriate.
- Managers should avoid imposing their own values and preferences on employees.
- Employees from cultures where dress and grooming habits significantly differ from our own can be required to change and conform to the standards of our country and the organization. However, there must be legitimate business reasons for requiring such conformity.

## Whistle-Blowing

Primarily because of employees' increased awareness of business activities' social impact and because of changing attitudes about loyalty and obedience to employers, employees are increasingly willing to express their views and concerns outside internal communication channels. Though business interests theoretically should always harmonize with society's welfare, this is not always the case. The boundaries of different groups' legitimate interests are usually fuzzy, and areas of conflict inevitably arise. Further, different groups may share common interests but have conflicting views about how those interests are best served.

Historically, employers have shown little tolerance for employees who go outside the organization to express concern about what is going on inside the organization. Employers have usually viewed these employees as being disloyal or worse, treasonous. However, the public often sees such employees as heroes, especially when allegations of wrongdoing prove correct and the public welfare was endangered. In recent years a number of laws have been passed to protect employees from reprisal when they "blow the whistle" about questionable practices. Clearly, employers should have open internal communication channels to address employees' questions and concerns. When such systems exist and work as intended, trust is high and employees are unlikely to seek an outside forum. However, even when internal systems are available, employees do not always use them. Out of either ignorance or intent, some employees will rely on external forums to communicate their feelings, opinions, and concerns. Such activities can embarrass employers, detract from images, and hurt business.

Though managers no longer have a free rein to discipline whistle-blowing employees, the right to discipline still exists. Dissident employees who go outside the organization and allege wrongdoings should be subject to discipline if one of the following conditions is satisfied:

- The employee's allegations or assertions were entirely or substantially incorrect.

- The employee's disclosure was based on differences of opinion rather than on something that was clearly wrong.

- The employee's motive was self-interest rather than standards of integrity and decency or the welfare of the organization, its customers and stockholders, or the public.

- The employee made no attempt to use internal channels to air the matter and it is subsequently determined that the employee had no valid reasons for bypassing internal channels.

- The employee breached a trust or confidence and disclosed information that by prevailing social standards was legal, ethical, and moral.

- The employee caused potential or actual damage to the organization and/or its employees by false or largely incorrect accusations.

## Medical Disability

Excessive absence for illness or injury is a persistent problem for employers. Though many cases are legitimate, some employees with medical problems stay away from work much longer than what may be considered normal. Other employees claim medical problems as an excuse for absence to avoid being subject to disciplinary action. Medical excuses for not feeling well, backache, nausea, and assorted minor ailments are easily obtainable anywhere in the country. This is not to imply that the medical profession openly legitimizes dubious ailments, only that medical practitioners seldom want to challenge a patient's claim or risk losing a patient's business. Some managers and many employees mistakenly believe that as long as a "doctor's note" substantiates the existence of illness or injury, no employee can be disciplined.

In our society we do not guarantee people jobs irrespective of whether they are able to work. Many forms of employer- and government-furnished insurance provide support to people who cannot work because of legitimate medical disability. But those who cannot

## Case   Betty Adair

Betty Adair is a computer operator in the company's data-processing center. Betty has worked at the company for eight years. She is a very capable person who has always received good performance reviews.

In the course of her day, Betty, like most other employees, regularly uses pencils, pens, file folders, and note pads while doing her work. On occasion Betty, and probably just about everyone else, has taken a pen, pencil, or note pad home. Employees usually take things home unintentionally or because they are going to work at home. The company allows and even encourages employees to do some work at home.

Management has always monitored the cost and use of office supplies, but because employees are basically trusted, strict controls on distribution and use of supplies have not existed. In the past year management has noticed a dramatic increase in the use of supplies and believes they are being taken for personal use. The problem has been repeatedly brought to the employees' attention. They have been asked to exercise personal responsibility and not take supplies home for personal use, but for the most part, management's pleas have fallen on deaf ears.

It was finally decided that stronger action had to be taken. The president sent a letter to all employees outlining the scope of the problem, how much money was being spent per employee on supplies, and how this figure was far higher than it should be. Numerous examples were cited. For instance, in the first nine months an average of seventy-five writing pads were used per employee. The letter went on to say that drastic action was necessary to stop the petty theft. Employees were put on notice that anyone taking so much as a pencil off the premises without permission would be fired, irrespective of their service record.

Yesterday, as she left with her attaché case in hand, Betty was stopped by a security guard who asked her to open her case. She at first refused but then complied. The guard found two 8½-×-11-inch note pads that appeared to be fresh out of stock. He reported what he found to higher authority.

In a disciplinary interview this morning, Betty maintained that she took the pads because she planned on doing some work at home. Betty is known to occasionally do work at home. When asked why she had two pads, Betty said, "I didn't want to run out of paper." Those who listened to her story are split about what to do. Half want to fire her as an example to others, and half want to give her a verbal reprimand for not having told her boss that she was taking the pads to do work at home. You have the deciding vote.

## Questions

1. How will you vote? Why?
2. Would you make a different decision if the president had not sent the letter to everyone, including Betty?
3. Where do you draw the line on petty theft?
4. If Betty is fired and she challenges the action in court, do you think she will win or lose? Why?
5. If Betty is fired, how will this affect the attitudes of other employees? Will she become a martyr?
6. If Betty is not fired, how will this affect other employees? Will employees feel that the president's letter is a joke?

work must step aside for those who are able and willing, and those who will not work must be moved out of the organization.

Managers are faced with two major challenges in dealing with claimed medical disability. The first is: How can it be determined if an employee's medical problem is bona fide? If it is not, medical excuses to cover recent absences can be invalidated and future excuses for the same condition not accepted. The employee would be subject to normal disciplinary action. The second is: What can be done if the employee has real medical problems that are causing partial or total disability? Despite valid reasons, employees who cannot adhere to reasonable, consistently enforced attendance standards and competently do their jobs are subject to corrective action, including dismissal.

Employers have a right to question the legitimacy of claimed illness or injury. Even where disability is obvious, employers can question the seriousness of the disability and the likelihood of complete recovery. Employers have a considerable investment in employees, and they must safeguard that investment. In many cases employers are paying the medical costs through insurance premiums, and in all cases employers are incurring such costs as lost productivity, payment of nonmedical benefits, more overtime to compensate for absence, and so on. Managers must know an employee's medical status in order to decide on the best course of action to follow.

An employee can be requested to have an examination by a medical practitioner with appropriate credentials and expertise in the area of illness or injury being investigated. Typically, the employee is asked to select a practitioner from a list of qualified professionals. Though management can choose the medical authority, it is questionable as to whether an employee can then be required to have an examination. If the employee is attempting to return to work, however, he or she can be required to submit to examination by the employer's medical counsel before being allowed to return. But if the employee submits to examination by a management-selected person, the employee could challenge the examiner's objectivity. If the employee is not attempting to return to work or a compensation claim is not being contested, the best course of action is to request the employee to select someone from an agreed on list of professionals. As an alternative, the local medical association could be asked to provide a list. If the employee refuses to cooperate, absences relating to the illness or injury in question should no longer be excused.

If the employee is examined and nothing is found to substantiate the illness or injury, the absence should not be excused. In fact, if the employee is in excellent medical health, any absence for reasons that are not obvious should be challenged and considered unexcused.

An entirely different matter exists when bona fide illness or injury is established. When dealing with such, the following should be considered:

- Is the employee's condition correctable by medication and/or surgery? As a condition of continued employment or keeping a particular job classification, an employee can be required to take medication or submit to corrective surgery. The employee's refusal would be grounds for corrective action, including removal from the job and even termination.

- Will convalescence rehabilitate the employee? If so, how long will it take and to what degree will the employee recover? If full recovery is likely, the length of time a disabled employee's job should be held for him or her is a function of many of the variables, including length and quality of service, policy and practice, and other factors outlined in Chapter 5.

- If a lengthy convalescence is required (a year or longer), it may be prudent to avoid guaranteeing the employee his or her job on return.

- Employees unable to meet attendance and performance standards can be removed from their jobs and even terminated. The action would be administrative and medical rather than strictly disciplinary. Any disciplinary action, especially removal from the job, must be based on unbiased, competent opinion and whatever possible clear fact.

- Progressive discipline, especially punitive discipline, would be improper for the employee whose absences are caused by real medical problems. For example, a three-day disciplinary suspension for an employee with a heart condition would serve no useful purpose. In fact, it could be quite harmful.

- In any displacement or separation action involving an employee who is partially disabled from accident or injury, management must prove the employee cannot satisfactorily do his or her job or do it without high risk of recurring or additional illness or injury.

- Management's decision about an employee's fitness to properly do his or her job can and should overrule medical experts' opinions. However, management must be able to substantiate a decision based on knowledge about the job and its environment.

- Job requirements often change, as do the physical and mental requirements needed to do them. Employees with known disabilities

## Case   Eric Svenson

Eric Svenson is the manager of administrative services. He has been with the company for eighteen years and is respected for his managerial skills. Eric fancies himself as something of a ladies man, and he often flirts with many of the women in the department. From time to time there have been rumors about his having made sexual advances, but his bosses dismissed these rumors as petty jealousy and idle gossip.

Jill Jenkins was recently hired into the department. She is twenty, single, and lives with her family. Eric immediately took a shine to her, which was not unusual because he took a shine to just about every young woman who came to work in administrative services.

This morning something very disturbing happened. Jill's father accosted the president as he got out of his car. He was quite upset and threatened to blow Eric's head off if he even looked at Jill crossways. It seems that Jill came home in tears yesterday and told her father that Eric had made repeated advances and threatened to have her fired if she did not have dinner with him. In Jill's mind there was every indication that dinner would just be for openers. The

who were performing satisfactorily but now can no longer do so because of changed requirements should be subject to removal.

• Whenever possible, deserving employees who are partially or permanently disabled should be offered positions commensurate with their present capabilities.

• If a partially disabled employee could satisfactorily perform his or her job with reasonable accommodation, employers should make reasonable adjustments to accommodate specialized needs.

## Incompetence

Incompetence has been and still is a common reason why employees are demoted and fired, but with increasing frequency, employers are being required to substantiate their actions. When taking corrective action the following guidelines should be used:

president is unaccustomed to such a reception and wants you to get to the bottom of this and recommend a course of action.

You start to investigate the incident and suddenly a flood of complaints about Eric's alleged advances comes forth. You interview Jill and conclude that she has exaggerated the incident and is overreactive. However, there is a basic truthfulness to her story. You interview Eric, and he brushes the incident aside as innocent flirtation. He says that he will apologize if it will settle the matter; if not, he has every intention of defending his reputation.

### Questions

1. What courses of action are available to you?
2. Should demoting Eric be given serious consideration? Why?
3. Should he be fired? Why?
4. Is Eric emotionally ill and in need of professional assistance?

• Performance must be documented, and written performance appraisals must reflect employees' actual performance.

• Evidence that raises and other rewards have been withheld or reduced as compared to what others receive should be documented.

• If no performance appraisal system is used, management must have records and other types of evidence to support allegations of incompetence.

• Before an employee is disciplined for inadequate job performance, management should be reasonably certain that the responsibility for such performance rests primarily with the employee.

• Where feasible and practical, demotion in lieu of termination should be used for long-term employees with prior satisfactory records of service.

• A record should be kept showing consistent treatment of other employees with comparable performance records. Inconsistencies in treatment may occur when policy has changed.

- The employee should be aware of his or her performance and have been given a reasonable opportunity to change behavior.

## Alcoholism

For various reasons alcoholism is a frequent direct or underlying cause of misconduct. Most often it shows up in attendance and job performance problems. Alcoholism is currently considered to be an illness, and approaches to discipline for alcoholism should be similar to those used to deal with medical illness. These include access to employee assistance programs, sickness and disability leave of absence, counseling, medical assistance, and coordination with organizations that specialize in rehabilitating alcoholics.

- The amount of time, money, and effort that management should expend in helping alcoholics should be a function of (1) the organization's prevailing attitudes toward employees and (2) employees' length and quality of service.
- Employees undergoing treatment can and should be required to make progress toward recovery. If reasonable progress has not been made within a stipulated period of time, consideration should be given to discontinuing rehabilitative efforts.
- As with any medical disability, at some point it may be necessary to remove the employee from his or her job and possibly terminate employment. The reason for termination may be medical disability or misconduct.

## Intoxication

- Supervisors and higher-level managers do not need extensive training to know when an employee is intoxicated, under the influence, or impaired to the degree that he or she cannot work safely and/or efficiently.
- Oral or written accusations should be limited to saying that the employee was impaired or under the influence of some intoxicant rather than saying that he or she was drunk.
- Under no circumstances should an employee who is under the influence be allowed to work.
- If the employee is barred from working, arrangements should be made to get him or her home safely. A taxi should be called, someone

should take the employee home, or someone should be called to come and get the employee. The employee should not be allowed to operate his or her own motor vehicle or to leave the premises unattended. If the employee does so and no attempts are made to stop him or her, the organization and individuals in authority on the scene could be held responsible for any injuries or damages resulting to the employee or others after he or she left.

## Drug Abuse Other than Alcohol

Employers generally feel that drug abuse is more serious than alcoholism. However, management should note that the 1973 Federal Rehabilitation Act prohibits discharging employees for drug or alcohol addiction unless their work is deficient. The trend appears to be toward treating all types and forms of drug abuse, including misuse of prescribed drugs, as bona fide illness.

## Fighting

Fighting is less likely to be encountered among white-collar employees than among blue-collar employees. Physical fights are more likely to occur at lower organizational levels, especially among employees who by conditioning have learned to settle their differences by physical means. In determining discipline, the following guidelines should be considered:

• Instigators and perpetrators should receive more serious discipline than victims.

• Assaults against supervisors and higher-level managers should be viewed as more serious than fights among coworkers. If physical attacks against supervisors are not viewed as being so serious that anything less than termination and even criminal prosecution is the exception, occurrences of such activities will tend to increase. This could seriously affect managers' ability to manage.

• In investigating fights, remember that the one who threw the first punch may not be the most guilty party.

• Employees, particularly those in managerial positions, should understand that it is better to walk away from a fight than to get involved in one. Even if struck, an employee should attempt to get away before striking back. This is not an act of cowardice. It is more prudent to seek justice by bringing charges under the organization's rules and the civil and criminal laws. However, there are limits to anyone's willingness and ability to avoid defending oneself. No one should have to withstand a battering. Self-defense is entirely appropriate, but it should be limited to neutralizing the attacker.

- The use of a dangerous weapon in a fight should be viewed as more serious than the use of fists only.

- The intensity of the altercation (for example whether there was one blow or a series of blows) should be considered in determining discipline.

- The effects of the fight in terms of injuries, effect on morale, safety, and relationships should be evaluated when determining discipline.

## Sexual Harassment

Increasingly and for many reasons, sexual harassment charges are being made against employers. For at least the next few years, the trend is likely to continue upward. The great majority of cases involve charges by women against men. Historically, organizations have tended to either ignore such charges or take them lightly. With aggrieved employees more frequently using the courts and government agencies to seek justice, employers are being compelled to take such charges seriously. When a sexual harassment charge is made, the following should be considered:

- As with all allegations of misconduct, a determination of the presence and degree of guilt must be made before discipline is determined.

- Investigations should be objective and thorough. In sexual harassment situations the emotions of the accuser and the accused can run high, thus causing overreaction and distortion of facts. Fact from fiction must be sorted out as well as possible.

- Sexual harassment may be symptomatic of emotional illness, and medical treatment as a form of constructive discipline should not be overlooked.

- Employers should have a well-communicated and understood policy regarding sexual harassment.

- Employees should understand that things said in jest may not be similarly interpreted. In determining the degree of guilt, motive is as important as what was actually said or done.

# Insubordination

Managers sometimes confuse insubordination with abusiveness, disrespect, or just plain questioning. Strictly defined, insubordination is the refusal to follow a legitimate directive.

- Employees do not have a right to refuse compliance with a legitimate directive unless they can prove compliance actually was (or they genuinely believed it was) dangerous to their safety and/or the safety of others.
- The practice in unionized organizations has been and still is "obey now, grieve later." The same practice should apply for nonunion employees.
- Reasons for refusal should be assessed before passing judgment.
- The degree of insubordination should be evaluated when considering discipline. Outright refusal should be considered more serious than failure to carry out an order or minimally complying with an order.
- If their concerns appear to be genuine, employees should be afforded some latitude to question orders or directives.
- Insubordination is a very serious matter. Before insubordination is charged, an effort should be made to ensure the employee understands the instruction, that it is an order, and the likely consequences for noncompliance.
- Abusive language and disrespect should be regarded as less serious than insubordination. When making a charge of abusive language, discretion should be used to differentiate between what is normal shop talk and what is clearly abusive. In determining what is abusive and what may be disrespect or normal shop talk, context, tone, body language, and intent are more important than actual spoken words.

# Misconduct off the Job

Contrary to what many people think, employees can be subject to discipline for after-hours misbehavior. An organization's image is important to its well-being. Those in higher-level positions are typically most closely identified with their employer's name and reputation. Disciplining an employee for misconduct off the job is proper if it meets any of the following conditions:

---

## Case   Anne Fagiano

Anne Fagiano is an operating room nurse in a medium-size community hospital. She is a dedicated professional with many years experience and a record of exemplary service. Some months ago Anne became increasingly concerned about Dr. Mary Landgrum's surgical techniques. She found they did not conform to standard medical practice, and in two instances she believed that the doctor's poor technique caused two patients to arrest on the operating table. Fortunately, both were revived by the quick work of others. She once detected alcohol on the doctor's breath while they were scrubbing for surgery. Another time Anne thought she may have been under the influence of some drug.

Dr. Landgrum is one of the most influential physicians in the community. Her peers believe she is brilliant, and her patients adore her. The hospital's management accommodates her every wish because her patients account for a substantial share of revenues.

Anne was finally motivated to bring her concerns to the hospital administrator and medical director. Both thanked her for her concern and, from all appearances, did nothing. After seeing a young patient arrest during a routine surgery for what she believed was Dr. Landgrum's mistake, she again brought her concerns to the medical director and administrator. An inquiry was made, and Dr. Landgrum was fully exonerated. Anne saw it as a whitewash and

---

• The conduct conflicts with the employee's job duties in such a way that the employer's legitimate business interests are jeopardized.

• The conduct renders the employee unable to perform his or her job, such as being confined to jail.

• The misconduct started on the job and carried over after hours.

• The conduct is so reprehensible that other employees are unwilling to work or are very uncomfortable working with the employee.

• The organization's image and/or its ability to effectively serve its customers could be or has been impaired. Keep in mind that when

coverup. She felt that the hospital was afraid of losing her business if she were disciplined. Anne was severely reprimanded and told in no uncertain terms to mind her own business.

Earlier this week, Anne saw Dr. Landgrum go into surgery in what she perceived to be a drunken state. This time she went to the local media and presented her case. The media gave it a full airing, and the hospital and Dr. Landgrum were furious.

Anne was called before a disciplinary review board chaired by the administrator. After the hearing, the vote was unanimous to fire her. Anne was fired, and she is taking legal action against the hospital. Dr. Landgrum is suing her for defamation of character.

### Questions

1. Was Anne justified in taking her complaint outside the hospital?
2. Did the hospital have a legitimate reason to fire Anne?
3. What if it later comes out that Dr. Landgrum has a chemical dependency problem?
4. How can organizations protect themselves from employees who indiscriminately air their grievances in public?

probable rather than actual injury is claimed, a higher degree of proof is required.

## Major Theft

Management has the right to fire and even criminally prosecute employees for major theft. Because this type of discharge is serious, a very high degree of proof should be required. Remember that labeling an employee a thief brands him or her for life. On the other hand, employees must understand that such behavior is intolerable and there is a high price to pay for such misconduct.

## Minor Theft

Most employers are willing to overlook a small amount of property loss resulting from misappropriation. The more employees take work home, the more likely they are to take some materials to facilitate doing the work. It is hard to determine whether the employee who takes a pad of paper home is doing it for business or personal use when his or her job involves writing. But employers should have a clearly stated policy regarding all degrees of theft, and employees should understand that pencils, pens, pads, wire, nuts and bolts, paper clips, and so on taken for personal use are not fringe benefits.

- Normally good employees should not be severely disciplined for a first offense of minor theft. An exception would occur where petty theft has become a problem and employees have been put on notice that management intends to crack down.
- Precise determination of where petty theft ends and major theft begins is impossible, but a clear difference exists between stealing a box of paper clips and stealing a typewriter.
- The employee's position with the organization, length and quality of service, reasons for stealing, admission of wrongdoing, sense of remorse, willingness to make restitution, and sincerity about changing behavior should be carefully considered before deciding how to treat the matter.
- Leniency should not be accorded repeat offenders.
- Consistent enforcement of policies regarding theft must exist to sustain terminations.
- Because termination for theft is serious and will impair an employee's chances of finding another job, considerable proof of guilt should be established before making a termination decision.

## Immoral Conduct

Changing social values and moral standards have altered the boundaries between what is moral and immoral. Even though they may not like or agree with them, employers would be wise to be open-minded about changing standards. Charging an employee with immoral conduct is extremely serious. In determining what is immoral conduct, the following considerations are offered:

- Prevailing social standards, specifically those in the community where business is conducted, should be used as a yardstick by which to judge employee conduct.

- Employee conduct off the job is none of the employer's business unless it falls within the scope of what was outlined earlier in this chapter.

- Criminal immoral conduct such as child abuse is more serious than legal conduct that conflicts with organizational values.

- Employers have no right to discipline employees for adopting unusual living arrangements, sexual relationships, or values and beliefs unless they clearly adversely affect the employer's legitimate business interests or affront community standards.

- Some types of immoral behavior may stem from character disorder or serious emotional illness. In such cases, if the employee is deemed worth saving, medical treatment should be considered as part of discipline.

## Dishonesty

Dishonesty is a catchall category for a broad range of misconduct. It can include lying, falsifying records and information, omitting information, accepting bribes and payoffs, covering up misconduct, misusing property, cheating customers, receiving stolen property, and much more. Firing an employee for dishonesty is on the same level as firing for theft; therefore, the same degree of proof should exist. In determining the degree of guilt and proper discipline, a number of factors should be considered:

- Was the dishonesty an oversight, lapse of memory, or deliberate act with intent to defraud? A deliberate act is far more serious than a mere oversight. Unintentional negligence or carelessness is not nearly as serious as deliberate dishonesty.

- Dishonest acts committed in the course of performing one's job are usually regarded as being more serious than ones committed outside the job.

- Dishonesty that causes injury to the employer is more serious than dishonesty that does not.

## Case  Lonnie Green

Dick Anderson manages a retail department store that caters to an affluent, older, conservative clientele. Most of his personnel are in the same age range as the clientele. Six months ago Dick decided to broaden the store's customer base and market merchandise that appeals to a younger, fashion-conscious market. The store still caters to its traditional customer base, but he recognizes that market potential is shrinking.

Dick added a number of fashion-conscious young people to his staff. Lonnie, one of the few black employees, was among those hired. He is very personable and competent, and his sales record puts him in the top 15 percent for the store. During the past two months, Dick has heard an increasing number of complaints about Lonnie's dress and appearance. At first he brushed them off, but they persisted. All came from senior staff and elderly conservative customers. A couple have turned in their charge cards. Lonnie's sales record has not been affected, and the people that come into the store often ask for him by name.

Lonnie's dress and appearance can be described as individualistic but professional. He wears an Afro and trimmed beard. His clothes are brightly colored but well coordinated. He wears his shirts open, often with a colored ascot.

Dick decided to talk to Lonnie in order to appease his

# Disloyalty

Disloyalty, like dishonesty, is a catchall heading that can embody a broad range of misconduct. It can include false, misleading, malicious, and slanderous statements about employers, supervisors, or associates; criticism of practices; working for competitors; conflict of business interest; uncooperativeness; and breach of confidentiality. Even in this period of increased employee rights, managers can still discipline disloyal employees who attempt to discredit their employers. In deciding an appropriate discipline, the following factors should be considered:

complaining staff and customers. He would like him to shave the beard, trim his hair, and wear clothing that is a little more conservative. Dick does not want to lose him, but he must do something about the mounting complaints.

Dick just brought Lonnie into his office and candidly told him about his concerns. Lonnie is not taking it well and is questioning Dick's motives and judgment. He cites his excellent record and claims that others are jealous and prejudiced. He says the older customers are simply stuffy. Dick knows there is a lot of truth in what Lonnie is saying.

### Questions

1. Does Dick have the right to discipline Lonnie?
2. Can Dick direct Lonnie to change his dress and appearance or face more serious discipline? If so, on what basis can he take such action?
3. What if Lonnie files a complaint alleging that Dick's discussion was racially motivated?
4. If Dick decides not to press the issue, what should he tell the complaining staff and customers?
5. Is there room for possible accommodation of both positions in this situation?

- The seriousness of the employee's disloyalty and its effect on the organization, employees, and customers.
- The employee's explanation for being disloyal. It is important to understand why the employee acted improperly.
- The degree of truthfulness should be evaluated in instances where statements have been made about the organization, its products or services, management, associates, and so on. Even if the employee's remarks are essentially correct, discipline is possible if the employee's motive was primarily self-serving, that is, to embarrass, discredit, or get even. If the employee had honest motives, such as a

## Case   LeAnne Harvey

LeAnne Harvey is a materials handler in a regional distribution center of a major toy manufacturer. She has been with the company for seven years and is an average employee.

The company has had a problem with employees coming to work drunk, drinking on the job, and smoking marijuana. A number of approaches to dealing with the problem have been tried without success. Recently, management decided to take drastic action and posted a notice informing all employees that anyone found to be in possession or under the influence of any nonprescription drug, hallucinogen, or alcohol would immediately be fired, regardless of his or her length and quality of service.

The notice had been in effect for three weeks when Cletus Howard, a supervisor, was driving a motor cart down the main aisleway and smelled the odor of burning marijuana in the air. He stopped to investigate and walked to a secondary aisle that parallels the main aisle. He saw a cloud of smoke in the air and LeAnne hurriedly leaving the area. As he walked toward where he first spotted LeAnne, the distinct smell of marijuana grew stronger. Cletus searched the area but did not find any discarded joints. He did find a couple of cigarette butts.

concern for the organization's well-being, safety and health, or the public interest, disciplinary action may be inadvisable and indefensible.

- Management should be extremely careful when disciplining employees whose actions are protected by law, even though it may view the act of publicly airing grievances as disloyalty. Many laws protect employees who allege that their employer is knowingly breaking the law.

- Managers are on shaky ground when disciplining employees who constructively criticize organizational policies and practices. However, employees are not free to openly speak out about whatever they do not like to anyone who is willing to listen. Employees should

Cletus reported what happened to Marian Schmidt, his supervisor. Marian and Cletus called LeAnne to the office and asked her if she had been smoking marijuana when Cletus spotted her. She denied doing so but admitted to smoking a cigarette, which is in violation of a company rule. Smoking in a nonauthorized area warrants discipline less than discharge for a first offense. LeAnne admitted to making a hasty exit when she saw Cletus because she knew that she was breaking a rule.

### Questions

1. What should Cletus and Marian do at this point?
2. To what extent can circumstantial evidence be used to support a charge?
3. Are there sufficient grounds to fire LeAnne?
4. If LeAnne is not fired and the word gets around that she was smoking marijuana, what does this do for management's credibility?
5. If Cletus and Marian recommend firing LeAnne, do you think upper management will support them? Why?

understand that when they go outside established internal channels to air grievances, they incur the possibility of being subject to discipline. On the other hand, employers must be more flexible in accommodating, listening to, and responding to employee criticisms.

## Carelessness, Negligence, Irresponsibility, and Accidents

Occasions will arise when employees are careless, negligent, or irresponsible. The best employees will sometimes make mistakes, even serious ones. Generally, employers should not fire employees for one careless mistake. However, employers do not have to wait for an irresponsible employee to accrue a history of screwing up before removing him or her from the job. In determining the right disci- pline, the following factors should be considered:

- The degree of carelessness, negligence, or irresponsibility and its potential or actual effect on others
- Whether the degree of responsibility inherent in the job was so high that one offense could warrant discharge
- Whether the act was willful or accidental
- Whether there were mitigating or extenuating circumstances, especially those beyond the employee's direct control
- The employee's willingness to admit being wrong, and his or her desire and ability to change behavior
- Whether this was an isolated incident or part of a pattern
- The employee's proneness to having or causing errors and acci- dents
- The extent to which the employee should have known better or should have been able to avoid the error

## Instigation and Troublemaking

The category of instigation and troublemaking includes rumor- mongering, back-stabbing, subterfuge, chronic complaining, unco- operativeness, argumentativeness, and abusiveness. Employees' rights to dissent and to air grievances must be carefully weighed against the employer's need to maintain order and efficiently con- duct business affairs. Responsive upward communication channels should exist so employees can constructively air their concerns and vent their feelings. Employers do not have to condone destructive dissent or retain troublemakers.

Though employees may disagree with decisions, policies, practices, procedures, and regulations that are legal and reasonable, they do not have the unrestricted right to air their feelings in ways that conflict with their employer's legitimate interests. Employees who are unwilling to conform to work practices and standards of conduct that are legal and reasonable are subject to discipline, including termination. Furthermore, managers do not have to continually lis- ten to or put up with chronic complainers and argumentative or uncooperative employees. As with all other types of misconduct, discipline should be tailored to the seriousness of the misconduct.

## Summary

The purpose of this chapter has been to provide managers with some thoughts to consider and guidelines to follow when handling many common types of misconduct. This information is certainly not meant to be all-inclusive. Management is largely an art, and detailed formulas rarely cover all aspects of different situations. However, throughout this book I have attempted to give managers the mental tools and demonstrate the basic ways in which they are used. Over time, success in using these tools when handling different types of disciplinary situations will enable managers to develop their own detailed methods and techniques. Much of what has been presented is time tested. Some of it is new, either because things have changed and old approaches no longer work or because new situations are being encountered.

## Concluding Remarks

Each of us wants to leave his or her footprint in the sand as we pass through this life. We want those who follow us to know we were here and have left something good behind. This book is one of my footprints in the sand. If in some small way what you have learned from reading this book contributes to your development, then my footprint will still be here after I am gone. By doing good with what you have learned, you will be making your own footprints. Thank you for taking the time to read this book.

## MORE CASES

### Case   Bob Jones

Bob Jones has been employed by the company for thirty-two years. He holds the highest classification in the machine department and is one of the most skilled employees. Although his formal education is limited, he is street smart and knows his work backward and forward.

Until about twelve years ago, Bob had an excellent employment record. In fact, he had twice received the employee of the year award. He had been offered a supervisory position a number of times, but each time he refused the promotion. About ten years ago it became apparent that Bob had a drinking problem. In recent years his service record has progressively deteriorated.

Bob is a rough sort of man and had a reputation as a fighter in his youth. It is known, although it cannot be proven, that he has threatened and beaten a number of employees. His friends are all troublemakers, and he appears to be their ringleader.

Bob has been placed on employment probation four times in the past six years. Each time he improved to the point where he was taken off probation. Last week word reached you that Bob had intimidated another employee. The employee is so afraid of Bob that he refuses to verify the incident. You have had enough of Bob's misbehavior and decide to take drastic action.

### Questions

1. Considering that Bob is an alcoholic, what do you intend to do about the situation?
2. Can you fire him and make it stick?
3. How will you get the threatened employee to file a complaint? Without a formal complaint, you have nothing to base any action on.
4. How will you protect the accusing employee from possible violence by Bob or his buddies?

## Case   Joel Siegel

You were recently hired as director of operations. One of the first things you did was announce a tightening of the attendance standards, which were loosely enforced by your predecessor. Joel is among the worst offenders. In reviewing his record, you find he was placed on probation five years ago for excessive absence. Joel improved for a while, but his record for the past year is worse than ever. You forewarned him and others with poor attendance that they faced termination if they did not improve.

In reviewing attendance for the past month, you noted that Joel has not improved. You decided to make an example of him for the others. You called him into your office and told him he was fired. Joel immediately challenged your decision. He said the attendance records were inaccurate and others in the unit with worse attendance are not going to be fired. He claims you are discriminating against him.

## Questions

1. What should you do at the moment?
2. What if there are minor errors in Joel's record? Should it make a difference in your decision given he is among the worst?
3. What if there are others with better records of service but worse attendance? Can you defend your firing of Joel?
4. What if the others with comparable records of service and attendance are not dealt with the same as Joel? Can you still defend your decision?

---

## Case  Paul Sakada

Paul Sakada is one of three second-shift supervisors at the company's heat-treating plant. There are sixty-eight employees working on the second shift in the plant. Paul and the other supervisors are thinly spread out. In fact, they often go the entire evening without seeing one another.

Last night one of Paul's employees, Larry Wilson, showed up for work in a disoriented state of mind. One look coupled with the overwhelming smell of liquor exuding from his body was enough to convince Paul that Larry was under the influence of alcohol and unable to safely do his job as a heat treat operator.

Paul exercised his authority and refused to let Larry clock in. He suspended him for his shift and ordered him to leave the premises. Larry left and, from all accounts, proceeded to go directly to a local bar frequented by employees. He continued drinking until the bartender refused to serve him any more. Shortly after leaving, Larry was involved in a serious automobile accident. From the police report, he was driving alone, strayed over the center line, and collided head-on with a car driven by a newly married couple. Both were killed. Larry is in fair condition and expected to survive.

### Questions

1. Did Paul do the right thing in refusing to let Larry clock in and go to work?
2. If Paul acted improperly, what should he have done? Why?
3. Can Larry disclaim responsibility for his behavior?
4. What is the company's potential liability in this case?
5. What is Paul's potential liability?
6. How do you think other employees will react on hearing the news of the accident?

---

## Case    Mike Juliano

Mike Juliano is the contracts officer for a large natural gas transmission company. As part of his job, he is the chief negotiator for land sales and rights-of-way. The job is very demanding and stressful. Mike is very competent and has an outstanding record of performance spanning more than twenty years.

A year ago, at age forty-eight, Mike suffered a heart attack. He was off from work for a month. When he returned, he was a different man. Though his physicians said that he made a full recovery and suffered no apparent permanent damage, Mike is afraid of another attack. His new attitude of "I'm not going to let this job kill me" has dramatically affected his performance. He refuses to work the extra hours his job regularly requires. He no longer aggressively negotiates land deals, and this is costing the company money.

His boss counseled him but did not succeed in reducing Mike's fears or changing his behavior. The company interviewed his physicians and reconfirmed his physical fitness to resume a normal work pace. The company's medical director spoke with Mike, but nothing to date has worked, and Mike's performance has not improved.

Nobody wants to fire Mike. He has too good a record and is a valued employee. Everyone feels that he has much to contribute and would like him to stay in his present position. However, everyone recognizes that things cannot keep going the way they are.

### Questions

1. What options are available?
2. What courses of action would you recommend? Why?
3. If Mike is offered a transfer to a less demanding position with a cut in pay but refuses, what should be done?
4. Do you think it's possible to get Mike to overcome his fear of having another heart attack?
5. Can companies develop guidelines for cases such as this, or must each one be handled on its own merits?

---

## Case   Earl Schumacher

Earl Schumacher is an executive with a major employer in the area. He is a real mover and shaker, and much of the company's success is owed to him. In his position, he is highly visible in the community. He frequently represents the company at civic and social events.

In the past six months it has become increasingly apparent that Earl drinks heavily at the various events he attends. At first, reports of his being drunk were brushed aside. However, the situation has worsened, and Earl regularly gets drunk and makes a fool of himself at the activities he attends. His conduct has become an embarrassment, and the president has decided that something must be done.

Before doing anything, she conducts a behind-the-scenes investigation of Earl's behavior at work. She finds that Earl is an outstanding role model at work. Except for his public drunkenness, Earl is a tremendous asset.

## Questions

1. If you were the president, what would you do? Why?
2. If the company has an employee assistance program, how can Earl be encouraged to utilize its services?
3. On what bases does management have a right to tell employees how to live their lives?
4. If Earl were in a less visible position with the company, would this affect the handling of his situation?

## Case  Nick Cramer

Nick Cramer is a teacher at a grade school located in a conservative community. He is thirty-one years old, a bachelor, and lives alone. He joined the district right out of college and, in all respects, is an excellent teacher. His young students adore him and his peers deeply respect him. He is quiet, unassuming, and regularly attends church.

Recently it was learned that Nick is gay. At first no one believed the rumors, but when they continued to mount, Nick was asked by one of his associates. Nick freely admitted his homosexuality. As the word spread, pressure on the board of education, the superintendent of schools, and Nick's principal mounted. People in the community with considerable political influence have demanded that Nick be removed from the classroom. A number of parents have requested that their children be taken out of his class.

Nick has defended his homosexuality by saying it is his preference and that we live in a more enlightened age. He further argues that he does not flaunt it and that his sexual preference in no way has affected or will affect his job performance. He also contends it is no one's business what he does off the job and that the system is infringing on his personal freedom.

## Questions

1. If you were Nick's supervisor, that is, the principal, what would you do in this case?

2. Do grounds exist to fire Nick? If so, what are they?
3. If Nick is not fired, what problems does this create for the board, superintendent, and school principal?
4. If Nick is fired and seeks due process in court, what do you think will be the outcome of his action?
5. To what extent can employees be subject to discipline for off-duty conduct?

## Case    Susan Fowler

Susan Fowler was hired as a secretary ten months ago. She passed the company's ninety-day probation period with flying colors. Susan is very popular and was an outstanding worker until four months ago, when she was in a serious car wreck. Two people were killed and Susan suffered severe head injuries. She was absent for six weeks.

When Susan returned, her boss and coworkers saw that her motor skills had deteriorated. Her coordination was not normal, and at times her thinking appeared to be confused. She has also become forgetful. All this has negatively affected her work. Everyone feels sorry for her, but it is obvious that she cannot handle her job responsibilities. The company has a long-term disability insurance program, but employees cannot participate in it until they have one full year of service. Also, it does not cover preexisting conditions.

Susan's doctors have been consulted to find out how permanent her condition is. One believes that she will make at least a 90 percent plus recovery in the next six months. The other feels that she will make little, if any, improvement.

### Questions

1. If the decision is made to terminate Susan, what should be the reason for the action?
2. What other options are available?
3. If Susan is left in her present position, how would this affect similar cases that might arise?

4. If it is learned that Susan is two months' pregnant, what bearing, if any, should it have on the disposition of this case?

## Case   Kay Rakowski

Kay Rakowski is a fifty-seven-year-old widow who has been with the company for thirty years. Until three years ago, her service record was excellent, but during the past three years, Kay's health has deteriorated. It started shortly after her husband passed away. Kay has been suffering from a variety of emotional and physical ailments. Her attendance pattern has been one of frequent periodic absence lasting from three to ten days.

For the first two years of widowhood, her total absence ran 10 and 12 percent, respectively. This year it is running at 15 percent, and everything indicates that it is going up. When she is at work, her performance is as good as ever.

Kay's supervisor has spoken to her a number of times. At first she was very understanding, but understanding has turned to frustration. She can no longer rely on Kay to be there when she is needed, and Kay's associates have grown increasingly tired of having to fill in for her when she is absent.

Kay's supervisor has decided that something must be done now. Kay has just returned from a week's absence.

### Questions

1. If you were Kay's supervisor, what is the first thing you would do?
2. Should Kay be required to submit to a complete medical evaluation? Why?
3. Should Kay be fired?
4. What are some of the options available? Which one would you choose? Why?

# Index